Hot Questions
Cold Storage

Architecture from Austria

The Permanent Exhibition
at the Az W

Angelika Fitz
Monika Platzer
Architekturzentrum Wien

Contents

Preface 4
Angelika Fitz
Karin Lux

Introduction 6
Angelika Fitz
Monika Platzer

Keep it Hot 12
Monika Platzer

Collections that Speak Back 18
Tom Avermaete

Cold Storage 24

Elements	38
Players	78
Planet	126
Capital	168
Habitat	222
Common Good	260
Image	298
Making-of	354

Tracing Spaces / Michael Hieslmair, Michael Zinganel
seite zwei / Christoph Schörkhuber, Stefanie Wurnitsch

Bibliography	375
Index	380
Authors	382
Colophon	383

Preface

Don't let the word "Zentrum" (center) in our name fool you. From the very beginning, the Architekturzentrum Wien's intention has been to build an impressive collection of Austrian architecture, an aim it has pursued since shortly after its establishment in 1993. In light of the pan-European architecture museum boom of the 1980s, the collection activity of the Az W filled a gap in the Austrian museum landscape and gave proper attention to the international significance of Austrian architecture. Meanwhile, the Az W possesses the most comprehensive documentation of twentieth and twenty-first century Austrian architecture and is the only museum in Austria entirely dedicated to the discipline. Nevertheless, we have kept the "Zentrum" in our name. The Az W is a dynamic point of convergence which bridges the worlds of architecture professionals and everyday experts through international themed exhibitions, symposia, workshops, tours, film series, and hands-on formats. The Az W is an open space, where one can experience a diversity of ideas and architectural views. The Az W is a place where the political nature of architecture and urban development is front and center, where we research, discuss, and show how these fields shape the daily lives of all people. The Az W is a change maker, advocating for a new ethics in architecture that will enable us and all other species to survive and hopefully live well on this planet.

What can architecture do? This question has guided Az W's activities under our leadership since 2017. What can be achieved through architecture? This question touches each and every one of us and is the inspiration for Hot Questions – Cold Storage, our new permanent exhibition. Our search for answers is firmly rooted in the present. Each of the exhibition's sections is prefaced by a Hot Question related, for example, to the impacts of globalization on our cities and their surroundings, the way we shape our dwellings, and how architecture can contribute to our survival on this planet. At the same time, the "Cold Storage" display gives visitors a glimpse of the extensive contents of our holdings.

While most architecture museums concentrate on the history of architecture and design, the Az W consistently maintains a social perspective in its collection activity. Above all, the more than 100 bequests, the one-of-a-kind photo archive, and the extensive project collections with their enormous quantity of objects and documents address not only art and cultural history, but also social, economic, and technological history. The objects in our archive range from models, photographs, and drawings via textile designs and furniture to rare books and historical documents. The Az W's previous permanent exhibition was opened in 2004 under the founding director Dietmar Steiner. At the time, our collection activity was just getting underway; consequently, the a_show relied mainly on secondary sources. One of our new director's main aims is to make the archives – which now hold the most important collection documenting Austria's contemporary architecture – accessible to the public in a permanent exhibition. It is, of course, only possible to present a small sample of the objects, one that ultimately constitutes about 0.5 percent of the entire inventory. This new permanent exhibition revolves around the inquiries into key objects – some prominent, some less well-known – and our thoughts about the potential and relevance of the collection, which will in the future be the point of departure for many more investigations. We were able to rely on the expertise of the Az W collections team, which, befitting the collection, conducts research on interdisciplinary and transnational approaches, as well as on the curatorial expertise of the entire institution, without which the Az W would not today rank among the world's most innovative institutions in architecture education.

The concept for the new permanent exhibition was developed by Angelika Fitz, the Az W's director, and Monika Platzer, who heads the collection. In their introductory text, they elaborate upon it. Monika Platzer is responsible for the curatorial implementation, and in her text, entitled "Keep it Hot," she discusses the emergence of the collection and the synergies between research, collection, and exhibitions. Tom Avermaete provides insight into the history of collection and exhibition strategies. He positions the new permanent exhibition in the current discourses on the decolonization of architecture and exhibition narratives. Karin Lux, our executive director, was in charge of remodeling and the complex implementation of the new exhibition premises. The new permanent exhibition must meet conservation demands for the next several years and create a suitable indoor climate for the objects on display and for the visitors. As a certified "green museum" and in keeping with our programmatic approach, we chose a nature-based and low-tech solution that combines mechanical and natural forms of air-conditioning, including automated night ventilation and special glazing, to reduce radiation and heat gain. The flexible and energy-saving lighting, the high-quality materials, and the new media equipment support the varied interventions and enhance the sensory-rich atmosphere and overall experience. The steel-plate modules from the old permanent exhibition were salvaged for a social project, which is, incidentally, portrayed in the new permanent exhibition.

We are convinced that this exhibition catalog will be a milestone both with regard to how architecture is presented and how the format relates to the permanent exhibition. The presentation is two-pronged, showing fine examples of Austrian architecture and pondering the underlying question as to the role of architecture in our society. The goal is to make visitors want to see more and to stimulate political discussion. The exhibition invites them to take their time and delve into topics, and sets a new global course, or as the architecture critic Christian Kühn writes in the Austrian daily *Die Presse* on the occasion of the opening: "With this exhibition Vienna has yet another top attraction on offer." And now you can take this marvelous show home with you in the form of a book.

Producing a book or an exhibition is always a collaborative endeavor. We would like to thank all the architects who have donated their archives to us. We also acquired a significant number of documents while putting together the permanent exhibition. This can be contributed to our continued collection efforts, the success of which we owe to the confidence of various architecture scenes and their protagonists. Of course, having the right design professionals is a prerequisite to presenting the concepts and ideas in a publication and exhibition. We selected Tracing Spaces (Michael Hieslmair and Michael Zinganel) and seite zwei (Christoph Schörkhuber and Stefanie Wurnitsch) and are grateful to them for their fine work. Above all, we want to thank the sensational Az W team and, in this case, particularly Barbara Kapsammer, Sonja Pisarik, Katrin Stingl, and Iris Ranzinger (the members of the collections team); Monika Platzer, the curator and head of collections; Andreas Kurz, who supervised the production; as well as the members of the workshop team and the education team. With the new permanent exhibition we show what architecture can do and what the Az W can accomplish as a museum!

Angelika Fitz, director
Karin Lux, executive director

Introduction

Hot Questions – Cold Storage. The Permanent Exhibition at the Architekturzentrum Wien

Angelika Fitz, Monika Platzer

The climate crisis, distributive justice, social cohesion, identity, and memory are vital themes in respect to our present and future, and they are closely intertwined with how we think about, design, plan, and build space. The Architekturzentrum Wien views the museum as a change maker and has created a place where burning questions can be explored in an overarching context – in its temporary exhibitions, in its research and education, and now also in the new permanent exhibition. While most international architecture museums concentrate on the history of architecture and design, the Az W consistently maintains a social perspective, even in its collection activity. It compiles, researches, and shows how architecture impacts people's day-to-day lives. It brings together various types of knowledge and in doing so counteracts the fragmentation of society.

As an architecture museum, the Az W has positioned itself as a future-oriented institution in which knowledge is not only collected but also shared. The guiding question in the work of the Architekturzentrum – "What can architecture do?" – is also an underlying question in the new permanent exhibition. An extension of this question is "What can collections accomplish?" Museum collections are much more than merely the debris washed ashore by the ebb and flow of history; their social relevance can be seen in the inquiry and illumination, in the relationship between a museum's research work and its collection mandate.

The Exhibition Practice of the Az W

Exhibitions are instruments of power; they are used to write architecture history. In the past they played an essential role in establishing who the master architects were or in contributing to the definition of a style. As a visual format, exhibitions provide an important contribution to the global spread of architectural ideas and images. At the same time, each exhibition is always the product of a history bound to a particular time and embedded in its institutional context. The Az W's curatorial orientation focuses not on style or mastership, but on the social dimension of architecture; that is to say, on the answers architecture is able to give to questions concerning society, culture, and the planet.

The permanent exhibition "Hot Questions – Cold Storage" also recognizes the need to scrutinize its own practice and contributes actively to building a museum of the future. The goal is to create a network linking scientific research and museum practice. At the core is an examination of the historical material from a specific point in time. In preparation for a critical and reflective examination of the inventory of the Az W collection, in 2017 we developed the new exhibition format known as SammlungsLab.[1] This orientation is marked by the new director Angelika Fitz[2] and her shift of the institutional focus from the question "What is architecture?" to "What can architecture do?" In the process of developing the new permanent exhibition, the SammlungsLabs served as instruments of curatorial research. By delving into the content of specific topics, we tapped the collection from a present-day standpoint, and in doing so discovered new interconnections, but also addressed gaps and omissions. The formats ranged from intensive critical engagement with the objects via cross-generational, oral-history projects to critical interpretations of the material, and they all seek to foster further research. A few intermediary results of this curatorial research found their way directly into the permanent exhibition as

View of the new permanent exhibition | Photo: eSeL.at – Lorenz Seidler

Concept development: Angelika Fitz and Monika Platzer | Visual protocol: Angelika Fitz, 2020

material groups, for example, objects that had been in use at a former Children's Town in Vienna and the research on a guild of designers and craftspeople named the Vorarlberger Baukünstler. But what is more important is maintaining a specific stance in the curatorial work with the collection.

As head of the collections, Monika Platzer was responsible for the curatorial implementation of the concept she and Angelika Fitz had developed. In her curatorial vision there is a constant overlap of the collection space and the exhibition space, whereby the cultural techniques of the selection and arrangement of the display objects elicit dialectical interaction. This stands in stark contrast to the archetypical image of collections as the accumulation of materials. According to Michel Foucault, collections are not merely items in storage spaces; inherent in them is a system of expression that warrants investigation. Historically, the institution of the museum is inextricably entwined with the collection objects, which, taken together, are built upon a connoisseurship and have consequently led to the formation of a canon.

Hot Questions – Cold Storage, the Az W's new permanent exhibition, signals our determination to confront the gaps and actively affirms, deconstructs, and sets the course. Nothing is taken for granted, our inquiry moves from the center to the periphery and vice versa; it spots gaps and is open to "guests" who interact with our holdings or inject a new framework of meaning. The silence of the cold storage is interrupted; the display objects are examined and juxtaposed from seven perspectives. The development of the seven questions reflecting these perspectives has to do with the research mandate of the Az W's collection work, on the one hand, and with our curatorial research in keeping with current temporary exhibitions, on the other hand. For example, the exhibition and publication Land for Us All (Az W, 2020)[3] show the urgency of bold measures for reducing land consumption – from the climate crisis and affordable housing to food security – and offer useful information by listing interest groups and property situations, pointing out alternatives, and encouraging self-reflection between personal interest and the common good. Some particularly clear examples from this exhibition, which has toured more than 20 communities in Austria to date, have been incorporated into the permanent exhibition.

Our reflective look at architecture history takes into account the fact that architecture and urbanism have in the past been and continue to be dominated by the interests of capital, and that they are deeply entwined in the political, social, and ecological crises of their times. This is made particularly clear in the exhibition's "Who shapes the city?" section. But architecture can also be part of the solution. Critical Care – Architecture and Urbanism for a Broken Planet (Az W, 2019)[4] set forth a new ethics in architecture and urbanism that seeks to ensure the survival of all human and non-human beings on this planet. Selected projects incorporate this ethics of care in the permanent exhibition.

A glimpse behind the scenes of complex social negotiation processes is another constant that runs through the Az W's exhibition practice. The exhibition and publication entitled Cold War and Architecture (Az W, 2019)[5] and the curatorial examination of building codes and regulations entitled Form Follows Rule (Az W, 2017)[6] exemplify this approach. Another section, "How is architecture produced?," elaborates on the discipline's localities, methodologies, and reference systems and thereby revisits some of the themes addressed in The Force is in the Mind – The Making of Architecture (Az W, 2008)[7]. And in dialogue with the Az W's gender-informed research – whose contributions and questions can be found at various other points in the permanent exhibition – female architects are presented in prominent solo exhibitions in a new Az W series that experiments with the format of the "solo show." Rather than focusing on master narratives, this segment – which began in 2018 by presenting the very first exhibition focused on the work of Denise Scott Brown,[8] and will be dedicated to Yasmeen Lari in 2023[9] – sheds light on new interconnections, "joint creativity," decarbonization, decolonization, and planetary perspectives.

Cold Storage – Hot Questions

Collections have the potential to change our habitual view of architecture. In the permanent exhibition, the Az W's depot makes its presence felt in a dynamic Cold Storage video installation that gives the visitor a glimpse into our collection storeroom. The spaces shown house a good share of Austrian architecture history in the form of more than 100 architects' archives and a comprehensive project collection. The collection's holdings range from architectural drawings, plans, and models via photographs, furniture, and design objects to rare books and a rich array of documents. Together with the comprehensive photo archives, the inventory spans multiple

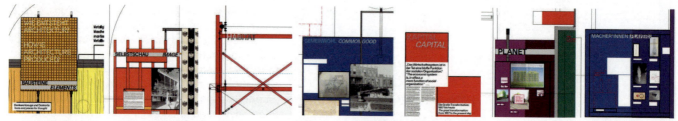

7 questions, 7 topics | Exhibition design by Tracing Spaces and seite zwei, 2021

fields, from art and cultural history to social, economic, and technological history. The Cold Storage installation focuses on the collection – not as a physical medium for storing the past, but as a future scenario for constantly thinking about and by means of architecture. In the "Cold Storage" installation, the collection is portrayed not as linear and encyclopedic, but as fragmentary with gaps and inconsistencies.

Grouped around this are the seven Hot Questions that breathe life into the Cold Storage. They range from the impacts of financial capitalism on our towns and cities, via reflection on how we want to live, to architecture's contribution to our survival on this planet. We see this set of questions as a discourse generator and point of departure for many other possible inquiries into the collection. With these Hot Questions we juxtapose the introspective examination of the Cold Storage with an outside view that brings contexts and ideas to the fore. Austria's building activity – with all its cultural, social, political, economic, and technical implications – is made clearly visible. The result is not a miniature walk-in storeroom with objects on display, but a look at the objects and materials from today's perspective. Transnational and multidisciplinary relationships are traced, overlooked facets come to light, and the familiar is brushed against the grain. Chronological order is clearly not a priority here; the narratives do not offer a linear account. Notions of multi-perspectivity and coexistence of ideas, aesthetic positions, architectural views, social and sociopolitical concepts have guided the process.

How is architecture produced? ELEMENTS
Here the focus is shifted to the places where architecture is produced. The depiction of various workspaces and the tools found in them – for instance, drawing instruments, slide rules, drafting templates, drafting sets, early computers, and modern interfaces for Building Information Modeling Systems – give the visitor a good idea of the various transformation processes that take place in the discipline, including born-digital items. Presented here side by side are digital pioneers such as Ottokar Uhl and Manfred Wolff-Plottegg, as well as outstanding draftsmen such as Bogdan Bogdanović and Heinz Tesar. The sliding panels can be pulled out to reveal a collage of sample materials prepared for a competition by Elsa Prochazka, along with several other tactile exhibits demonstrating experiments with color, material, and construction. The "useful trip" favored by architects, which can be traced back to the Grand Tour in the nineteenth century, is documented in our collection in the form of extensive film footage and slides. In the permanent exhibition, visitors can travel to the southern Cyclades with Bernhard Rudofsky, to the World Fair in Brussels with Karl Mang, to John Lautner's spectacular buildings and construction sites in Los Angeles, to Palm Springs with Hans Dieter Smekal, to China with Roland Rainer, to Iran with Djamshid Farassat, to Moscow with Hans Puchhammer, and to Norway with Johannes Spalt.

Who gets involved? PLAYERS
Over the decades, the (mostly male) narrative perspectives have become consolidated into master narratives. The field of gender studies has opened up new perspectives and prompted scholars to pose new questions, such as those involving misrepresentations in the canon. Two Barbie dolls have been included in the permanent exhibition as provocative wildcards for missing perspectives: Architect Barbie and Builder Barbie. The Barbie doll version of femininity was developed in 1959 as an alternative to the classic doll intended to prepare girls for their role as a mother. With the "I Can Be Anything" series, Barbie breaks into typically male professions. Although today the gender ratio at schools of architecture is balanced, on construction sites, women in hard hats are still in the minority. Of the 3,383 licensed architects in Austria, 2,782 are men and only 601 are women.

In contrast, between the first and second world wars, women had already begun to gain a foothold in photography. With the acquisition of Margherita Spiluttini's photography archive, the Az W came into the possession of one of the most important photographic collections on Austrian architectural works. Spiluttini has documented more than 4,000 buildings and objects and – like Friedrich Achleitner and his archive – has helped shape the perception of Austrian architecture. Among other things, she set in motion a lasting process of change in the reception of postwar architecture, and the photographic careers of those buildings now categorized as mid-century modern architecture were launched single-handedly by Margherita Spiluttini.

Architecture history is a construct. Architects become canon makers through narratives about themselves. They themselves become history, and the exhibition format is instrumental in this process. From the 1960s on, the exhibition carousel started to spin around the fin de siècle with the "rediscovery" and enthroning of "turn-of-the-century Vienna." The permanent exhibition shows prominent and lesser known curatorial projects by Hans Hollein and arbeitsgruppe 4. The concept "Wiener Moderne" was construed as something uniquely Austrian, and after 1945 many architects tried to find ways to perpetuate that creed.[10] Austrofascism and National Socialism, in contrast, didn't factor into Austria's identificatory self-image.

How can we survive? PLANET
Dealing with nature as a result of urbanization and the repercussions of urbanization on society in its historical dimension have been topics of the discipline of environmental history for quite some time. In the twenty-first century, attaining socially sustainable and resource-saving architecture became the key topic in architectural discourse and architectural practice. A new look at the collection and the inclusion of such fields as landscape planning, climate engineering, and biology provides a more open view of the built connections between humans

and nature. By the 1960s, a change in awareness had taken place among architects – from Haus-Rucker-Co to Friedensreich Hundertwasser – who recognized the reckless consumption of raw materials and responded with ideas alternating between utopian and dystopian. In light of the climate crisis, projects like the Donauinsel (Danube Island) in Vienna – a large-scale recreational space resulting from an ingenious combination of flood control measures and an understanding of qualities of open space – and the early solar houses now appear all the more prescient. More recent solutions range from such "green technology" proposals as the prototype of a bioreactor facade by SPLITTERWERK to Anna Heringer and Martin Rauch's reintroduction of loam as a building material. In civil society initiatives – whether historical, such as gentle urban renewal, or current as in the efforts by Bodenfreiheit [Land Liberation], a non-profit organization in Vorarlberg – architects are joining forces with activists to repair the future.

Who shapes the city? CAPITAL

Although buildings may not directly reflect sociopolitical events, they do serve as a sociopolitical means of communication. Always manifested in architecture are not only design aspects but also an imaginary society. In the eyes of the Viennese economist Karl Polanyi, all human economic activity is embedded in social relationships. Published in 1944, his book *The Great Transformation* is now more relevant than ever and refutes Margaret Thatcher's neoliberal claim that "[t]here is no such thing as society!"[11] All the more reason for including it at the beginning of the "Who shapes the city?" section in the form of two opposing ideological models – the capitalist city and the anti-capitalist city. To illustrate this dichotomy, we jump from the Gründerzeit in the nineteenth century to finance capitalism in the twenty-first century and visit their opposing models from Red Vienna to the various new collectives.

In nineteenth-century Vienna, the interplay of migration and politics became both palpable and comprehensible. Austrian Jews were granted equal rights by the December Constitution (1867) and henceforth allowed to acquire land. The ensuing emancipation and will to integrate on the part of the Jewish community aroused antisemitic resentment, as can be seen in the nicknaming of the Ringstrasse as "Zion Street in New Jerusalem." Economic crises such as the stock market crash of 1873 fueled the continuous rise in political power of Karl Lueger, whose term of office (1897–1910) as mayor of Vienna was characterized by an anti-liberal and antisemitic stance. The so-called "Annexation" of Austria to the German Reich in 1938 paved the way for the murder and expulsion of thousands of Austrians, among them countless architects. From 1945 on, an invitation to return was extended to only a small number of Jewish expatriates. Even today, the lack of sources still makes it difficult to clearly show the Jewish contribution to the culture of building in Austria. All the more striking is the inclusion in the permanent exhibition of two architects, whose material tracks led them into the Az W collection via circuitous route: Leopold Ponzen (1892, Vienna – 1946, Shanghai, China) and Karl Dirnhuber (1889, Vienna – 1953, Birmingham, UK).

How do we want to live? HABITAT

In this segment of the exhibition, models built over the course of more than 100 years rotate in a continuous loop. They show how places where we live become social practice arenas and formal testing grounds, producing ever new relationships between the public and private realms. One major objective of the permanent exhibition is to present not only avant-garde designs of homes, but also practical alternatives to the freestanding single-family dwelling. And maybe our interactive living-space questionnaire will encourage visitors to envision new housing concepts for living with others.

Who provides for us? COMMON GOOD

The turn of the twentieth century marked the modernization of a charitable welfare system, the beginning of a public health system as a fundamental human right. The control of epidemics through hygienic improvements and the belief in an interplay between architecture and health confirmed the municipal administrations' conviction that they were responsible for caring for their citizens from cradle to grave. All this led to the development of new typologies.

In Red Vienna, children became synonymous with the "modern-day person" and the focus of a large-scale campaign to implement new social and health policies – and these technical advances didn't stop at funeral culture. Cremation was considered a socially just, hygienic, and progressive alternative to burial. As the practice was strictly rejected by the Catholic Church, Austria's first crematoria were erected in cities governed by the Social Democratic party. The interrelationship between politics, legislature, and social transformation was most evident in the construction of schools. Since the introduction of compulsory education under Empress Maria Theresia in 1774, school construction has been under the control of the state. Thus, educational spaces have been and continue to be ideologically biased elements of control.

Who are we? IMAGE

As a symbolic construct, the landscape plays an important role both in the way Austria sees itself and in how it is seen by others through the prism of tourism. At the 1937 World Fair in Paris, the transparent shell of the pavilion by Oswald Haerdtl became a vessel that exalted the photographic collages of panoramic Alpine roads, making the landscape a symbol of the nation. In the rooftop extension by Coop Himmelb(l)au, the provocative corner solution is a new take on the baroque dome and awakens the desire to celebrate space – a characteristic that, according to Wolf Prix, has for centuries distinguished Austrian architecture and made it distinctive. The intricate project was showcased as one of the key works in the 1988 exhibition Deconstructivist Architecture at the Museum of Modern Art in New York.[12] In this case, global cultural processes intertwine with local historical traditions.

This makes clear that an exclusively national historical perspective doesn't suffice and that architecture must always also be seen in the context of global processes. Identity assignments are constructs that fluctuate with the wind of cultural policy. For instance, the confessional openness that had prevailed under the Austro-Hungarian monarchy – despite the dominance of the Catholic Church – was not reintroduced until after 1945. In 1912, the Habsburg monarchy took a pioneering stance when it officially recognized Islam as a religious community with equal rights. The Austrian half of the monarchy supported an initiative to erect a mosque in Türkenschanzpark, though Austria's first mosque to explicitly represent its function wasn't built until the 1970s. In 2013, Bernardo Bader won the distinguished Aga Khan Award for his Islamic Cemetery in Vorarlberg. A mock-up of the cemetery's ornamental facade is on display in the permanent exhibition.

Discourse and Fascination

The protagonists of our permanent exhibition are objects, models, drawings, furniture, and textiles – including material from both prominent and less well-known projects, as well as from historical and current ones; in fact, the most recent project in the permanent exhibition is still under construction. Many of the exhibits are being shown here for the first time. The some 400 items on display are organized in seven sections corresponding to the seven Hot Questions. As the Cold Storage's bounty suggests, this amounts to a little less than 0.5 percent of our collection inventory. Each of the selected objects is given a literally custom-designed presentation in the permanent exhibition. The way the objects are displayed intrigues the visitors, encouraging them to welcome spontaneous encounters and stray from a linear path through the multifaceted exhibition in which the display objects are subject to an ongoing contextualization by our burning questions and in this way connected to the present. And not least, the objects themselves pose questions to each other. By juxtaposing objects that span epochs, styles, and ideologies, we give them a voice. They step out of their given project contexts and develop commonalities or discrepancies. They challenge each other and shake the foundations of the canon. We hope that visitors will leave the permanent exhibition with more questions than they came with.

What crystallized during our briefing with the designers was the desire to develop diverse environments for the varied narrative threads and the breadth of material. Neither can architecture history be comprehended without its context, nor can our conceptual approach be neutralized in a white cube or a homogeneous modular system. The seven visual thematic clusters with their subsections were arranged in variable spatial configurations by the two offices making up the design team: Tracing Spaces and seite zwei. The concept allows visitors to choose their own paths through the exhibition. Hierarchies are avoided, and the exhibition design uses colors, differentiated lighting, and material characteristics to accentuate the mediality and materiality of the display objects.

Research and presentation enter into a reciprocity. Our methodological approach aims at bringing history to the fore and activating it for the present day. With the permanent exhibition at the Az W we do not write a new narrative over existing knowledge; rather, through the exhibition we expand our approach and take other perspectives and protagonists into consideration. It is a permanent exhibition that tackles two tasks: it shows great examples from Austrian architecture history and ponders the basic question as to the role of architecture in society. It shows both what architecture can do and the potential of an architecture collection.

1   SammlungsLab #1: The Terrassenhaus. A Viennese Fetish? 10/19/2017–1/8/2018, curators: Lorenzo De Chiffre, Monika Platzer; SammlungsLab #2: Stadt des Kindes. On a Failed Utopia, 4/17–5/28/2018, curator: Monika Platzer; SammlungsLab #3: Roland Rainer. (Un)Disputed. New Findings on the Work (1936–1963), 10/20/2018–1/7/2019, curators: Ingrid Holzschuh, Waltraud P. Indrist, Monika Platzer; SammlungsLab #4: Hans Hollein unpacked. The Haas-Haus, 6/13–8/9/2019, curator: Mechthild Ebert; SammlungsLab #5: Vorarlberg – An Intergenerational Dialogue, 12/5/2019–2/10/2020 and 5/19–9/5/2020 at vai, Dornbirn, curator: Sonja Pisarik.

2   Dietmar Steiner was the founding director of the Architekturzentrum Wien and headed it from 1993 to 2016. Angelika Fitz has served as director of the Az W since 2017.

3   Land for Us All, 12/9/2020–7/19/2021 exhibition at the Az W; from 2020 to 2022 shown at more than 20 venues in Austrian cities and communities; curators: Karoline Mayer, Katharina Ritter; publication: Karoline Mayer, Katharina Ritter, Angelika Fitz, Architekturzentrum Wien (eds.), *Boden für Alle* (Zurich, 2020).

4   Critical Care. Architecture and Urbanism for a Broken Planet, 4/25–9/9/2019 exhibition at the Az W; from 2020 to 2021 shown at venues in Berlin, Dresden, Zurich, Dornbirn, Antwerp; curators: Angelika Fitz, Elke Krasny; publication: Angelika Fitz, Elke Krasny, Architekturzentrum Wien (eds.), *Critical Care. Architecture and Urbanism for a Broken Planet* (Cambridge, MA, 2019).

5   Cold War and Architecture, 10/17/2019–2/24/2020 exhibition at the Az W; curator: Monika Platzer; publication: Monika Platzer, Architekturzentrum Wien (eds.), *Cold War and Architecture. The Competing Forces that Reshaped Austria after 1945* (Zurich, 2020).

6   Form Follows Rule, 11/23/2017–4/4/2018 exhibition at the Az W; curators: Martina Frühwirth, Karoline Mayer, Katharina Ritter.

7   The Force is in the Mind. The Making of Architecture, 10/16/2008–2/2/2009 exhibition at the Az W; curator: Elke Krasny; publication: Elke Krasny, Architekturzentrum Wien (eds.), *The Force is in the Mind. The Making of Architecture* (Basel, 2008).

8   Downtown Denise Scott Brown, 11/22/2018–3/24/2019 exhibition at the Az W; curators: Jeremy Eric Tenenbaum, Angelika Fitz, Katharina Ritter; publication: Jeremy Eric Tenenbaum with Denise Scott Brown, Angelika Fitz, Katharina Ritter, Architekturzentrum Wien (eds.), *Your Guide to Downtown Denise Scott Brown* (Zurich, 2018).

9   Yasmeen Lari. Architecture for the Future, 3/9/2023–8/16/2023 exhibition at the Az W; curators: Angelika Fitz, Elke Krasny, Marvi Mazhar; publication: Angelika Fitz, Elke Krasny, Marvi Mazhar, and Architekturzentrum Wien (eds.), *Yasmeen Lari. Architecture for the Future* (Cambridge, MA, 2023).

10   x projects by arbeitsgruppe 4. Holzbauer, Kurrent, Spalt (1950–1970), 3/4–5/31/2010 exhibition at the Az W; curators: Sonja Pisarik, Ute Waditschatka; publication: Sonja Pisarik, Ute Waditschatka, Architekturzentrum Wien (eds.), *arbeitsgruppe 4. Wilhelm Holzbauer, Friedrich Kurrent, Johannes Spalt. 1950–1979* (Salzburg, 2010); Architektur in Wien um 1900, 5/20–8/23/1964 exhibition at the Österreichisches Bauzentrum, Liechtenstein Garden Palace, Vienna, curators: arbeitsgruppe 4; Traum und Wirklichkeit. Wien 1870–1930, 3/27–10/6/1985 exhibition at the Künstlerhaus Wien, curator: Hans Hollein.

11   Margaret Thatcher in an interview: "Aids, education and the year 2000!" for *Woman's Own*, October 31, 1987, https://www.margaretthatcher.org/document/106689 (accessed August 28, 2022).

12   Wolf D. Prix, Thomas Kramer (eds.), *Prinz Eisenbeton 6: Rock over Barock. Young and Beautiful: 7+2* (Vienna 2006); Philip Johnson, Mark Wigley, *Deconstructivist Architecture*, exh. cat. Museum of Modern Art, New York, 6/23–8/30/1988, (New York, 1988).

Keep it Hot

Programmatic Thoughts on the Collection of the Architekturzentrum Wien

Monika Platzer

Museum collections are distribution nodes, they serve as points of departure for questioning the past, present, and future and making these visible.

Like many of the European architecture museums, in its collection activity, the Architekturzentrum Wien is nationally oriented. New approaches are now needed to reveal the economic and cultural cross-border interconnections that have existed throughout the territorial changes Austria has undergone over the centuries.[1]

View of Hall 5 at the depot in Möllersdorf | Photo: Az W

In present-day research, viewing the collection from a strictly national perspective is obsolete.[2] Approaches gleaned from global history help to overcome the Eurocentric scope of national history and open new perspectives for a boundary-crossing transnational historiography. Once history is denationalized, two things happen: first, the overproportionate male power relationships and interpretational sovereignty of the global north become apparent, and second, the thought space opens up to a plurality of narrations, which diverges from the master narrations and illustrates the otherwise suppressed cross-cultural and transregional worlds of experience of many ethnic groups.

As a result, museum institutions take on a new role, going from self-appointed, purportedly "neutral/objective" observers to active players. Museums and exhibition halls are no longer satisfied with merely imparting contexts and effects, but are prepared to face up to the political and societal contexts in which the institutional conditions of their activity are embedded. In addition to their significance as historical sources, the materials found in collections are also always proof of strategic choice made by the originator, the legal entity, and the collecting institution. They are pieces of evidence that express an act of will. The scientific discourse addresses and reflects upon sociopolitical contexts and power relationships. In addition to writing collection and exhibition history, museum practice also always writes architecture history.

Looking Back

In 1979, accompanying the paradigm shift from the modern to the postmodern age and hand in hand with the increased interest in historical sources and in architecture per se, the International Confederation of Architectural Museums (ICAM)[3] was founded. The first convention of the international panel of professionals dedicated to the research and promotion of architecture was held in Helsinki and prompted the founding of countless architectural institutions, including the Canadian Center for Architecture (CCA) in Montreal (1979), the Institut français d'Architecture (IFA) in Paris (1981), the Deutsches Architekturmuseum (DAM) in Frankfurt (1983), the Netherlands Architecture Institute (NAI, today: Het Nieuwe Instituut, Museum voor Architectuur, Design en Digitale Cultuur) in Rotterdam (1988), and the Estonian Museum of Architecture in Tallinn (1991).

In 1993, in the slipstream of these new architecture museums and through the support of the City of Vienna and Austrian Federal Government, the Architekturzentrum Wien (Az W) was founded, and through the diverse programming efforts of its founding director Dietmar Steiner (until 2016) it soon took on a role model function.

From the beginning – as is reflected in its founding postulate "Das Architekturzentrum ist ein Zentrum der Architektur" – the Az W has viewed itself as a place focusing on vital themes and present-day architecture. Nonetheless, the last of the four programmatic pillars defined in the founding phase (present architecture, discuss architecture, publish architecture, archive architecture) implied a potential focus on collection.

These declarations were soon put into action, and just one year later, the archive of Oswald Haerdtl (1899–1959) was taken over for processing by the architect Adolph Stiller. With the acquisition of the archive of a pronounced protagonist of Viennese Modernism, the Az W announced it would be launching a programmatic series with a focus on Austrian Modernism. This became the theme for 1999 with retrospectives of Hans Steineder, Erich Franz Leischner, and Oswald Haerdtl.[4] The ambiguity of the word "weg" in the motto "Weg mit der Moderne?" left room for interpretation. Did it mean "Away with Modernism?" or "A path with Modernism"? Questions raised by the exhibition and catalog focused on the continuities and discrepancies within the architects' œuvres as well as the interplay between the changes in the political circumstances, local power structures, and aesthetic orientations.

An initial milestone on the road to becoming an architecture museum was the exhibition Architecture in the 20th Century –

Austria, which the Az W (curators: Otto Kapfinger, Dietmar Steiner, Adolph Stiller, Kurt Zweifel) presented in collaboration with the Deutsches Architekturmuseum (DAM) on the occasion of the Frankfurt Book Fair in 1995, when Austria was the guest of honor. To this day, it remains the most comprehensive portrayal of Austrian twentieth-century architecture shown abroad. At the same time, the exhibition laid the foundations for the project collection of the Az W, which has continued to expand steadily along the lines of our exhibition program.[5]

When the City of Vienna transferred the Friedrich Achleitner Archive to the Architekturzentrum Wien in 1999, it not only helped the Az W to continue expanding its scientific competence, but the digitalization project comprising more than 22,000 object index cards and more than 66,000 photo negatives also laid the cornerstone for our digital collection management. From the 1960s on, Friedrich Achleitner rose to the position of chronicler of a systematic compilation of Austria's built environment. Achleitner's multiple-volume guide continues to shape our knowledge and understanding of recent Austrian architecture and consolidates a canon upon which architecture historiography is still based today, although Achleitner himself maintained a critical view of it throughout his lifetime.

In March 2004, the Architekturzentrum Wien celebrated the opening of the first phase of the a_show, which, once completed in October 2005, would present a survey of architecture in Austria in the 20th and 21st centuries arranged in eleven thematic-chronological episodes (Prologue, Red Vienna, Landscape, Power, Reconstruction, International, System, Utopia, Collage, The Present, Housing). In terms of content, the permanent exhibition focused on specific features or developments in Austrian architecture from 1850 to the present, condensing these into a visual anthology.[6] Curated by Gabriele Kaiser and Monika Platzer, the a_show remained in place until 2021, providing a concentrated and comprehensive cross section of Austrian architectural practice for more than 17 years and serving in this way as one of the pioneers of this presentation format among the specialized museums both in Austria and abroad.[7]

A groundbreaking policy decision and new approach in the a_show saw the incorporation of Austrofascist and National Socialist architectural production into the overall narrative. Addressing the political changes – from the end of the First Republic to Austrofascism and National Socialism to postwar reconstruction – led to surprising insights about Austrian Modernism, and rather than revealing discrepancies, it brought continuities to light. The selected materials were generated from the resources of the Friedrich Achleitner Archive, an inventory in which object-specific primary and secondary materials had been compiled over the course of decades. In contrast to this, with the twentieth-anniversary exhibition Az W Gold – The Collection in 2013, the Az W put its own activity and holdings front and center for the first time by presenting original material, including plans, drawings, models, furniture, and photographs – all from its own archives.[8]

Following the founding phase, structural challenges caused delays in the implementation of the Az W's mandate to collect the archives of Austrian architects.[9] On May 5, 2008, the Az W hosted the "Evening of the Collection" with prominent protagonists of Austrian architecture, kicking off an active collection strategy of acquiring archives that continues to this day. Less than one percent of the then "unknown collection," which is kept in a storehouse outside of Vienna – in Möllersdorf – was shown in the exhibition Az W Gold.[10] Along with the many highlights from the collection, narrations gave visitors an in-depth look behind the scenes of our collection practice, showing them where the archives come from, how they are stored and

View of the former permanent exhibition, entitled a_show. Austrian Architecture in the 20th and 21st Centuries, which was shown at the Az W from 2004 to 2021 | Photo: Pez Hejduk

processed, and how we work with the protagonists, including those of our most recent acquisitions. The narratives were tied together by the motto "Bringing background to the foreground and making it visible." Meanwhile, the collection has grown steadily and the inventory consists of the following:

Analogue collection:
    approx. 100 architects' archives
    approx. 400 individual projects
    Friedrich Achleitner Archive
    Margherita Spiluttini Photo Archive (100,000 photographs)
    Karin Mack Photo Archive (2,000 photographs)

Virtual collection:[11]
    Encyclopaedia of Architects (1,700 entries)
    Architecture Archive Austria (2,600 entries)
    Soviet Modernism 1955–1991 (650 projects)

Thinking with the Collection
In the Az W Collection, the concept of architecture is interpreted broadly. Along with the work, its authorship, and all the aesthetic and building cultural dimensions we dedicate ourselves to multidimensionality and plurality. We do not view collecting architecture as a monothematic activity; in our minds, the role played by clients, users, critics, politicians, and legal entities is as important in the development of architecture as the role played by architects. These interlocking relationships, schools of thought, power structures, as well as continuities, discrepancies, and ideologies can be seen in the countless design drawings, sketches, technical drawings, models, visual media, biographical

documentation records, theoretical texts, and even official letters, documents, bookkeeping records, and correspondences. Along with the creative and architectural aspects of the origin and realization of "built culture," the Az W follows a collection strategy that transcends the usual bounds of the discipline of architecture and in addition to architecture history always also reflects contemporary, social, political, migration, global, economic, and technological history.

Researching and Exhibiting
Let us go back to the birth of our collection. The few women who were present at the "Evening of the Collection" were architects' wives or partners or, at best, responsible for the back office. Over the years, the (mostly male) narrative perspectives have been consolidated into master narratives. The field of gender studies has helped to open up new perspectives and pose new questions to architecture, such as those involving misrepresentations in the canon. There is a great desideratum for women role models in architecture history. It is, therefore, astonishing that, despite the structural discrimination, researchers at the Margarete Schütte-Lihotzky Center – our partner in the project "Vienna's Pioneering Women in Architecture" – have found documentation of more than 200 women who were enrolled in Austrian architecture schools prior to 1938.[12] Bringing these architects to light and realigning the canon is one of our long-term research goals. In 2022, for instance, we hosted the international workshop that focused on rediscovering Ella Briggs (1880–1977), an outstanding proponent of modernism who worked in Austria, the United States, Germany, and Great Britain.[13]

Our objective, however, is not to focus on women architects, that is to say, not necessarily to include projects by women in the master narrative. Our main concern is raising consciousness about social inequalities – for example, the strict patriarchal system that denied women access to the education system. The investigative look at architecture schools in the new permanent exhibition shows the structural disadvantage of women architects and reveals the continuing effects of a gender-specific discrimination in procedures for professorship appointments. The first woman to be appointed professor of architecture in Austria was Eda Schaur, who accepted this position at the Institute for Structure and Design at the University of Innsbruck in 1995; shortly thereafter Nasrine Seraji (1996–2001) was appointed professor at the Academy of Fine Arts Vienna.

With our collection, we make an active attempt to connect with those academic discourse formations reflected in our exhibition narratives, events, or our own research projects. At the moment, we are conducting three research projects at national and international levels, for which the Az W collection serves as a research partner. The research project financed by the EU entitled "Communities of Tacit Knowledge: Architecture and its Ways of Knowing (TACK)" gathers ten major academic institutions, three leading cultural architectural institutions, as well as nine distinguished architecture design offices. Collaboratively these partners offer an innovative PhD training program on the nature of tacit knowledge in architecture. This silent and non-formalized knowledge is a highly relevant set of instruments that connects intellectual and practical work and supports relationships between various disciplines and fields of science.[14] The research project "Transnational School Construction" headed by Maja Lorbek investigates transnational knowledge exchange in the field of school construction between Austria, Slovenia, and the German Democratic Republic after 1945.[15] In many of the architects' bequests there are numerous "gray items," meaning typescripts and manuscripts from legal entities and individuals which had not been available to the public. Entire bundles of unsorted documents and conference reports of the School Building Commission, which was established in 1951 within the International Union of Architects (UIA), have meanwhile been processed in our inventory. They document countless instances of intensive international exchange among architects. Particularly after 1945, architecture became a collective project, and overarching formulations of questions led toward a transnational history of architecture, a history of transfer, as well as a history of differences and similarities.[16]

In architecture, the themes antisemitism and racism and the accompanying question as to the responsibility of the architects continue to be very hotly debated issues both in the public sphere and among fellow professionals. Taking the Austrian capital as an example, in 2015 we examined the Third Reich's broad spectrum of construction and planning activity and presented some of our findings in the exhibition Vienna. The Pearl of the Reich. Planning for Hitler.[17] The exhibition was based on material never before presented to the public consisting of plans, photographs, and documents compiled by the architect and urban planner Klaus Steiner over the course of decades and turned over to the Az W in 2011 for scientific processing. The identity construct of the "Second Republic" of Austria, which sees itself as the victim of National Socialism, has delayed the process of working through the past in Austria – as compared to Germany. By mapping source documents and

"Evening of the Collection," attended by several of Austria's protagonists in the field of architecture, May 5, 2008 | Photo: Az W

biographical traces, Ingrid Holzschuh, Waltraud P. Indrist, and Monika Platzer, the curators of the exhibition Roland Rainer. (Un)Disputed. New Findings on the Work (1936–1963),[18] attempted to shed light on the scientific discourse as well as the political objectives of the institutions and players involved. Along a timeline, historical events (the current events of the day), official directives (instruments of National Socialist policy), institutional histories (Deutsche Akademie für Städtebau, Reichs- und Landesplanung und Technische Planung Ost), architectural control elements (urban planning concepts), and biographies of key players are juxtaposed with Roland Rainer's own biography. Through the comparison of manifold sources, Roland Rainer's life and work are for the first time examined in connection with the Nazi research machine and his biography mapped within the complex web of interrelationships. The line of reasoning and questions produced by our investigative approach to the exhibition have subsequently earned us a grant for a research project in collaboration with the Academy of Fine Arts Vienna.[19]

This method of mapping – the unweighted juxtaposition of plans, concepts, statistics, correspondences, and visual media – continues to be applied in the permanent exhibition. This produces a multi-perspective view of architecture that is not based solely on the objectness, but gives various frames of reference equal consideration, thus allowing a broader range of interpretation of architecture.

Source mapping in the exhibition entitled Roland Rainer. (Un)Disputed. New Findings on the Work (1936–1963) | Photo: Az W

This brings up the question as to the existence of an "unpolitical" architecture, science, and culture per se. Culture, science, and politics have always been closely intertwined. A not insignificant share of architects see themselves as a driving force in reform and support political agendas indirectly or directly through their professional work. This focuses attention on the sociopolitical activity of architects. In this context the mechanisms of inclusion and exclusion – of legitimization and delegitimization, of the assignment of value and meaning – come to the fore as aspects which the permanent exhibition investigates in detail under the headings: "The Pendulum Swings: Migration and Politics," "Emancipation and Antisemitism," "Gender Firewall," and "Symbols of Power."

Center Stage – the new permanent exhibition's discursive discussion program – offers the opportunity to delve deeper into various themes from an aesthetic, historical, social, or political perspective and opens the door to the new and different beyond the confines of the exhibition.

Outlook and Lived Practice
The Az W collection sees itself today as an indispensable stock of evidence for object-related basic research. The collection practice of the founding phase – summarized by the shorthand title "Archiving Architecture" – was based on the activities of "collecting and preserving" as well as "making accessible and researching." Over time, these were expanded to include a third aspect: "networking and mediating." In other words, we generate social knowledge of architecture based on the questions developed from the material.

The focus is not on remembering and preserving individual experiences, but on the ever fructifying process of confronting research perspectives and questions that have relevance today. The idea is not to interpret the past from a present-day vantage point, nor is it to shift the focus away from the historical toward the contemporary. For this, the cultural historian Lynn Hunt coined the term "presentism,"[20] in which she sees the expression of moral superiority.

Our understanding of history is an approximation of the past that remains open to contemporary developments. Under the new director[21] our work on the collection will continue to be informed by current themes and will be made available to the public in temporary exhibitions and education programs.

In the permanent exhibition, the historical narrative is always presented in dialogue with diachronic layers of time and diverse protagonists. Many of the themes – for example, gender, globalization, social inequality, the planet, racism, and white supremacy – have long been omitted from the history of architecture. In order to track down, identify, close, and address these gaps in the collections, new approaches, categories, and descriptive systems are necessary. We see Hot Questions – Cold Storage as an initial step in calling into question our own conception of history, evaluating the related collection processes, and adapting them to new challenges. In my lived practice and as the head of collections and curator of the permanent exhibition, I negotiate the interdependencies of collecting and curating, inclusionary and exclusionary principles, and the construed and the contradictory. Taken together, my curatorial activity for the permanent exhibition produces spaces for supplements or corrections, which, in turn, stimulate or call for new areas of collection, because – as is often the case – the question arises whether it is a matter of the collection of the future or the future of the collection.

The pressure on the collection practice to present fragmentary content and the increased prevalence of digital material emphasize the cultural-political relevance of collection strategies more than ever. Collections straddle a line between truth and fiction. In the critical reflection of one's own archiving and collecting activity one recognizes that the focus must be not on the task of preservation but on a process of selection that addresses the following questions: How can structural diversity be expressed materially and made accessible? What does the recontextualization of the canon mean to us today? And why are collections so eminently important?

In the making: Preparation for the new exhibition | Photo: Az W

1   The Austro-Hungarian monarchy 1867–1918, the First Republic 1918–1938, the "Annexation" of Austria into the German Reich 1938–1945, the Second Republic 1945–1955 under allied occupation, Austria's neutrality from 1955 on, Austria joins the European Union 1995.

2   Julia Angster, "Nationalgeschichte und Globalgeschichte. Wege zu einer 'Denationalisierung' des historischen Blicks," in *Aus Politik und Zeitgeschichte* 68, 2018, 9–16, www.bpb.de/shop/zeitschriften/apuz/280566/nationalgeschichte-und-globalgeschichte/ (accessed August 29, 2022).

3   On the history of the ICAM see: Monika Platzer, ed., "ICAM 30 years," special issue, *icamprint* 03, January 20, 2009, https://icam-web.org/publications/icam-print-03/ (accessed 8/29/2022).

4   Monika Platzer, Architekturzentrum Wien (eds.), *Viel zu modern. Hans Steineder Architekt. 1904–1976*, exh. cat. Architekturzentrum Wien, 2/24–4/5/1999 (Salzburg, 1999); Erich Bernard, Barbara Feller, Karl Peyrer-Heimstätt, Architekturzentrum Wien (eds.), *Amt Macht Stadt. Erich Leischner und das Wiener Stadtbauamt*, exh. cat. Architekturzentrum Wien, 6/16–8/2/1999 (Salzburg, 1999); Adolph Stiller, Architekturzentrum Wien (eds.), *Oswald Haerdtl. Architekt und Designer. 1899–1959*, exh. cat. Ausstellungszentrum im Ringturm, 6/5–9/15/2000 (Salzburg, 2000).

5   Annette Becker, Dietmar Steiner, Wilfried Wang (eds.), *Architektur im 20. Jahrhundert Österreich*, exh. cat. Deutsches Architekturmuseum, 10/14/1995–1/14/1996 (Frankfurt am Main); Shedhalle, 5/24–8/10/1997 (St. Pölten), (Munich, 1995).

6   Gabriele Kaiser, Monika Platzer, Architekturzentrum Wien (eds.), *a_show. Architecture in Austria in the Twentieth and Twenty-first Centuries*, 2nd edition, (Zurich, 2016); 2nd stage: opening on 9/15/2004, 3rd stage: opening on 10/12/2005.

7   Ulf Gronvøld, "Permanent Architecture," in Monika Platzer (ed.), Permanent Exhibitions, *icamprint* 01, 2005, 14–23.

8   Az W Gold. The Collection, 3/21–7/22/2013, exhibition at the Az W.

9   The first decade was marked by structural measures in respect to building and human resources and at the same time the course was being set for an ongoing operation with permanent funding, which would for the first time make continuous programming possible.

10   Curators of the exhibition: Sonja Pisarik, Monika Platzer, Katrin Stingl, Ute Waditschatka.

11   Az W, Encyclopaedia of Architects, https://www.azw.at/en/articles/collection/encyclopaedia-of-architects/ (accessed August 29, 2022); Az W, Architektur Austria Gegenwart, https://www.azw.at/de/artikel/sammlung/architektur-austria-gegenwart/ (accessed August 29, 2022); Az W, Soviet Modernism 1955–1991, https://www.azw.at/de/artikel/sammlung/sowjetmoderne-1955-1991/ (accessed August 29, 2022).

12   Research project "Vienna's Pioneering Women in Architecture," Margarete Schütte-Lihotzky Center (Christine Zwingl, Sabina Riss, Carmen Trifina) in cooperation with the Az W (Monika Platzer), https://architekturpionierinnen.at/ (accessed August 29, 2022).

13   International workshop "Rediscovering Ella Briggs – The Challenge of Writing Inclusive Architectural Histories for Women Who Broke the Mold," concept and organization: Elana Shapira, Despina Stratigakos, Monika Platzer, 6/9/2022 at the Az W, www.azw.at/wp-content/uploads/2022/07/Ella-Briggs_International-Workshop_June-9_2022_Final.pdf (accessed August 29, 2022). A publication with Princeton University Press is forthcoming.

14   Research project "Communities of Tacit Knowledge: Architecture and its Ways of Knowing (TACK)" in conjunction with the Marie Skłodowska-Curie Research Program Horizon 2020 (no. 860413), duration: 2020–2023, academic partner: ETH Zürich, Delft University of Technology, KTH Royal Institute of Technology, Oslo School of Architecture and Design, University of Wuppertal, Politecnico di Milano, Academy of Fine Arts Vienna, University of Antwerp, University College London, Leibniz University Hannover; non-academic partners: Het Nieuwe Instituut, Vlaams Architectuurinsitut, Architekturzentrum Wien, Architecten Jan De Vylder Vinck, Korteknie Stuhlmacher Architecten, Spridd, De Smet Vermeulen architecten, Cityfoerster, One Fine Day architects, SOMA Architecture, Onsite studio, Haworth Tompkins, https://tacit-knowledge-architecture.com/ (accessed August 29, 2022).

15   FWF research project "Transnational School Construction" (P 33248), duration: 2020–2024, Maja Lorbek, University of Applied Arts Vienna (leader), Oliver Sukrow, Technische Universität Wien (national research partner), Monika Platzer, Architekturzentrum Wien (institutional research partner), Susanne Rick, Architekturzentrum Wien (scientific staff), https://transnationalarchitecture.org/ (accessed August 29, 2022).

16   See: "Cold Transfer. Architecture, Politics, Culture. Germany – Austria – Switzerland after 1945," symposium 1/24–1/25/2020 at the Az W, www.azw.at/de/termin/cold-transfer-architektur-politik-kultur/ (accessed August 29, 2022).

17   'Vienna. The Pearl of the Reich.' Planning for Hitler, 3/19–8/17/2015, exhibition at the Az W; curators: Ingrid Holzschuh, Monika Platzer; publication: Ingrid Holzschuh, Monika Platzer, Architekturzentrum Wien (eds.), *'Vienna. The Pearl of the Reich.' Planning for Hitler* (Zurich, 2015).

18   SammlungsLab #3, 10/20/2018–1/7/2019.

19   Research project supported by the Austrian Science Fund (FWF) "Ambivalences of Modernity. The Architect and City Planner Roland Rainer Between Dictatorship and Democracy" (P 34938-G), duration: 2022–2024, Angelika Schnell (leader), Ingrid Holzschuh, Waltraud P. Indrist, Susanne Rick, Academy of Fine Arts Vienna, Monika Platzer, Architekturzentrum Wien.

20   Lynn Hunt, "Against Presentism," in: *Perspectives on History*, 5/1/2002, www.historians.org/publications-and-directories/perspectives-on-history/may-2002/against-presentism (accessed August 29, 2022); see also: Barry Bergdoll, "Exhibiting History in a Period of Presentism, or should we still be collecting archives?," lecture, icam 17 (Montreal/New York 2014).

21   The concept for Hot Questions – Cold Storage was developed by Angela Fitz, who has been the Director of the Az W since 2017, and Monika Platzer, who is a curator and heads the Az W's collections.

Collections that Speak Back:

Decolonizing the Architecture of Narratives and Holdings

Tom Avermaete

In the past few decades, we have become wary of the collections maintained by architectural archives and museums. It is no longer possible to think of collections as records that neutrally reflect an architectural or urban design practice. Instead, we have learned to look at them as carefully constructed assemblages that are meant to articulate, for instance, a heroic narrative about their producers. The instrumentality of collections

G. Wingendorp | Museum Wormianum | Leiden, 1655 | The Wellcome Collection

in shaping a particular image of architects and urban designers – but also their complicity in maintaining canonical viewpoints and narratives – has been revealed and scrutinized. Conventional collections have increasingly become typified as "compromised sources of knowledge" that urgently need thematic revision and expansion.

In reaction to these critical perspectives, strong calls for decolonizing the archive and de-centering the collection narrative have gained traction. This has not only resulted in initiatives for new collections pertaining to previously underrepresented actors such as female architects or urban designers. It has also altered the acquisition and presentation policies of several collecting institutions.

Against this background, it is no coincidence that the exhibition Hot Questions, Cold Storage confronts us with one of the most important concerns for contemporary museums and archives: How do the perspectives that we have today relate to the collection items and their histories? In other words, how can we think of the relationship between the manifest values of current narratives and the latent meanings of historical holdings?

Of Narratives and Collections

In order to address such issues, it is worthwhile to explore the age-old relation between narratives and collections by looking at two prototypical exhibitions. The first is the so-called Wunderkammer, a collection of curiosities assembled by the Danish antiques collectors and physician Ole Worm in 1655 as part of his Museum Wormianum.[1] Worm's collection was driven by curiosity. It has no predetermined narrative but is rather an associative assemblage of elements.[2] Worm himself entitled his collection rerum rariorum. His associative way of collecting transpires in the curation of the exhibition, which seems to be a free accumulation of different elements. The second example is the Eastern Zoological Gallery in the British Museum in London, designed by architect Robert Smirke (1823–1828) and with objects provided by chemist Charles Hatchet and physician and naturalist Hans Sloane. Scientific development drove the composition of this collection. Consequently, the pieces in the exhibition are arranged to exemplify the scientific theories of biological evolution of the day.

These two exhibitions represent two curatorial regimes. In Ole Worm's Wunderkammer, shells are placed next to figurines, and the remains of animals feature beside jewellery and tools. Worm's museum exemplifies an open approach to collecting and presenting. The observer is invited to make associations and connections across objects and shelves, between human and non-human species, and between nature and culture. The objects in the British Museum's zoological gallery illustrate a preexisting theory of evolution. Following well-established scientific narratives, the so-called lower species of shells and fish are situated on the lower shelves. The birds are located in the middle, and the presumably most noble of all species, the human being, is at the very top of the wall. The presentation of the different objects is firmly situated in scientific discourse. Visitors to the exhibition were not meant to associate freely, but rather to understand the various objects in the semantic frame of evolutionary theory (including a hierarchy of animals) commonly held during the nineteenth century. Worm's Wunderkammer and the British Museum's zoological gallery illustrate the difference between what I refer to as the "associative" and "discursive" ways of collecting and exhibiting that informed many museums and galleries in the nineteenth century.

The Dominance of the Discursive

Similar curatorial attitudes are discernible in the field of architecture. British architect John Soane's collection of cork and plaster scale models is a case in point.[3] Assembled between 1800 and 1834 following personal experiences during his grand tour in the South of Europe, the collection contains models of buildings and ruins that had impressed him. Soane's model room is a typical example of an associative way of collecting and presenting architecture. Models of Pompeii and Paestum figure next to other ancient sites.

In the nineteenth century, another approach to exhibiting architecture became predominant. With the emergence of the first galleries and museums exclusively dedicated to architecture, a more discursive mode of curating architectural collections emerged.[4] This was, for instance, the case when in 1806, the French theorist and architect Jacques-Guillaume Legrand inaugurated "a complete museum of architecture" in Paris, which offered a visual history of the art of building during

The British Museum's Great Zoological Gallery | London, 1845 | Wood engraving | The Wellcome Collection

the classical period.[5] Based on a selection of architectural casts and artefacts from the Parisian École d'Architecture, as well as on the architectural models and images assembled by artist and architect Louis-François Cassas, the exhibition in the museum confirmed a well-established historical narrative. It mainly validated the canonical discourse on the evolution of classical architecture, as argued by architect and professor Jean-Nicolas Louis Durand in his book *Recueil et parallèle*, published in 1801.[6]

This discursive way of organizing architectural exhibitions would remain the rule throughout the twentieth century. The first exhibitions of the Schusev State Museum of Architecture, founded in 1934 in Moscow, were primarily based on established narratives of Russian architecture and contributed to the further canonization of neo-classical architects such as Vasili Bazhenov and Matvey Kazakov.[7] In the presentations of the permanent collections of the Finnish Architecture Museum, inaugurated in 1956, or the Dutch Architecture Institute (NAi), which was established in 1993, this strong relation between canonical architectural histories and the presentation of collections continued to be the dominant curatorial paradigm.[8] Time and time again, collections were presented as the sheer affirmation of the narratives that critics and historians had previously produced.

In the past decades, however, our historical narratives have increasingly come under scrutiny. Architectural historians and theoreticians have questioned, problematized, and discarded the conventional ways of narrating architecture and have called for revised perspectives. These revisions not only fundamentally alter the canonical histories of architecture, but also affect the way that we present and exhibit architectural collections.

Death of the Author

A first revision relates to the notion of the author and authorship. Indeed, well into the twentieth century, the idea of approaching architecture through the perspective of heroic male authors was well-established. Very often, architectural historiography professed that the agency of the design and realization of buildings lay with individual architects, who seemed to single-handedly propel these processes. In the past decades, however, we have realized that this singular understanding of the architect as the heroic leading actor in the built environment does not correspond to the urban and architectural realities.

As a result, this perspective on authorship has been amended in two ways. First, under the influence of several waves of feminism and gender studies, scholars have expanded historiographic views to include previously marginalized actors, including females, gays, and queers, in the center of our histories. The work of Dolores Hayden, Hilde Heynen and Gulsum Baydar, and of Jane Rendell, Barbara Penner, and Iain Borden, to only name a few, have radically changed our understanding of who participates in the production of the built environment and how cultural predispositions play a decisive role.[9]

The exhibition Hot Questions, Cold Storage participates in this expansion of authorship. It not only surfaces a variety of so-called "other" categories of stakeholders, but also problematizes the hierarchic relations that various actors maintain. For instance, in the section "Who shapes the city?" under the header "All citizens are equal before the law," we learn from Lina Loos about gender inequality in legal urban matters; she advises being "adamant that women who bring furniture and an apartment into a marriage should have their ownership documented so that in case of divorce she is not simply shown the door."[10]

A second way we have amended perspectives on authorship is by moving histories of architecture beyond the agency of the architect. We have come to realize that the appearance of buildings and neighborhoods is equally dependent on the agency of other actors, including politicians, commissioners, constructors, and, of course, inhabitants. The many encounters, confrontations, and collaborations between these different actors seems to be generative of new buildings and neighborhoods.

Telling our histories as the complex and ambiguous negotiation between these different actors seems to be an adequate way to reflect the intricacy of the production of the built environment. Hot Questions, Cold Storage offers such an idea of multi-authorship in which politicians, critics, surveyors, and citizens all figure as producers of architecture and the city, next to architects. Policy maker Hugo Breitner – a retired bank director subsequently appointed Vienna's lead councillor for financial policy who introduced a tax on luxury goods that profoundly influenced the city's housing stock – is but one example of how the built environment is understood as a multi-authored matter. Throughout the exhibition we learn that the development of architecture culture in Austria does not depend on individual actors, but rather emerges from the contact zones between a variety of human and non-human actors.

John Soane | Model room | Engraving, 1835 | Courtesy of Sir John Soane's Museum London

Death of the Centre
In addition to questioning the idea of authorship, recent decades have also brought an in-depth critical reflection on the geographical definitions that we have projected on architecture culture. Numerous are the examples of architectural studies that have taken the nation state and its borders as point of departure. Publications with titles like *Brazil Builds, New Japanese Architecture, or A Hundred Years of Dutch Architecture 1901–2000* are commonplace.[11] In the past few decades, however, we have learned that architecture culture is not a matter that is constrained by nineteenth century circumscriptions of nation states. On the contrary, studies have demonstrated that architecture and urban design are transnational and cross-cultural matters. Recently, several global architectural histories have emerged that are no longer organized solely according to national or regional categories, but relate the design and thinking of architecture to broader processes and flows.

The books on global architecture by Francis Ching, Vikram Prakash and Mark Jarzombek; Kathleen James-Chakraborty; and Richard Ingersoll and Spiro Kostoff are good examples of such cross-cultural analysis.[12] These studies render an alternative image of architecture culture in which people were travelling across geographies: think of the architects, but also commissioners and craftspeople working outside the confines of their home nations. Similarly, architectural ideas, concepts, and even materials embarked on mediated or actual voyages through geographies. This is also the case for the many of the protagonists that figure in Hot Questions, Cold Storage. Under the headers "Who are we?" and "More than a Small Nation" we are confronted with figures such Bruno Kreisky, who was named the first Minister of Foreign Affairs after Austria regained independence in 1955 and not only helped to propel Kurt Waldheim to the position of secretary-general of the United Nations (1971–1981), but also secured the commission for a so-called UN City in Vienna for the Austrian architect Johann Staber. Though it was erected on national territory, the architecture of this new UN neighborhood was clearly a transnational matter.

Death of the Synchronic
A last big change in our perspectives on architecture relates to what can be labelled as the transition from the synchronic to the diachronic. For a very long time, architectural studies have had the tendency to present architecture in a synchronic and linear manner. From Nikolaus Pevsner's *Pioneers of Modern Design* (1960) to Leonardo Benevolo's well-known architectural history of modern architecture (1998) – in three tomes engaging with "the industrial revolution," "the modern movement," and "the postwar conflicts" – architectural history has been written as an evolutionary narrative.[13] Time and again, architectural culture has been depicted as the outcome of gradual and linear development of key moments, be it artistic, technological or social.

Recent scholarship opens a different perspective. It invites us to look upon phenomena in a more diachronic fashion. The study *Imperfect Health*, which is concerned with the recurrent question of the medicalization of architectural space trough time, and the publication *Casablanca-Chandigarh*, which focuses on the discrepancies of simultaneous urban realities from a comparative perspective, are good examples.[14] Such diachronic approaches to architecture culture can also be found in the exhibition Hot Questions, Cold Storage, in which perennial questions such as '"How do we want to live?" do not illustrate progressive development, but rather speak about periodically recurring issues and viewpoints. Indeed, time and time again, architects and other actors in Austria have asked and re-asked these fundamental questions, right until today.

Hot Questions, Cold Storage illuminates how the perspectives that have been introduced in the last few decades to revise the canonical historiographies of architecture also offer the opportunity to rethink the relationship between narratives and collections. The exhibition rearranges the rapport between hot questions and cold storage by asking seven distinct questions: Who shapes the city? Who gets involved? How is architecture produced? Who provides for us? How can we survive? Who are we? How do we want to live? This frame of recurrent questions enables new assemblages of the material contained in the Az W archives. It illustrates how incomplete answers, or possibly more questions, are embedded within the collections.

Reflexivity, or the Collection as Counterstatement
Collections, however, do not so easily lend themselves to being framed in a particular narrative, nor in a set of seven questions, irrespective of how open they may be. Rather collections speak back to frames. Directly, or indirectly, they have the capacity to offer a counterstatement to the narrative in which they are situated.

This becomes visible in the section entitled "Elements." Within the frame of "Inspiration," we find survey documents about building in the Kathmandu Valley by Carl Pruscha (1975) and anonymous construction in northern Burgenland by Ronald Rainer (1961).[15] Looking at these publications, it is clear that they functioned as sources of inspiration for designers.

Still, they also raise questions about their construction of an exotic "other" that allowed the reader-architects to understand their own positions as more sophisticated, complex, or even superior to the others. This is what I call the reflexivity of the collection; the capacity of the different pieces that are exhibited to criticize and even contradict the frame in which they are located in the first place. This "speaking back" typically opens new alleys of thought. It raises further questions.

The reflexivity of the exhibition, however, extends further still. Regardless of their age, when presented in an exhibition, collections have the capacity to reach beyond their original time frame. One of the main sections of Hot Questions, Cold Storage asks "Who shapes the city?" While the exhibition tackles the question by focusing on capitalist and anti-capitalist tendencies – including the context of Red Vienna at the beginning of the twentieth century – it also holds up a mirror to our current situation. As a reflection, the exhibition problematizes not only the declining role of the state in the production of the contemporary city, but also questions the enduring role of capitalism in its various declinations. In addition, it invites us to reflect upon the capacity of other actors, beyond state and market, to produce the city.

Re-assembling Narratives and Collections
Exhibitions also have another capacity: they can spatially re-assemble perspectives. Contrary to a book, which has a certain linearity and which always places one concern, or view, before the other, an exhibition has the ability to spatialize items and thereby create a certain simultaneity and co-existence of perspectives. This is an essential capacity. After all, the revised perspectives I have introduced – questioning authorship, geographies, and synchronicity – are not hierarchical. On the contrary, they are all important and must be considered simultaneously to construct new narratives on architecture and the city.

This re-assembling capacity seems to be at work in Hot Questions, Cold Storage. The exhibition allows the visitors to consider a set of questions at once, for example: Who are we? How is architecture produced? Who shapes the city? They may also imagine – visually and intellectually – new connections between these issues. This polyperspectivity allows visitors to simultaneously consider different vantage points and confronts them within the single space of the exhibition.

The ability to re-assemble also affects the difference between associative and discursive ways of exhibiting; between Ole Worm's Wunderkammer and the British Museum's zoological gallery. Regarding the exhibition at hand, it seems that this distinction is no longer valid. To put it differently, it appears that in Hot Questions, Cold Storage, the associative and the discursive modes have begun to work together. Clusters of discourses, in the form of seven perennial questions, spark the associations of the visitors. These associations, in turn, will question the exhibition's narrative and thereby suggest new connections, fields of tension, and ways of looking at architecture.

In between an associative and discursive way of presenting collections, a new idea emerges in Hot Questions, Cold Storage; the idea of the exhibition as an investigation. The investigation I refer to is not that of the Az W's curators, scholars and collaborators, but rather of those visiting the exhibition. In the end, that is what a collection can do: it can speak back to the visitors and, as such, provide a basis to ask new hot questions.

1   For an introduction to the work of Ole Worm, see for instance: Rafael Romero Reveron and Luis A. Arráez-Aybar, "Ole Worm (1588–1654) – anatomist and antiquarian," *European Journal of Anatomy* 19, (2015), 299–301.

2   A description of the various elements can be found in Ole Worm's book: Ole Worm, *Museum Wormianum, Seu Historia Rerum Rariorum, Tam Naturalium, Quam Artificialium, Tam Domesticarum, Quam Exoticarum, Quae Hafniae Danorum in Aedibus Authoris Servantur* (Lugduni Batavorum: Apud Iohannem Elsevirivm, 1655).

3   For an introduction to Soane and his scale models, see: Peter Thornton and Helen Dorey, *Sir John Soane: The Architect As Collector, 1753–1837* (New York, 1992); Margaret Richardson and John Taylor, *Soane's Cork Models* (London, 2011) and Mary Anne Stevens, *John Soane, Architect: Master of Space and Light* (London, 2015).

4   For an introduction to the architecture museum, see for example: Werner Szambien, *Le Musée D'Architecture* (Paris, 1988).

5   This collection was described in: Louis-François Cassas and Jacques-Guillaume Legrand, *Collection Des Chefs-D'œuvre De L'architecture Des Différens Peuples: Exécutés En Modèles* (Paris, 1806).

6   Jean-Nicolas-Louis Durand: *Recueil et parallèle des édifices de tout genre, anciens et modernes, remarquables par leur beauté, par leur grandeur ou par leur singularité, et dessinés […]* (Paris, 1801).

7   For a short history of the Schusev State Museum of Architecture and the role of exhibitions, see: https://art.1sept.ru/article.php?ID=200401204 (accessed June 10, 2022).

8   The history of the Dutch Architecture Institute (NAi) is described in: Sergio M. Figueiredo, *The Nai Effect – Creating Architecture Culture* (Rotterdam, 2016).

9   Dolores Hayden, *The Grand Domestic Revolution: A History of Feminist Designs for American Homes, Neighborhoods, and Cities* (Cambridge, MA, 1982); Hilde Heynen and Gulsum Baydar, *Negotiating Domesticity: Spatial Productions of Gender in Modern Architecture* (London, 2005); Jane Rendell, Barbara Penner, and Iain Borden, *Gender Space Architecture: An Interdisciplinary Introduction* (London, 2009).

10   Lina Loos, "We Women," 1948.

11   Philip L. Goodwin, *Brazil Builds: Architecture New and Old 1652–1942* (New York, 1943); Udo Kultermann, *New Japanese Architecture* (New York, 1967); Sergio U. Barbieri and Leen Van Duin, *A Hundred Years of Dutch Architecture, 1901–2000* (Amsterdam, 2003).

12   Francis D. K. Ching, Mark Jarzombek, and Vikramaditya Prakash, *A Global History of Architecture* (Hoboken, NJ, 2007); Kathleen James-Chakraborty, *Architecture Since 1400* (Minneapolis, 2014); Richard Ingersoll and Spiro Kostof, *World Architecture: A Cross-Cultural History* (New York, 2015); and Tom Avermaete, Klaske Havik, and Viviana D'Auria (eds.), "Crossing Boundaries: Transcultural Practices in Architecture and Urbanism." *OASE Architecture Journal* 95 (Rotterdam, 2015).

13   Nikolaus Pevsner, *Pioneers of Modern Design: From William Morris to Walter Gropius* (Harmondsworth, Middlesex 1960); Leonardo Benevolo, Vera Vicari, and Jacques Vicari, *Histoire De L'architecture Moderne*, T.1: Révolution Industrielle, T.2: Avantgarde Et Mouvement Moderne, T.3: Les Conflits Et L'après-Guerre (Paris, 1998).

14   Mirko Zardini and Giovanna Borasi, *Imperfect Health: The Medicalization of Architecture* (Montréal: 2012); Tom Avermaete, Maristella Casciato, Takashi Homma, and Yto Barrada, *Casablanca Chandigarh – A Report on Modernization* (Zurich, 2014).

15   Carl Pruscha, *Kathmandu Valley – The Preservation of Physical Environment and Cultural Heritage* (Vienna: 1975); Roland Rainer, *Anonymes Bauen Nordburgenland* (Salzburg, 1961).

Cold St

The architects' archives contained in our collections are resonant with Austria's architectural history. Az W's holdings – which also include project-related archives and extensive photographic archives – form the basis for our engagement with topics which intersect with art and cultural history, as well as with social, political, economic, and technological history. The items in the collections range from architectural drawings, plans, models, and photos, via furniture and household objects to rare books and archival materials. In line with the contents of these collections, the Az W has set up interdisciplinary and transnational architectural research. The seven Hot Questions posed in our permanent collection bring the Cold Storage to life.

We invite you to take a look at the Cold Storage. A collage of images provides a glimpse of the extent of our collections – a body of knowledge not linear and encyclopedic in its structure, but fragmented, with gaps and cracks. The aim is to present the collections not as sedimentation of times past, but as a scenario for a future that encourages us to think of and about architecture.

orage

-001

001-M	S-297-001-M	S-297
001-M	S-159-001-M	S-159
001-P	N05-003-001-P	N05-0
002-M	S-208-002-M	S-208
001-M	S-190-001-M	S-190
004-P	S-069-004-P	S-069
001-M	S-192-001-M	S-192
001-M	S-194-001-M	S-194
001-M	S-195-001-M	S-195
001-M	S-196-001-M	S-196
006-P	N10-076-006-P	N10-0
001-A	N10-016-001-A	N10-0
001-F	N10-020-001-F	N10-0
001-M	S-152-001-M	S-152
001-K	S-150-001-K	S-150
001-P	S-513-001-P	S-513
001-P	N06-194-001-P	N06-1
001-M	S-197-001-M	S-197
001-M	S-198-001-M	S-198
001-M	S-199-001-M	S-199
001-M	S-200-001-M	S-200
001-M	S-201-001-M	S-201
001-I	S-005-001-I	S-005
001-M	S-155-001-M	S-155

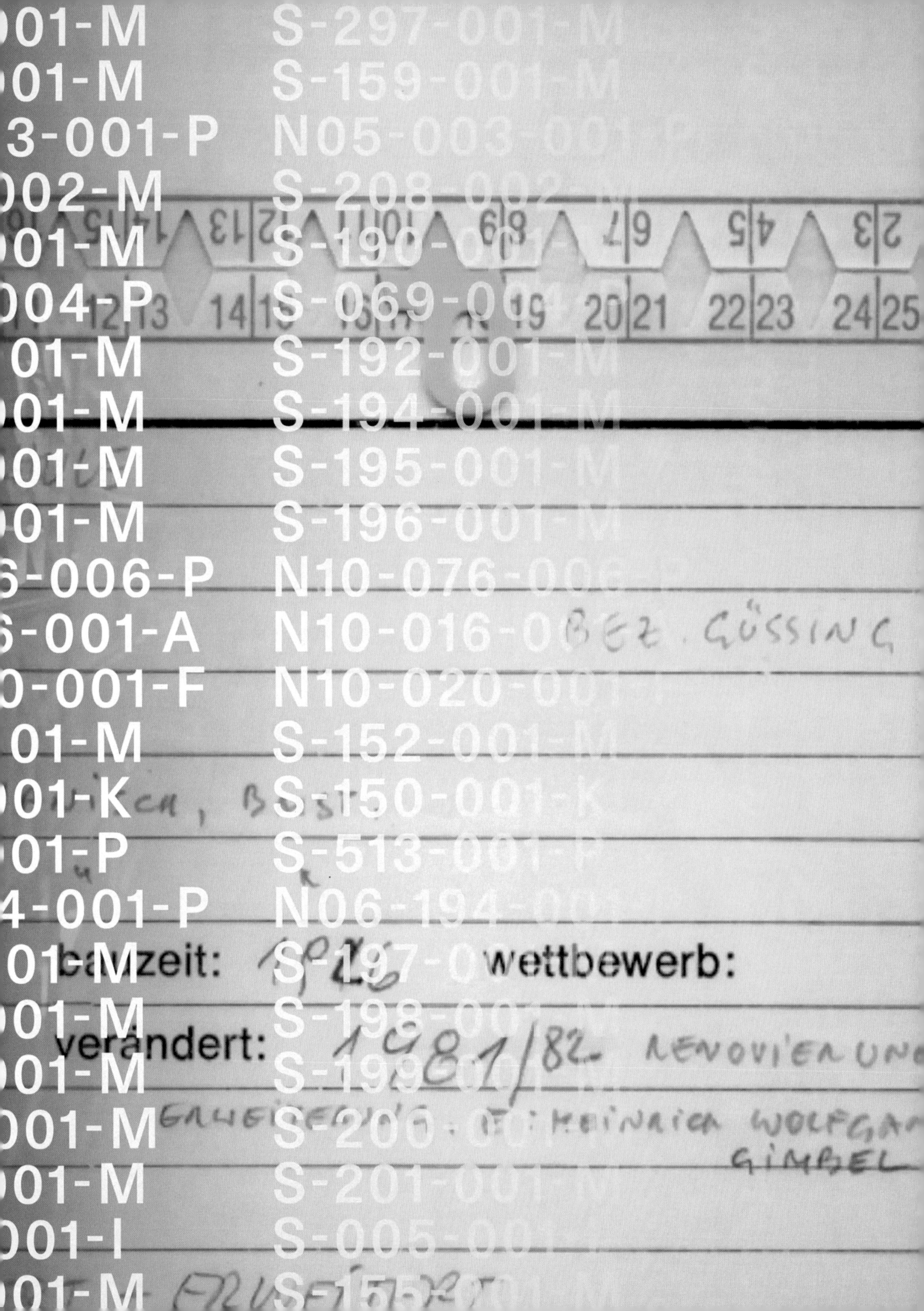

2	3	4	5	6	7	8	9	10	11	12	13	14	15	16	17	18	19	20	21	22	23	24	25	

S-297-001-M
S-159-001-M
N05-003-001-P
S-208-002-M
S-190-001-M
S-069-004-P
S-192-001-M
S-194-001-M
S-195-001-M
S-196-001-M
N10-076-006-P
N10-016-001-A   BEZ. GÜSSING
N10-020-001-F
S-152-001-M
S-150-001-Kch, B
S-513-001-P
N06-194-001-P

bauzeit: S-197-0 wettbewerb:

S-198-001-M

verändert: 1981/82 RENOVIERUNG

GRUEISEGG S-200-001 HEINRICH WOLFGANG
GIMBEL

S-201-001-M
S-005-001-I
S-15?-001-M   ERUSE

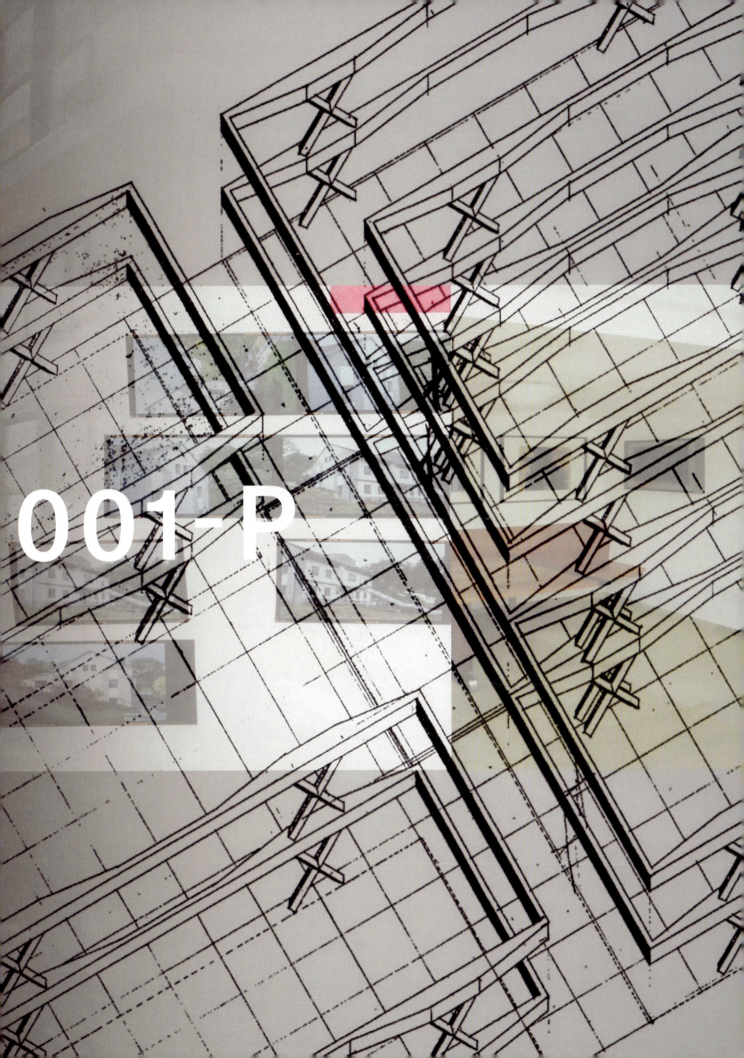

Elemen

How is
archi
produ

Tools and Places for Thought	40
Architects' Studios	52
Drawing	56
Bogdan Bogdanović	57
Heinz Tesar	60
Syntax of Building	62
Color	62
Construction	63
Reinforced Concrete	64
Building Components	65
Material	66
Inspiration	70
Genius Loci	70
The Useful Trip	72
Anonymous Architecture	74

Tools and Places
for Thought

The atelier, the office, and the studio are spaces where thought processes are nurtured and building programs are scrutinized. Where architecture comes into being and where it becomes concrete. As an unmediated instrument to record one's thoughts, the pencil is facing increased competition from digital drawing programs. By the same token, slide rules, drawing sets, templates, technical pens, triangular scales, and rulers are things of the past. The design and representation techniques of architecture are closely linked to the history of technology, and today most projects are even "born digital." Ottokar Uhl and Manfred Wolff-Plottegg are two of Austria's computer pioneers. They saw new opportunities for processes of democratization and de-subjectification in an architecture generated by algorithms. Pichler & Traupmann demonstrate how Building Information Modeling (BIM), a three-dimensional tool which is increasingly becoming the standard mode of cooperation for the persons involved in the project, can be employed when adaptations or additions are made to existing buildings.

Thonet swivel office chair,
from Wilhelm Cermak's atelier | Wood, steel

Drawing tools:
lettering templates, furniture templates, curve templates, ink pens, pencils, compass |
Photos: Az W

Elements Tools and Places for Thought 42

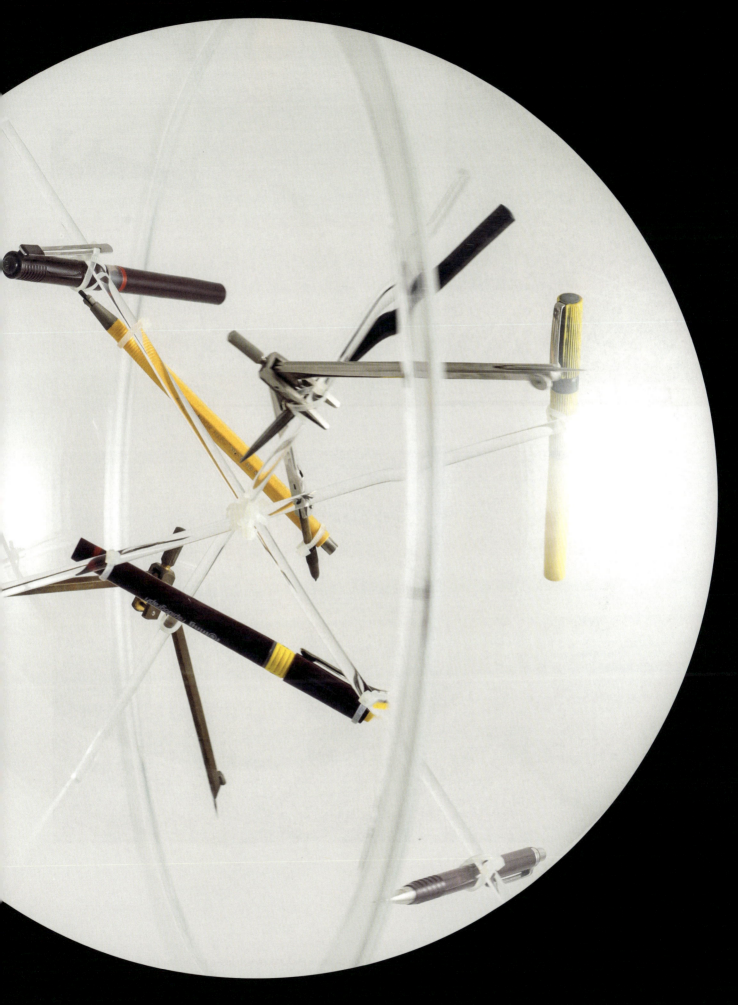

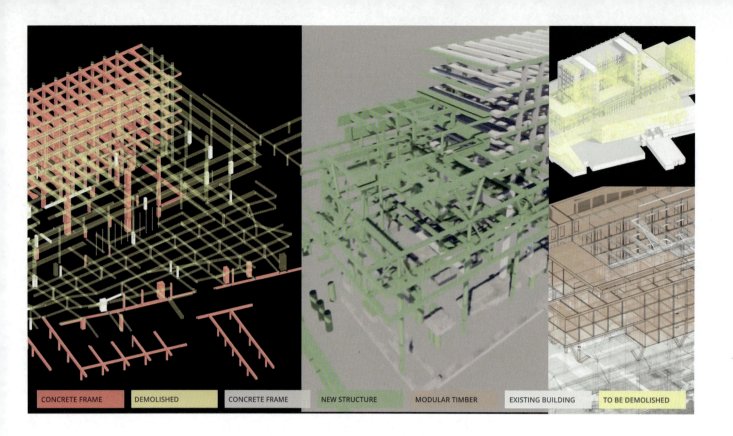

Pichler & Traupmann Architekten (Christoph Pichler, Johann Traupmann) | Raiffeisen Quartier (RAIQA) | Adamgasse 1–7, Innsbruck, Tyrol, 2019 | BIM / NO BIM, 2021 | Film stills

Pichler & Traupmann Architekten
(Christoph Pichler, Johann Traupmann)
Raiffeisen Quartier (RAIQA)
Adamgasse 1–7, Innsbruck, Tyrol, 2019
BIM / NO BIM

The crux of Pichler & Traupmann's prudent concept involved re-using the reinforced concrete structure of an existing building. Situated within the hybrid district – made up of spaces for the service industry, cultural institutions, and a hotel – the building was given a distinct spatial identity. Based on an intelligent model which is activated via a Cloud Platform, BIM unifies multidisciplinary data from all of the construction trades to produce a digital representation of the object: first of the planning process, then of the design, and ultimately of the actual building and its operation.

The film provides a glimpse of the BIM-aided planning process for Innsbruck's Raiffeisen Quartier.

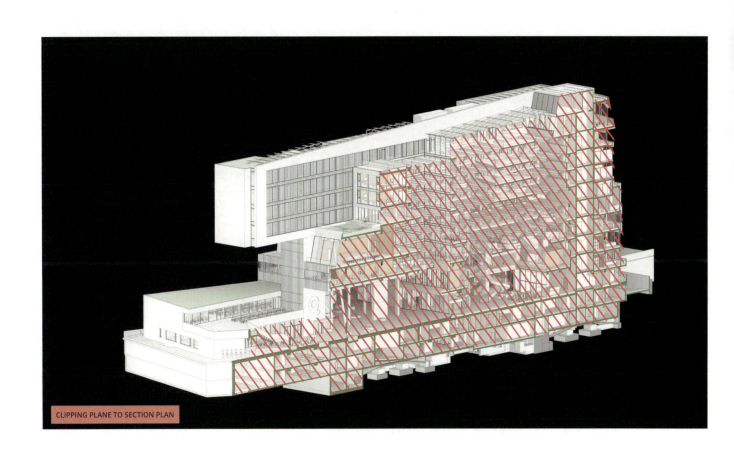

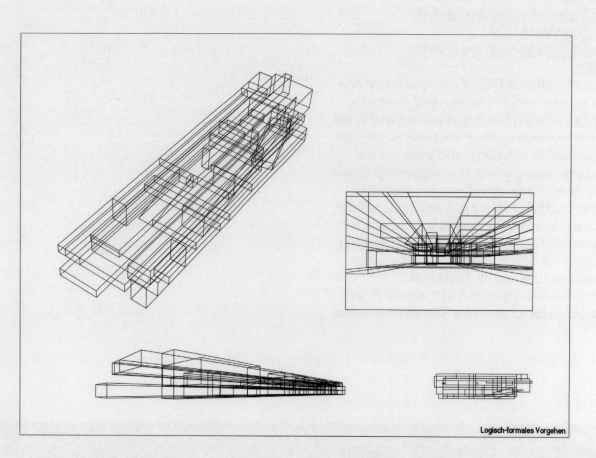

Logisch-formales Vorgehen

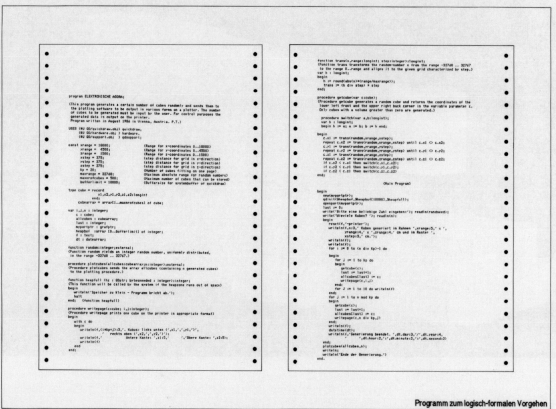

Programm zum logisch-formalen Vorgehen

Ottokar Uhl | Competition, Central Station and ZKM Center for Art and Media Karlsruhe |
Schwarzwaldstrasse/Ebertstrasse/Poststrasse/Ettlinger Strasse, Karlsruhe, Germany, 1986 |
Program for "logical-formal process" | Ink on translucent paper

Elements Tools and Places for Thought 46

Ottokar Uhl
Competition, Central Station and
ZKM Center for Art and Media Karlsruhe
Schwarzwaldstrasse/Ebertstrasse/Poststrasse/
Ettlinger Strasse, Karlsruhe, Germany, 1986

The task was to plan the development area consisting of the Central Station and of the ZKM Center for Art and Media Karlsruhe as in a user-oriented process, both with respect to construction and the spaces created. Corresponding to the future-oriented building problem, Ottokar Uhl decided to delve into computer technology. His concept for the competition: to submit not a finished building, but instead a procedure for a processual, interdisciplinary, and open approach to planning. Instead of perspectival drawings with a vanishing point, in this approach, after the parametrical data has been entered, contours accumulate; accordingly, processes and relations of the building components are expressed.

<u>Ottokar Uhl, Franz Kuzmich, Paul Tavolato
"Computer-aided Design and Decision-making"
research project, 1984–1988
Apple Macintosh Plus Computer, Systemsoftware 5.1, produced 1986–1990</u>

MBP, a computer program supporting participative processes, was the result of the research project for subsidized housing entitled "Computer-aided Design and Decision-making". The program, based on a software adaptation for the S.A.R. design method, was developed in the Netherlands for Apple IIe by the Stichting Architecten Research.

The MBP system is a CAD application for two-dimensional drawings with integrated cost estimation software. It comprises three programs: one to be used by the future residents to help them plan their apartments; another to generate the primary structure (structural-tectonic prerequisite to constructing a building); and a third program to develop the building-component catalogue, which includes drawings, specifications, and different price categories of the individual building components.

The last two of these programs were used by the architects in consultation with the residents and constitute the basis for the subsequent apartment planning. The participative system was conceived to run on two computer models: the Macintosh XL (Macintosh Desktop System) and the Macintosh Plus and SE systems. It generates simple, to-scale plans and lists of the building components to be employed. The apartment-planning program is self-explanatory: it does not require specialized training.

The users are encouraged to test a variety of floor plan configurations so that they will arrive at the best solution – ideally situated at the interface of necessities and opportunities for individual development. Ottokar Uhl considered the respective participant's involvement and experience in the process particularly valuable. The computer system allows the future residents to become active in planning their homes.

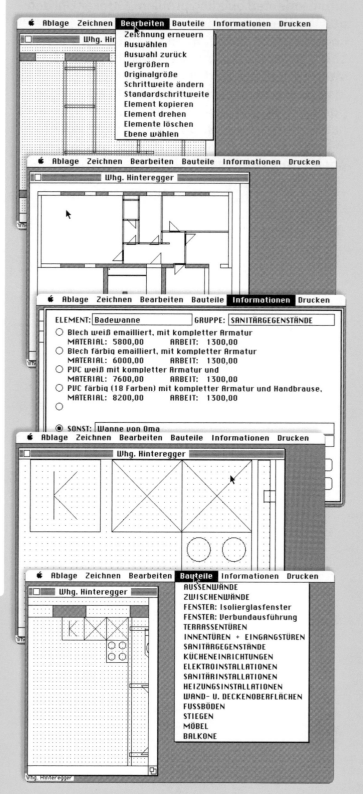

Elements   Tools and Places for Thought

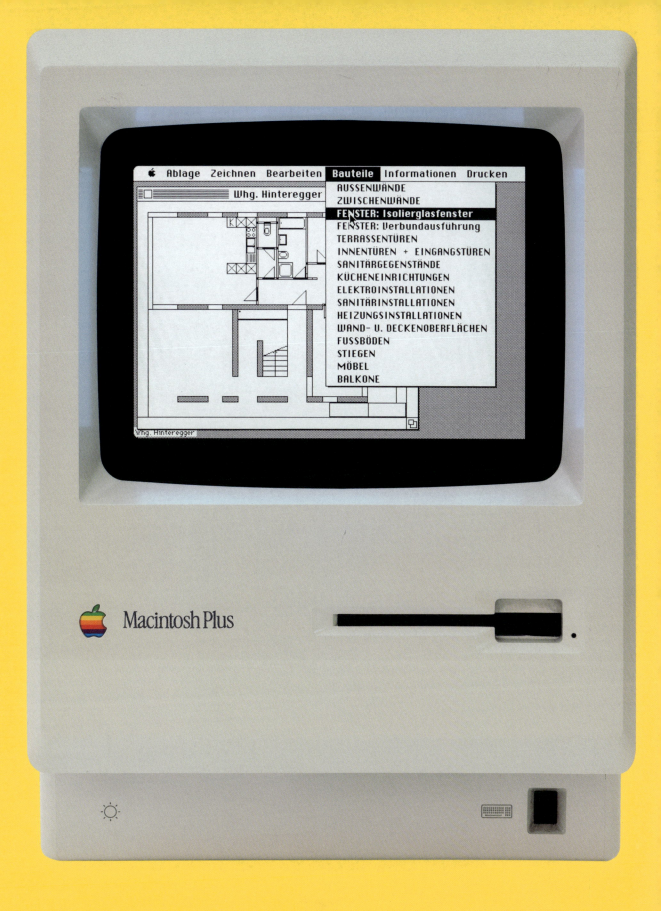

Ottokar Uhl, Franz Kuzmich, Paul Tavolato | "Computer-aided Design and Decision-making" research project, 1984–1988 | Apple Macintosh Plus Computer, Systemsoftware 5.1, produced 1986–1990 | Reconstruction: Richard Hilbert, Barbara Kapsammer, Iris Ranzinger, 2021 | Film stills

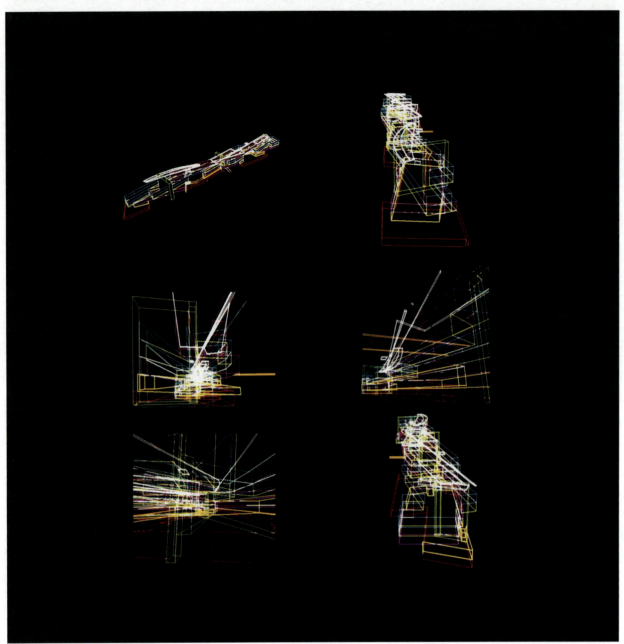

Manfred Wolff-Plottegg | RESOWI Universität Graz competition | Styria, 1985 | Wireframe perspectives | Print on cardboard

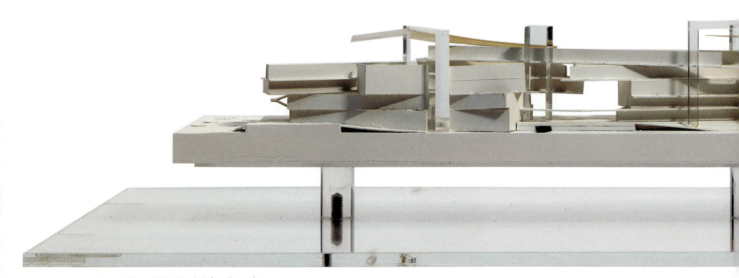

Model with superimposition of the levels | Cardboard, paper

Manfred Wolff-Plottegg
RESOWI Universität Graz competition, Styria
1985

Manfred Wolff-Plottegg used a script of Fortran, a programming language, to compute the complex spatial program for the RESOWI campus. The computer's processing power was also employed to develop the project's form. By employing algorithms, the program creates a system consisting of contours, distribution of floor space, and superimpositions. Repeated interactions with the machine lead to an extrusion, which is depicted graphically by means of wireframes, thereby defining the spaces. By transferring the design process to an algorithm, Wolff-Plottegg sought to liberate the architecture discipline from subjectivity and transform it from within.

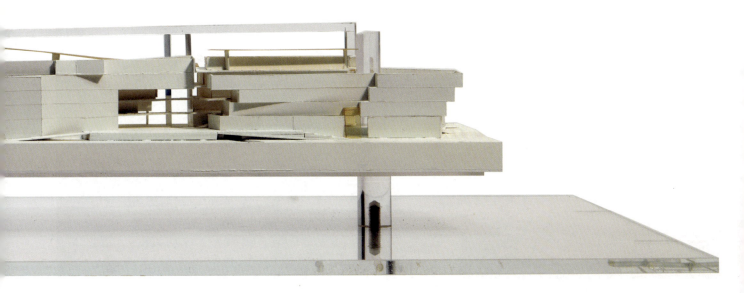

Architects' Studios

Rob Krier, Vienna | Photo: Christoph Panzer, 2020

Franz Kiener, Vienna | Photo: Christoph Panzer, 2013

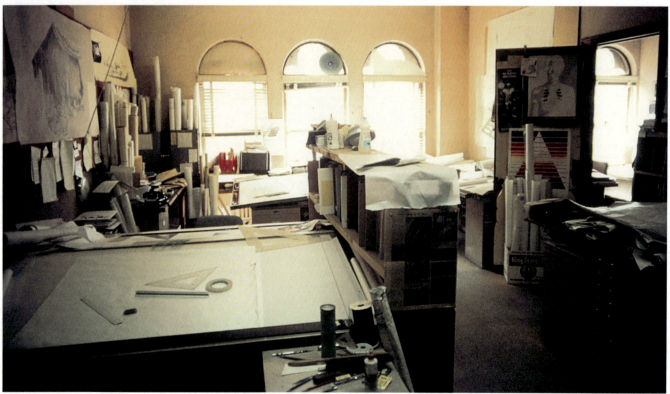

John Lautner, Los Angeles, USA | Photo: Hans Dieter Smekal, 1973

Hans Hollein, Vienna | Photo: Studio Hollein, about 1970

Raimund Abraham, New York, USA | Photo: Studio Abraham

Elements　　　　　　　　　　　　　　Tools and Places for Thought　　　　53

Margarete Schütte-Lihotzky, Vienna | Photo: Margherita Spiluttini, 2000

Anton Schweighofer, Vienna | Photo: Pez Hejduk, 2008

Johannes Spalt, Vienna | Photo: Pez Hejduk, 2007

Hanno Schlögl, Innsbruck | Photo: Günter Richard Wett, 2020

Hans Puchhammer, Vienna | Photo: Christoph Panzer, 2013

Elsa Prochazka, Vienna | Photo: Elsa Prochazka, 2021

Elements   Tools and Places for Thought   55

Drawing

The drawing was and, to a certain extent, still is a fundamental medium with which architects communicate their thoughts to clients and builders. In the act of drawing, a dialogue between hand and eye is established. The media philosopher Vilém Flusser refers to the drawing as a gesture with which a "phenomenalization of thought" takes place. For Bogdan Bogdanović, drawing was always inseparably linked to telling. Bogdanović ascribed his abstract forms to the trove of subconsciousness. In Bogdanović's view, the most fundamental question was always, "What does a work want to tell us?" And not, "What does the author want?" Heinz Tesar's drawn and written notations are part of his search for "pre-architectures" of the subsequent form-giving. The drawing becomes the spark that ignites the design process.

Bogdan Bogdanović

While drawing

While drawing

In the study

While drawing

Sharpening a pencil

Elements · Drawing

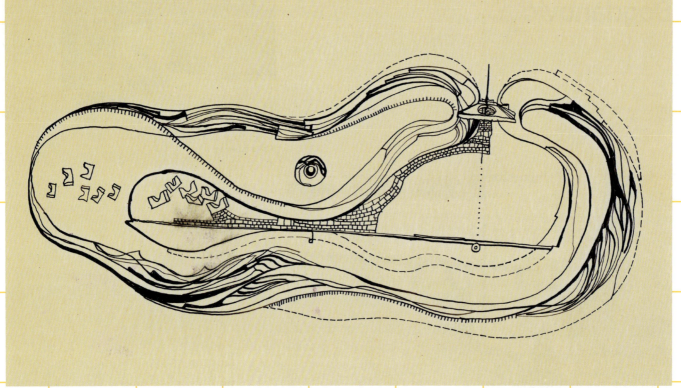

Bogdan Bogdanović | Slobodište Commemorative Site | Kruševac, Serbia, 1960–1965 | Ideography | Pencil and ink on translucent paper

"Yes, I need this pen in my hand and also these contours, which come into existence under my hand. [...] In this way I learn – time and again – to listen to my hand. [...] I am certain that not a single drawing was originally planned to turn out as it did." (Bogdan Bogdanović)

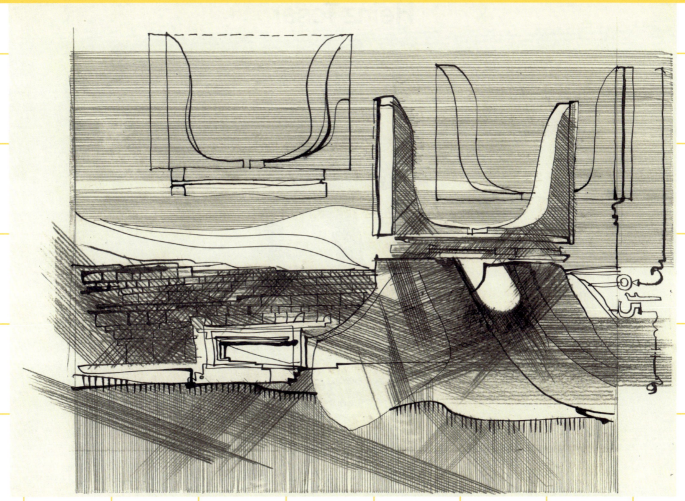

Bogdan Bogdanović | Slobodište Commemorative Site | Kruševac, Serbia, 1960–1965 | Post-construction studies | Felt pen and pencil on sketch paper, ink on translucent paper

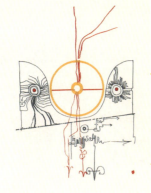

Vignettes of the Kruševac wing motif | Print, photocopy

Proportion studies | Ink, colored pencil and wax crayon on tracing paper, pencil on tissue paper

Heinz Tesar

Heinz Tesar | Notre-Dame du Haut (1950–1955) by Le Corbusier | Ronchamps, France | Sketch, 1963 | Ink brush on paper

Heinz Tesar | Museum Beaubourg (Centre Pompidou) | Paris, France | Sketch, 1972 | Ink and watercolor on paper

Heinz Tesar | House between two hills | Sketch, 1973 | Ink and watercolor on paper

Heinz Tesar | Playhouse study | Spatial sequence, 1973 | Ink and watercolor on paper

"The drawing is the body's thought, notations in notebooks are the incomplete diaries of the architect."
(Heinz Tesar)

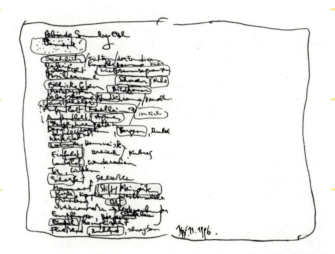

Heinz Tesar | Essl Collection Building | Notation, November 16/17, 1996 | Ink on paper

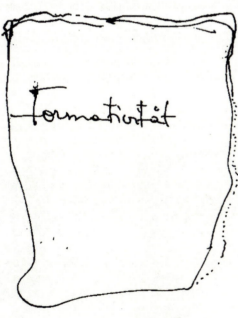

Heinz Tesar | Formativity | Notation, 2001 | Ink on paper

Elements — Drawing

Syntax of Building

"Color in architecture, a medium as robust as the floor plan or the cross section. Better yet: polychromy, a component of the floor plan and of the cross section itself." (Le Corbusier, 1936)

Josef Hoffmann, Oswald Haerdtl | Figaro Bar, 1927 | Portal, elevation | Pencil, watercolor and aluminum foil on paper | Drawing: Oswald Haerdtl

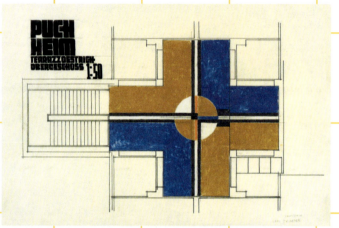

Hans Steineder | School Sisters Grade School and Middle School | Maria Theresien Strasse 5, Attnang-Puchheim, Upper Austria, 1934–1935 | Terrazzo color scheme, upper level | Ink and colored pencil on translucent paper

Color

Oskar Putz | Kix Bar | Bäckerstrasse 4, Vienna I, 1986 | Color concept | Ballpoint pen and opaque paint on paper; mounted on cardboard

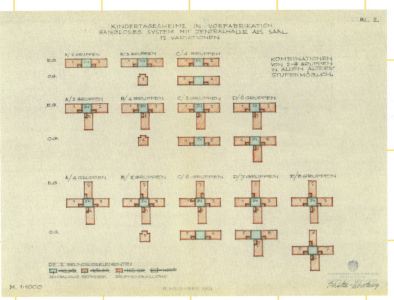

"The expression of the structure is not a matter of technology, but rather a matter of form and atmosphere."
(Elsa Prochazka)

Margarete Schütte-Lihotzky | Modular system: prefabricated daycare centers, 1964–1965 | Floor plan diagrams with cardinal directions and building-massing combinations, November 15, 1964 | Whiteprint with pencil and colored pencil

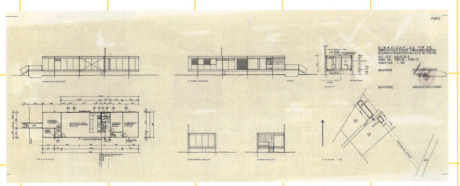

Roland Rainer | Lignostahl prefabricated houses, 1962–1964 | Permit plan for a house in Haiming (Ötztal), Tyrol | Ink on translucent paper

Roland Rainer | Lignostahl prefabricated houses, 1962–1964 | Advertising leaflet

Construction

Ottokar Uhl | Demountable church | Siemensstrasse 24, Vienna XXI, 1960–1964 | Photo of construction site and Mero System (model) | Metal

Elements   Syntax of Building   63

Reinforced Concrete

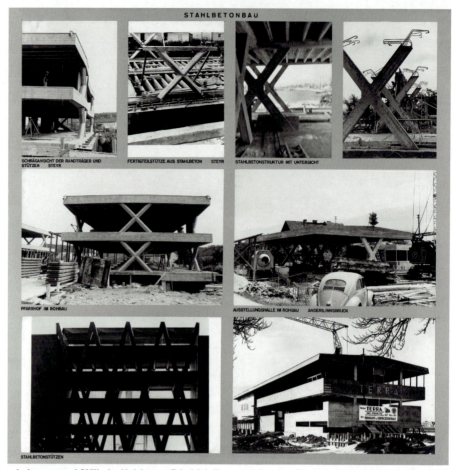

arbeitsgruppe 4 (Wilhelm Holzbauer, Friedrich Kurrent, Johannes Spalt) | arbeitsgruppe 4. 1951–1964 (exhibition title), Volksheim Kapfenberg, May 5–7, 1967, Styria | Exhibition panel of reinforced-concrete construction | Photos mounted on aluminum panel

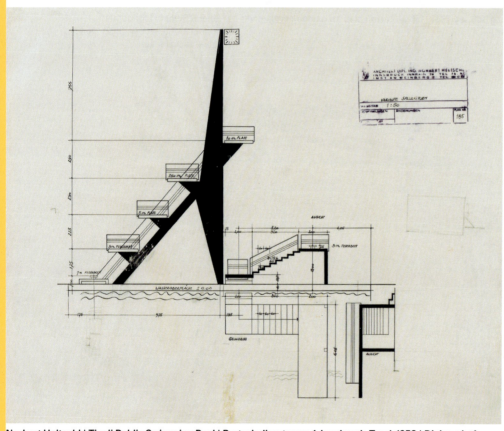

Norbert Heltschl | Tivoli Public Swimming Pool | Purtschellerstrasse 1, Innsbruck, Tyrol, 1958 | Diving platform, variant | Ink and pencil on translucent paper

Elements   Syntax of Building   64

Building Components

Manfred Wolff-Plottegg
Trautenfels from the vantage point of building components, 1993

Manfred Wolff-Plottegg's interventions at Schloss Trautenfels challenge users' expectations. Door and stair as the normed, unambiguously defined elements: the door as adjustable element for closing and opening and the stair as a building component that produces a fixed connection between two levels for moving upward and downward. In the hybrid Türtreppentreppentüre (Door-stair-stair-door), both the rules and the use are deconstructed. The door leaves are not only anchored to the wall, but also to the floor, and at the same time fulfil the function of a stair, even though they make no contribution to getting from Point A to Point B. In the closed position, the two stairs interlock as a door and alter their function.

Manfred Wolff-Plottegg | Schloss Trautenfels | Pürgg-Trautenfels, Styria, 1988–1989 | Model of Türtreppentreppentüre (Door-stair-stair-door) | Plastic, wood, metal; movable stair components

"I am not a designer, I just change rules." (Manfred Wolff-Plottegg)

"Following the renovation of Schloss Trautenfels in 1991/92, the camera was mounted on movable building components: sliding-door entrance, sliding cashier window, hallway door, WC door, toilet lid, flush button, toilet-paper roll, door handle, elevator, handrail, and Türtreppentreppentüre (Door-stair-stair-door). In this manner, a record is made of what the building components see each day (even though they don't have eyes)." (Manfred Wolff-Plottegg)

Manfred Wolff-Plottegg | Trautenfels from the vantage point of building components, 1993 | Film stills

Elements   Syntax of Building

"every material possesses its own language of forms, and none may lay claim for itself to the forms of another material. for forms have been constituted out of the applicability and the methods of production of materials. they have come into being with and through materials. no material permits an encroachment into its own circle of forms. whoever dares to make such an encroachment notwithstanding this is branded by the world a counterfeiter." (Adolf Loos)

Material

Elsa Prochazka | Competition (second phase) Konzerthaus Wien | Lothringerstrasse 20, Vienna III, 1994 | Material samples for the "service wall" in the foyer | Wood, stainless steel

Anka Dür, Anna Heringer, Martin Rauch, Sabrina Summer | Room for Birth and Senses | Hittisau, Vorarlberg, 2020 | Shingle cladding, painted | Courtesy of Anka Dür

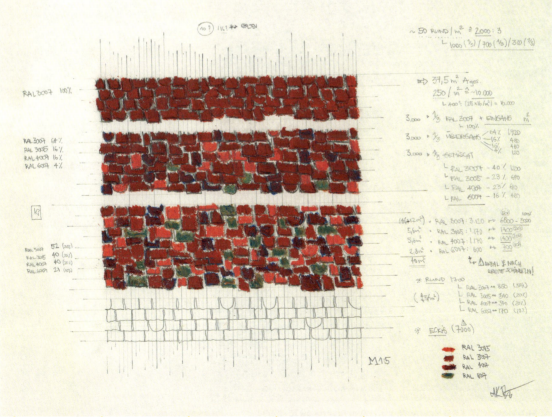

Shingle cladding, color specification | Wax crayon on paper | Drawing: Anka Dür

Elements Syntax of Building 67

Heinz Tesar | Essl Museum | Aufeldgasse 17–23, Klosterneuburg, Lower Austria, 1996–1999 |
Vacuum-formed relief, 2012 | Polystyrene

Tesar tests the limits of architecture and art. His vacuum models are autonomous spatial figures and haptic revelations of thought processes.

Inspiration

Genius loci

The drawings are based on personal memories and refer to the respective site-specific landscape.

Walter Pichler engages in a dialogue with his grandfather's smithy in Eggental/South Tyrol – a place Pichler was forced by political circumstances (South Tyrol Option Agreement, 1939) to leave at the age of five.

Günther Domenig's first Steinhaus sketches for the property he inherited from his grandmother on the north shore of Lake Ossiach in Carinthia are inspired by the particular mountain formations of the Möll Valley.

Both are searching for the final form: Walter Pichler's inspiration is the search for the lost sense of belonging in his grandfather's workshop in the middle of a narrow valley. Günther Domenig makes reference to the craggy landscape of the surroundings that is reflected in the jagged architecture of the Steinhaus.

Walter Pichler | House next to the smithy | Unterbirchabruck, Deutschnofen, Bolzano, Italy, 1995–2002 | Sketch 1995 | Pencil, ink, watercolor on paper

Günther Domenig | Steinhaus | Uferweg 31, Steindorf am Ossiacher See, Carinthia, 1982–2008 | In homage to Grandmother | Sketch | Whiteprint on cardboard

The Useful Trip

Le Corbusier, Iannis Xenakis | Philips pavilion | World Exposition | Brussels, Belgium, 1958 | Slide: Karl Mang, 1958

Vernacular Architecture in Iran, 1974 | Film still: Djamshid Farassat

The World as Garden, China, 1973 | Slide: Roland Rainer

Pirha, Santorini, Greece | Stairs to the harbour | Photo: Bernard Rudofsky, 1931

Field trip to Norway, master class for interior architecture and industrial design, University of Applied Arts Vienna, 1975 | Film still: Johannes Spalt's class

To architects, trips are tools of learning and sources of inspiration. The first expeditions are usually undertaken on field trips as students.

Anonymous Architecture

Engelbert Zobl | *LA Life*, prizewinning short film documenting Los Angeles street scenes, 1968 | Film stills

Elements   Inspiration

The inclination toward anonymous architecture is one of the discipline's major themes. Interest in vernacular design illustrated the efforts to derive architectural form directly from the local conditions and day-to-day habits. Anonymous architecture stands for a socially viable architecture and paves the way for themes such as regionalism, sustainability, townscape cultivation, historic preservation, and gentle urban renewal.

Roland Rainer | [Anonymous Architecture in North Burgenland], Salzburg, 1961

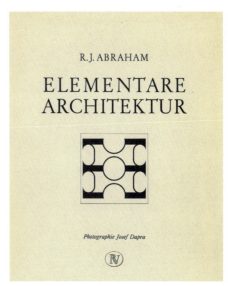

Raimund Abraham, Josef Dapra | [Elemental Architecture], Salzburg, 1963

Carl Pruscha | *Kathmandu Valley – The Preservation of the Physical Environment and the Cultural Heritage* | A Protective Inventory, volume 1, second edition, Kathmandu, 2015 (1974)

Engelbert Zobl
LA Life
Prizewinning short film documenting Los Angeles street scenes, 1968
    Understanding the everyday, the presumedly untamed growth, as a component of city planning was the outstanding achievement of the 1972 study by Robert Venturi and Denise Scott Brown, published in cooperation with Steven Izenour, entitled *Learning from Las Vegas*. In 1968, Engelbert Zobl, who studied under Denise Scott Brown at UCLA, and his camera made a pass through the melee of pedestrians, neon signs, and traffic – capturing the atmospherics of everyday architecture. The trivial, the supposedly ugly, and the socially marginalized come together in a Technicolor poem about urbanity.

Literature

Tools and Places for Thought
pp. 40–55

Elke Krasny, Architekturzentrum Wien (eds.), *The Force Is in the Mind – The Making of Architecture,* exh. cat. Architekturzentrum Wien, 10/16/2008–2/2/2009 (Basel 2008).

Teresa Fankhänel, Andres Lepik (eds.), *The Architecture Machine. The Role of Computers in Architecture*, exh. cat. Architekturmuseum der TU München, 10/14/2020–1/10/2021 (Basel 2020).

Ottokar Uhl, "Eine Sprache sprechen," in: *ARCH+* 77, 1984 (theme: Computer-Aided-Design).

Franz Kuzmich, Paul Tavolato, Ottokar Uhl, "CAD-Einsatz zur Mitbestimmung im Wohnbau," in: Fred Margulies, Günter Hillebrand (eds.), *Neue Automatisierungstechniken. Chancen für Klein-und Mittelbetriebe* (Vienna 1986), 249–254.

Manfred Wolff-Plottegg, *Hybrid Architektur & Hyper Funktionen* (Vienna 2007).

Manfred Wolff-Plottegg, *Plottegg – Architecture Beyond Inclusion and Identity is Exclusion and Difference from Art. The Work of Manfred Wolff-Plottegg* (Basel 2015).

Manfred Wolff-Plottegg, http://plottegg.tuwien.ac.at/ (accessed June 2, 2022).

Robert Venturi, Denise Scott Brown, Steven Izenour, *Learning from Las Vegas* (Cambridge, MA 1972).

Engelbert Zobl, https://www.engelbert-zobl.com/ (accessed June 2, 2022).

Drawing
pp. 56–61

Vilém Flusser, *Gesten. Versuch einer Phänomenologie* (Düsseldorf 1991).

Ivan Ristić, Architekturzentrum Wien (eds.), *Bogdan Bogdanović. Memoria und Utopie in Tito-Jugoslawien*, exh. cat. Architekturzentrum Wien, 3/5/–6/2/2009 (Vienna 2009).

Heinz Tesar, Liesbeth Waechter-Böhm, *Heinz Tesar* (Vienna/New York 1995).

Winfried Nerdinger (ed.), *Heinz Tesar. Architektur*, exh. cat. Architekturmuseum der TU München, 9/29/2005–1/8/2006 (Milan 2005).

Matthias Boeckl, *Heinz Tesar. Zeichnungen* (Stuttgart 2003)

Syntax of Building
pp. 62–69

Katharina Krenn, Wolfgang Otte, *Schloss Trautenfels. Von der Burg zum Museum* (Trautenfels 2018).

Elsa Prochazka, *architectureality. Raum & Designstrategien* (Basel 2018).

Inspiration
pp. 70–75

Ruth Baumeister, Ruth Froschauer (eds.), *Die nützliche Reise (Thesis, Wissenschaftliche Zeitschrift der Bauhaus-Universität Weimar* 1), 2003.

Players

Why not pink?	84
Gender Firewall	86
K. k. Kunstgewerbeschule	87
Technische Hochschule Wien	87
Akademie der bildenden Künste Wien	88
Technische Hochschule Graz	88
Archetypes	89

Canon Makers — 96
    Poetic Systematist:
    Friedrich Achleitner — 96
    Surveyor:
    Margherita Spiluttini — 104

Initiators of a Brand: Vienna around 1900 — 110

Stars are Born: Biennale Venice, 1980 — 114

Protagonists — 116

Ott*ilie Wagner

Hans*ine Hollein

Hermann*a Spalt

Frieder*ike M...

Players 80

Roberta Kramreiter

Rolanda Rainer

Johanna Schleitner

Adolfine Loos

Players

"Why have there been no great women architects?"

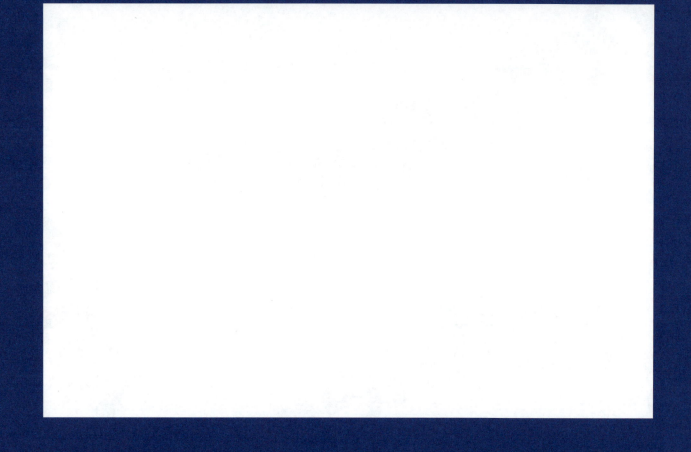

"Had I known that everyone would only talk about this damned kitchen, I would never have invented it!"
(Margarete Schütte-Lihotzky)

Margarete Schütte-Lihotzky in her appartment | Franzensgasse 16, Vienna V, 1967–1969 | Photo: Margherita Spiluttini, 1981

Writing history is never an entirely objective endeavor. The selection and interpretation of the material is made by persons who have themselves been shaped by the respective course of events. For decades the narrative's (usually male) vantage point on master narratives had solidified. Gender Studies has opened up new perspectives and new inquiries into architecture, including, for example, omissions in the canon. Linda Nochlin's 1971 essay "Why Have There Been No Great Women Artists?" examines the systemic discrimination in the art system. These analyses can be carried over to architecture.

Players

Why not

Barbie-Edition "I Can Be …" "The builder," 2017

pink?

Barbie-Edition "I Can Be …"
"The architect," 2011

Architect Barbie is part of the "I Can Be …" edition, whose aim is to motivate girls to take up professions in which women are strongly under-represented. Co-initiators of Architect Barbie are the architecture historian Despina Stratigakos and the architect Kelly Hayes McAlonie. The 2011 presentation of the new toy was followed by controversies about the right "look" for architects. Wearing a dress and high heels and carrying a pink drawing tube, Barbie did not correspond to the self-image of architects, who tend to see themselves wearing all-black. The idea is to reinforce girl power and put up resistance to any type of stereotyping. More than 400 girls took part in the accompanying workshops, which provided information about what being an architect entails. In 2017, the next doll to be presented was Builder Barbie, donning a pink hardhat and are wearing pants and sturdy shoes. Women wearing hard hats are still a rarity at construction sites, while at architecture schools there is parity between the sexes. Nonetheless, to this day there is an imbalance among Austria's self-employed architects – of the 3,383 architects with a license, 2,782 are men and just 601 are women.

Gender Firewall

In the history of architecture there is a dearth of female role models. Despite the various hurdles, more than 200 women were enrolled in architecture schools in Austria before 1938. Shining a light on these architects and finding a place for them in the canon is one of the focal points of our research.* At the same time, assessing educational institutions reveals the systemic disadvantages women architects faced and exposes the discrimination that has had a lasting effect when, for example, it comes time to appoint a new full professor. It was not until 1995 that the first woman was named to that position at the University of Innsbruck: Eda Schaur taught at the architecture faculty – and headed its newly established Institute for Structure and Design – for seventeen years.

One year later, Nasrine Seraji was named full professor at Vienna's Academy of Fine Arts (1996–2001).

* Research project entitled "Vienna's Pioneering Women in Architecture" (phase 1: 2021–2022; phase 2: 2022–2023), Margarete Schütte-Lihotzky Zentrum (Christine Zwingl, Sabina Riss, Carmen Trifina) in cooperation with the Az W (Monika Platzer), https://architekturpionierinnen.at/ (accessed July 7, 2022).

K. k. Kunstgewerbeschule

[Arts and Crafts School Vienna]

(today: Universität für angewandte Kunst [University of Applied Arts])

Established in 1867, the degree program was open to women from the beginning.

In 1873, the first four women enrolled in the architecture studio led by Josef Storck (1868–1898). When the new building on the Ringstrasse was inaugurated, two additional architecture studios were established, one headed from 1877 to 1912 by Hermann Herdtle, and the other from 1877 to 1905 by Oskar Beyer. Herdtle did not allow women to enroll in his studio. Each new academic year, there were a few women present in Oskar Beyer's studio. In 1880, Anna Peyscha of Brno (Moravia) was the first to receive an ex-matriculation certificate for successful completion of the seven-year degree program. During the first decades, the architecture studios at the Kunstgewerbeschule were primarily engaged with the design of interiors. Other courses focused on figural drawing in the classical tradition, as well as on embroidery and lacework. Ella Baumfeld (md. Briggs), began her artistic education from 1901 to 1906 at Koloman Moser's painting studio. Ten years later, she attempted to study architecture at Vienna's Technical College.

Josef Hoffmann (1899–1937)

From 1905, most of the female students attended Hoffmann's architecture class, where 1916/17 three quarters – 15 of the 20 students – were women. Arts-and-crafts designs and fabric patterns had priority. The education did not cover any subject matter on building technology. Therefore, for the graduates it was more difficult to gain access to the architecture profession, as well as to the licensing exam. Female auditors who had already had vocational training before studying in Hoffmann's class were: Olga Fricke, architect, Nymburg an der Weser, Germany (1908); Erika Paulas-Schuller, master builder diploma, Zürich (1909–1910); Ernestine (Erna) Kopriva completed her degree in 1919 under Hoffmann and in 1928 became an instructor in his class. From 1945 to 1960, Kopriva led the class and the ateliers for fabric prints and wallpaper.

Heinrich Tessenow (1913–1919)

In addition to the architecture class, Tessenow introduced coursework in building tectonics. After a year in Hoffmann's class, Regine Weinfeld, Warsaw, transferred to Tessenow's architecture class and graduated in 1914. She was followed by Elisabeth Nießen, Bielitz (1913–1917), and Hilda Friedenberg, Cronberg im Taunus (1914–1918). Students who attended the building tectonics course: Klothilde Drennig von Pietra-Rossa, Semlin in Slavonia; Hilda Friedenberg, Cronberg im Taunus; Ernestine Kopriva, Vienna; Maria Trinkl, Vienna; Margarete Lihotzky, Vienna; Elisabeth Nießen, Bielitz; Juliana Rysavy, Hranice, Czech Republic; Alice Hauber, Vienna; and Gertrude Morgenstern, Brno.

Oskar Strnad (1914–1935)

Beginning in 1909, Strnad taught the class on morphology. From 1914, he headed an architecture class. In 1917, there were three female students in his class who would graduate: Klothilde Drennig von Pietra-Rossa, Semlin, Slavonia (1915–1918); Margarete Lihotzky, Vienna (1915–1918); and Hertha Ramsauer, Vienna (1914–1918, architecture and painting classes). Through 1935, Gertrude Morgenstern, Brno (1916–1920), Alice Hauber, Vienna (1916–1921), and 13 more women successfully completed Strnad's program.

The first full professor and head of an architecture class was Zaha Hadid, from 2000 to 2015.

Technische Hochschule Wien

[Technical College Vienna]

(today: Technische Universität Wien [University of Technology Vienna])

1818 founded as "k. k. polytechnisches Institut in Wien"

As of April 7, 1919, women were allowed to enroll as full-time students at the Technische Hochschule. Ella Briggs became one of the first auditors (1916–1918). To finish her degree, she transferred to the Technische Hochschule München. From 1917 to 1919, Grete Heimerich (md. Metzger) audited courses as auditor at the college's Bauschule. In September 1919, she enrolled as a full-time student and passed the first state examination on July 12, 1921, with the highest marks possible. At 22 years of age, having passed the second state examination, Helene Roth became the first – and youngest – woman to complete her architecture degree. She initially enrolled as auditor in the fall semester of 1921/22 and, as of the spring semester 1922, as a full-time student. She took the second state examination on December 20, 1926. Brigitte Kundl (md. Muthwill), studied from 1929 to 1934, and in 1935, with her project "A municipal airport for Vienna," became the first woman to receive a doctorate. Hermine Frühwirth completed her doctorate that same year with the project "Vienna's secular buildings during the reign of Maria Theresa and Joseph II" at the Technische Hochschule Wien. By 1947, a total of seven women had received a doctorate in architecture. In fall 1940, even before receiving her degree in architecture, Edith Jurecka (md. Lassmann) worked as research assistant at the chair of building theory. After graduating in July 1941, she continued to work in academia, receiving a position as assistant professor. When nearing completion of her degree in November 1941, Ilse Weschta (md. Koci) became a research assistant at the chair for building art and building surveys, and in February 1942, after completing her thesis examination, became an assistant professor. In 1963, Elfriede Tungl, a civil engineer, became the first woman at the Technische Hochschule Wien to complete her post-doc requirements.

In 1996, Sigrid Hauser became the first woman at the faculty of architecture and spatial planning to complete her post-doc requirements. In 1999, Françoise-Hélène Jourda became the first woman to be appointed to a full professorship; she remained in that position at the Technische Universität Wien's faculty of architecture and spatial planning, department of spatial design until her death in 2015.

Akademie der bildenden Künste Wien

[Academy of Fine Arts Vienna]

Established in 1688 as private art academy
On June 14, 1920, the ministry of the interior and education demanded that women be accepted beginning with the 1920/21 academic year. For more than twenty years, the Akademie resisted the petitions seeking to open the course of study to women. Between 1920 and 1938, total of sixteen women studied architecture. In the 1920s, six of them took up their studies, but did not complete their degrees. Between 1920 and 1923, Helene Duczyńska, Wilhelmine Ohmann, and Hilary Pacanowski attended the master class headed by Friedrich Ohmann (1904–1923). During the mid-1920s, Edel Sparre and Charlotte Zentner attended the master class headed by Peter Behrens (1921–1936), and Maria Eckenstorfer, the one headed by Clemens Holzmeister (1924–1938 and 1949–1961). During the 1930s, women in Clemens Holzmeister's master class were the first to complete their degrees: Martha Bolldorf-Reitstätter (1930–1934), Susanne Banki (1933–1936), Irene Hitaller (1935–1938), Isabella Hartl (1935–1938), Margarete Hoffmann (1936–1938), Josefine Kraus (1936–1938), Grete Weiss (1936–1938), and Victoria Maier (1937–1939), the majority of them with high marks. The first female assistant professors at the architecture master classes were Elisabeth Baudisch (she began in 1953, working under Lois Welzenbacher) and Erika Zangerl (she began in 1953, working under Roland Rainer).

In 1995, Marta Schreieck was the first woman to be named guest professor in architecture. The first full professor in architecture was Nasrine Seraji (1996–2001), the second was Farshid Moussavi (2002–2005).

Technische Hochschule Graz

[Technical College Graz]

(today: Technische Universität Graz [University of Technology Graz])

1811 founded as "Joanneum"
As of 1897, women were permitted to study as full-time students at the philosophy faculty of the Karl-Franzens-Universität Graz. On April 7, 1919, Otto Glöckel's decree enabled women to enroll as full-time students in the architecture programs at the technical colleges in Graz and Vienna. In 1925, Anna-Lülja Praun was the first woman to enroll in the architecture program at the Technische Hochschule Graz; in 1934, Hertha Rottleuthner-Frauneder was the first to complete the degree program. She was one of about 70 women to graduate from the Technische Hochschule Graz between 1919 and 1950. In 1945, Lorle Herdey was the first woman to be hired as associate professor; she was employed at the department of building-art and design, which was headed by Fritz Zotter.

In 1991, Karin Wilhelm became the first woman to be named full professor; in that capacity she taught history of art and architecture for ten years at the Graz University of Technology. In 1998 Irmgard Frank was appointed full professor for interior design and design at the Technische Universität Graz. As head of that department she remained at the university until 2018.

Archetypes

"Do we truly need a 'true' sex? With a persistence that borders on stubbornness, modern Western societies have answered in the affirmative." (Michel Foucault)

Günther Feuerstein's grappling with roles assigned in architecture based on gender has its roots in C. G. Jung's exploration of archetypes. Feuerstein examined the origins of elementary forms with male and female attributions that have archetypical presence in the collective consciousness of every human being. Time and again, gender-specific basic forms have been invoked by architects as point of departure for a design. In contrast to this approach is a free, autonomous architecture which distances itself from the predominant normative gender categorizations and stereotypes.

With their implementation of a birthing room in Hittisau, Anka Dür, Anna Heringer, Martin Rauch, and Sabrina Summer self-confidently went a step further. By employing loam and a uterus-shaped protective shell, their design allows for an archaic corporeal experience that – on account of the trend toward economizing medicine – is seldom available to present-day women.

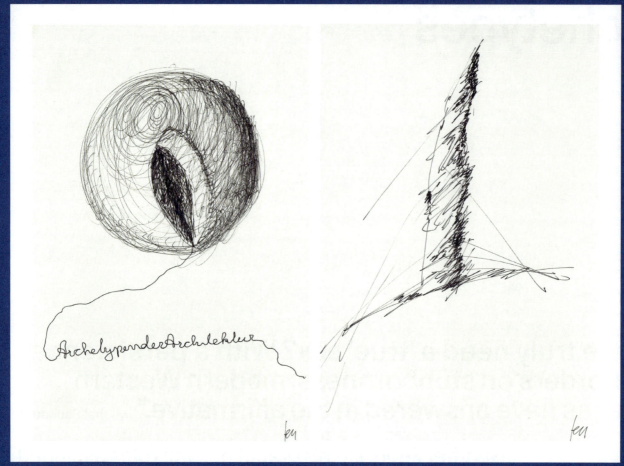

Günther Feuerstein | Archetypes in Architecture sketches, 1978 | Ink on paper

Hermann Czech | Kleines Café | Franziskanerplatz 3, Vienna I, 1970–1985 | Fields of association, the floor, 1977 | Felt pen and colored pencil on paper

Hermann Czech | Kleines Café | Franziskanerplatz 3, Vienna I, 1970–1985 | Floor detail

Players · Archetypes

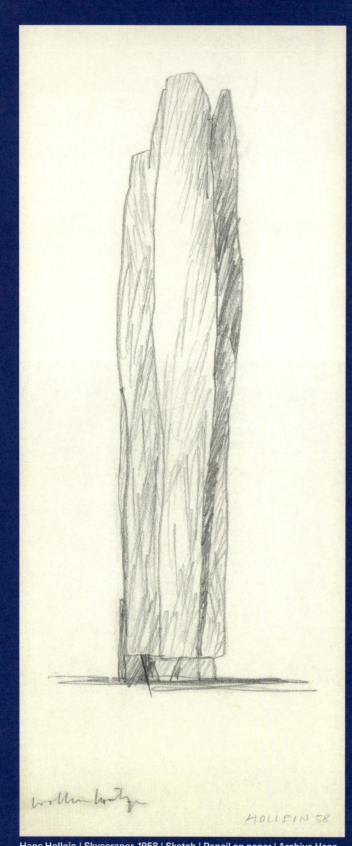

Hans Hollein | Skyscraper, 1958 | Sketch | Pencil on paper | Archive Hans Hollein, Az W and MAK, Vienna

Günther Domenig, Eilfried Huth | Multipurpose hall at the School Sisters Convent in Eggenberg | Georgigasse 84a, Graz, Styria, 1973–1977 | Sectional perspective, 1978 | Ink on translucent paper

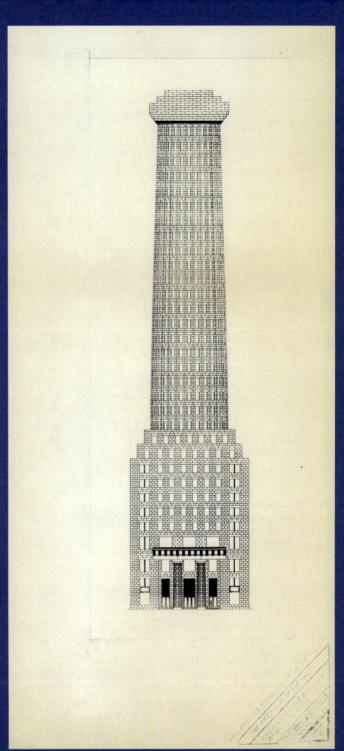

Adolf Loos | The Chicago Tribune Column, Michigan Avenue/Austin Avenue/St. Clair Street, Chicago, IL, USA | Facade with stone pattern, 1922 | Whiteprint | Archive Hans Hollein, Az W and MAK, Vienna

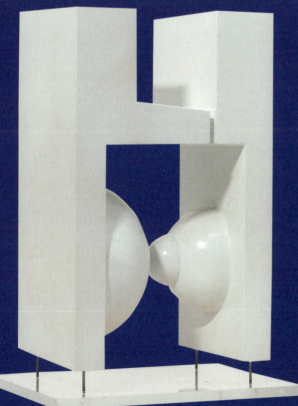

Heinz Tesar | Homotypes, glove, 1969 | Wood model

Players Archetypes 93

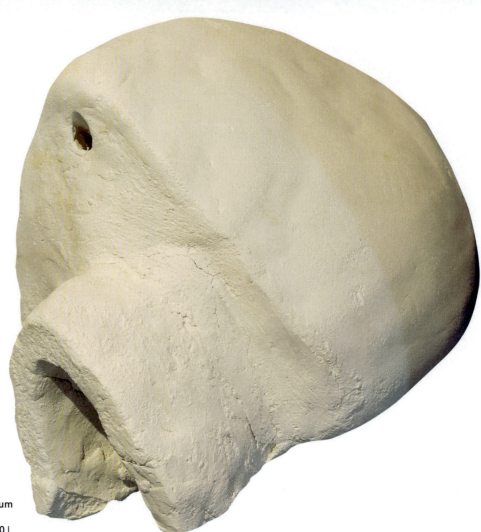

Anka Dür, Anna Heringer, Martin Rauch, Sabrina Summer | Clients: Frauenmuseum Hittisau, IG Geburtskultur a-z | Room for Birth and Senses, Hittisau, Vorarlberg, 2020 | Clay model: Anna Heringer

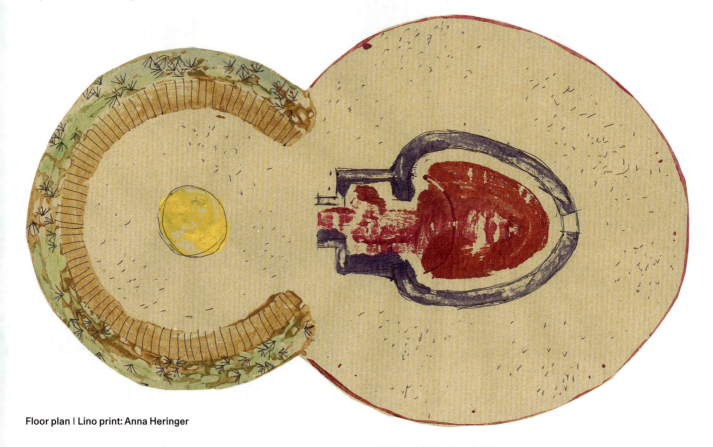

Floor plan | Lino print: Anna Heringer

Players   Archetypes   94

Anka Dür, Anna Heringer, Martin Rauch, Sabrina Summer | Clients: Frauenmuseum Hittisau, IG Geburtskultur a-z | Room for Birth and Senses, Hittisau, Vorarlberg, 2020 | Studies of movement | Photo: Frauenmuseum Hittisau/Katharina Rohner

Anka Dür, Anna Heringer, Martin Rauch, Sabrina Summer
Room for Birth and Senses
Hittisau, Vorarlberg, 2020

This crowd-funded prototype for a sensual birthing space located near the Frauenmuseum Hittisau directs attention to the atmosphere in which children are born. The archaic loam building is conceived of as a contemporary alternative to a hospital's delivery room and illustrates the close synergy between the human body and the space around it.

Canon Makers

Poetic Systematist: Friedrich Achleitner

The Achleitner Archive comprises:
22,340	index cards (buildings and objects)
2,690	index cards (architects)
66,500	photo negatives
37,800	slides
13,800	photo prints
570	drawings
250	fieldwork plans

1,030 books, pamphlets, catalogues, magazines (in some cases, all per annum issues of magazines such as *Profil, Der Bau, Der Aufbau, Perspektiven, Bauforum*), topographically classified boxes of material

In the mid-1960s, with his boxes of index cards, Achleitner began his systematic survey of Austria's built environment. The first of the five-volume *Österreichische Architektur im 20. Jahrhundert* [Austrian Architecture in the 20th Century] appeared in 1980. With the exception of Lower Austria, the guides covered all of the federal states. For many years these volumes set the standard of knowledge and comprehension of Austrian architecture. Achleitner thereby solidified a canon upon which – to this day – architectural historiography is based. Regarding the phenomenon of "how we perceive what we see changes over time," he reflected retrospectively on his work and encouraged colleagues to think in other categories and to fill in the stories that have yet to be told.

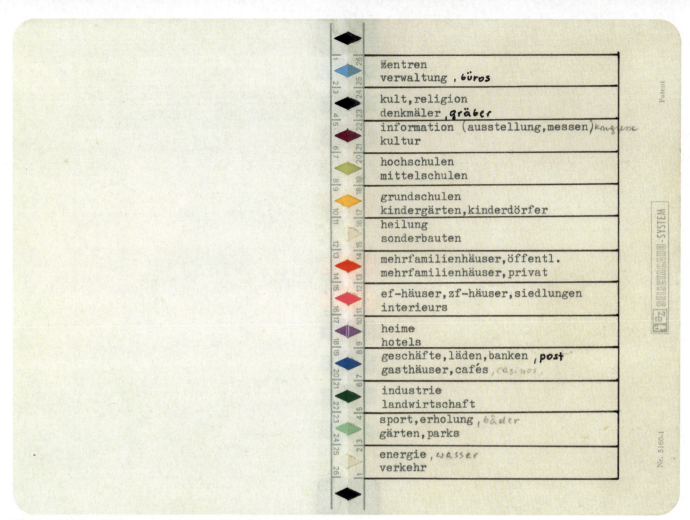

Friedrich Achleitner | Index card, color code for the building typologies

Friedrich Achleitner | Architecture guide
Österreichische Architektur im 20. Jahrhundert
[Austrian Architecture in the 20th Century],
five volumes, Salzburg, 1980–2010

The Achleitner system: the use of index cards for the preparation of the architecture guides facilitated a multi-phased selection process. Consequently, only a fraction of the material which was amassed made its way into the guide. Once the selection had been made, the work was done directly in the guide's layout template in a precisely calculated ratio to the font size. Page by page, the grid was filled, and illustrations were inserted in between, introducing a further layer of evaluation. The first step in the selection was limited to collecting the data: object, architect, construction firm, building data, addresses. In the second step, a brief text was added. As third step, one image was chosen to illustrate the building. Finally, a more elaborate text and additional illustrations were appended to buildings Achleitner deemed especially noteworthy.

Volume I: Upper Austria, Salzburg, Tyrol, Vorarlberg, 1980
Volume II: Carinthia, Styria, Burgenland, 1983

Volume III/1: Vienna, districts I–XII, 1990
Volume III/2: Vienna, districts XIII–XVIII, 1995
Volume III/3: Vienna, districts XIX–XXIII, 2010

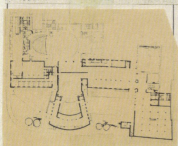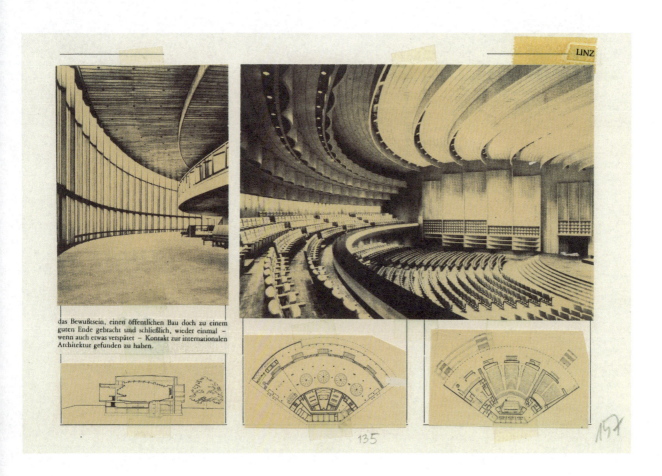

Volume I: Upper Austria, Salzburg, Tyrol, Vorarlberg, 1980 | Examples of layout templates (mounted)

DORNBIRN

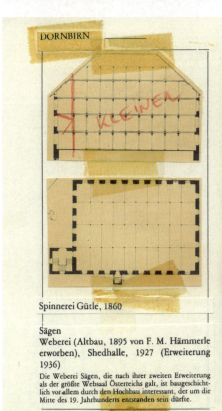

Spinnerei Gütle, 1860

Sägen
Weberei (Altbau, 1895 von F. M. Hämmerle erworben), Shedhalle, 1927 (Erweiterung 1936)

Die Weberei Sägen, die nach ihrer zweiten Erweiterung als der größte Websaal Österreichs galt, ist baugeschichtlich vor allem durch den Hochbau interessant, der um die Mitte des 19. Jahrhunderts entstanden sein dürfte.

Steinebach
Ab 1846 permanenter Ausbau, Webereihochhaus, E + A: Sepp Hämmerle, 1862
Hauptkontor, E: Hugo Schlösser (Stuttgart), 1937 – 39

Sägerstraße 1, Büro-, Wohn- und Lagerhaus F. M. Zumtobel, E: Hans Feßler, 1930

Steinacker 19, Ziegelei Joh. Nep. Rhomberg Nachf., Trockenspeicher, um 1885 – 90

Seltenes Exemplar eines Trockenspeichers mit einer eindrucksvollen Zimmermannskonstruktion. Die Höhe des Speichers ist ebenso selten und dürfte aus Platzmangel entstanden sein.

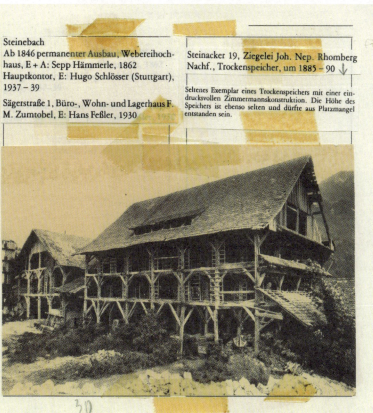

VOMP

VOMP
Volksschule, E: Günther Norer, MA: Margarethe Sentobe, 1972 – 1975

Die räumliche Konzeption der Schule könnte man als eine Art Brennpunkt verstehen, in dem sich viele Aspekte des Umraumes vereinen und in dem die Räume der Schule wieder auf diesen zurückstrahlen. Man kann behaupten, wenn man von den üblichen Fragen des Maßstabes und der Einbindung in die bauliche Situation des Dorfes absieht, daß in der Halle der Schule, durch die Lage der Klassen und Vorbereiche, der Wege und Verbindungen, der Ebenen und Galerien, der verschiedenen Schwellenbereiche und Raumfolgen, durch das Hereingreifen des gläsernen Grabendaches und der Lichtführungen eine landschaftliche Situation ihre räumliche Verdichtung erfährt, womit umgekehrt dem Benützer der Schule ein Erlebnisraum geboten wird, der gerade diese Beziehung zum Außenraum steigert und intensiviert. Mit diesem Schulbau wurde in Tirol eine neue Ebene der Auseinandersetzung erreicht, die jedoch bis jetzt nicht weitergeführt wurde.

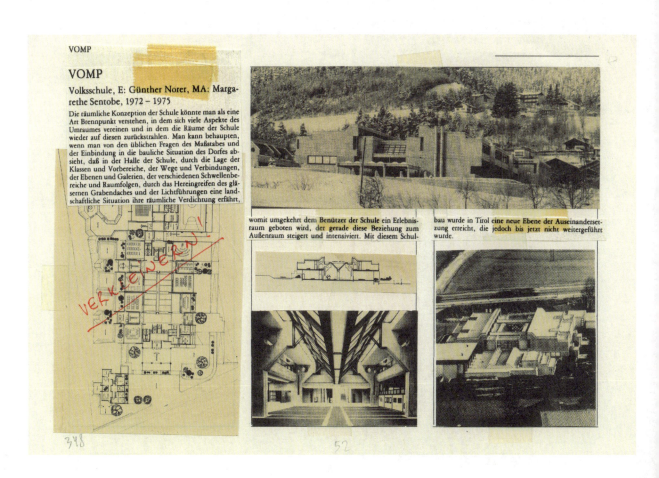

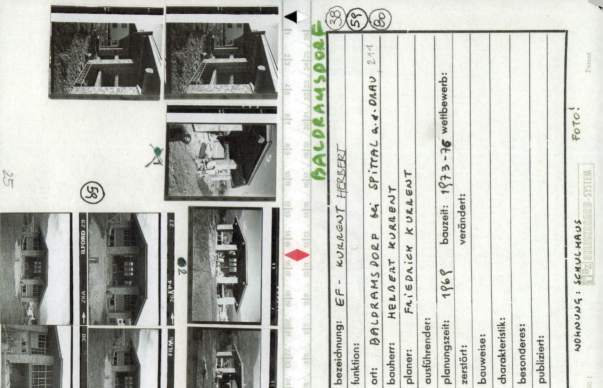

BALDRAMSDORF

1	bezeichnung:	EF - KURRENT HERBERT
2	funktion:	
3	ort:	BALDRAMSDORF bei SPITAL a.d. DRAU 211
4	bauherr:	HERBERT KURRENT
5	planer:	FRIEDRICH KURRENT
6	ausführender:	
7	planungszeit:	1968 bauzeit: 1973-76 wettbewerb:
8	zerstört:	verändert:
9	bauweise:	
10	charakteristik:	
11	besonderes:	
12	publiziert:	

WOHNUNG : SCHULHAUS   FOTO!

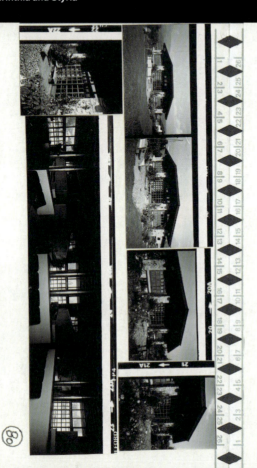

Forschungsinstitut und Rechenzentrum der Oesterreichisch-Alpine Montangesellschaft
Leoben, Peter-Tunner-Straße
Architekten: Dipl.-Ing. Günther Domenig, Dipl.-Ing. Eilfried Huth
Statik: Dipl.-Ing. N. Deutschmann
1970 bis 1972
Verbaute Fläche 1680 m², umbauter Raum 23 900 m³, Gesamtkosten zirka 64 Millionen Schilling. Klare funktionelle Trennung der Baugruppen (Forschung, Rechenzentrum, Büros). Trennung der Funktionsgruppen auch hinsichtlich Schall- und Schwingungstechnik. Konstruktion: Institut und Rechenzentrum Stahlbauweise; Bürotrakt stützenfrei vom Kern des Stahlskelettes abgehängt. Deckenkonstruktion Fertigteile; Fassade vorgehängt; Trennwände vorfabrizierte Polyestereinheiten.
1 Forschungszentrum (Hallentrakt), 2 Rechenzentrum, 3 Büros

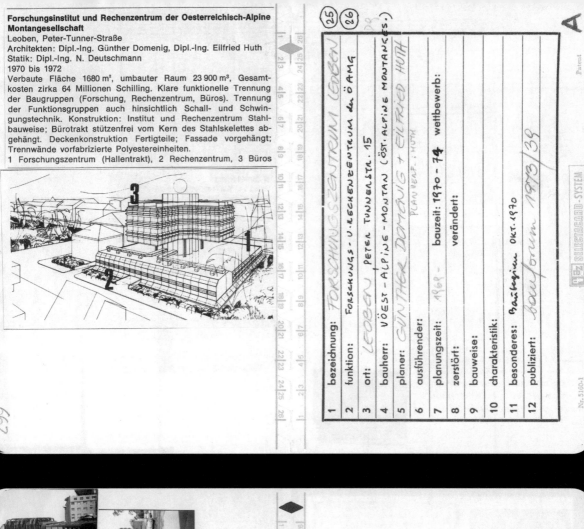

1 bezeichnung:	FORSCHUNGSZENTRUM LEOBEN
2 funktion:	Forschungs- u. Rechenzentrum der ÖAMG
3 ort:	LEOBEN, PETER TUNNERSTR. 15
4 bauherr:	VÖEST-ALPINE-MONTAN (ÖST. ALPINE MONTANGES.)
5 planer:	GÜNTHER DOMENIG + EILFRIED HUTH
6 ausführender:	PLANVERF.: HUTH
7 planungszeit:	1968 – bauzeit: 1970–74 wettbewerb:
8 zerstört:	verändert:
9 bauweise:	
10 charakteristik:	
11 besonderes:	Baubeginn OKT. 1970
12 publiziert:	bauforum 1973/38

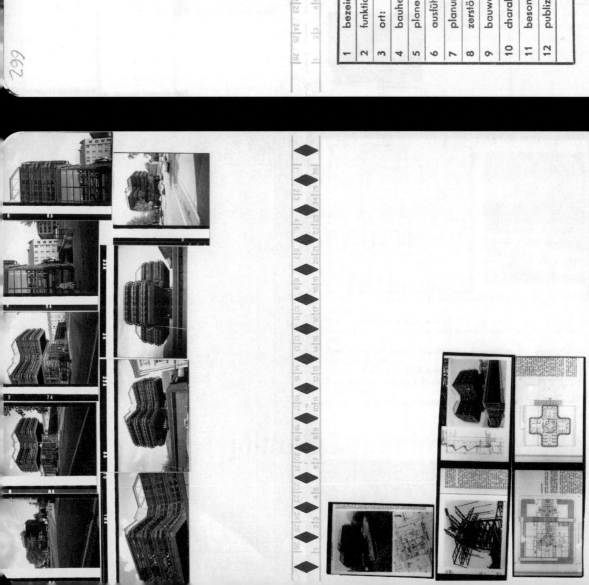

Kurt Schlauss | Underground streetcar loop and passageway at Schottentor, "Jonasreindl" | Vienna I, 1959–1961 | Photo: 1991

Franz Wallack | Grossglockner High Alpine Road | Heiligenblut, Salzburg, Carinthia, 1930–1935 | Photo: 2002

Surveyor: Margherita Spiluttini

Josef Maria Olbrich, Marcus Geiger | Secession painted red, 1998 | Vienna I, 1897–1898 | Photo: 1998

Margherita Spiluttini's photo archive is one of the most important collections of photographs on the production of architecture in Austria covering the period from 1980 to 2005. Commissioned by important architects and theorists, Margherita Spiluttini documented more than 4,000 buildings and objects. The focus of her photography lies in the documentation of contemporary architecture, including works from around the globe. In addition, she made studies of urbanistic sites and anonymous architecture and engaged with historic buildings and art in public space. As Spiluttini's series on postwar architecture demonstrates, her way of seeing initiated sustainable transformation processes in the critical discourse. An inventory of the some 100,000 photos she took over the years – mostly large-format, sheet-film slides – has been compiled. It is available on the Az W website.

Margherita Spiluttini Fotoarchiv, https://spiluttini.azw.at/index.php (July 2, 2022)

Oskar Putz | KIX-Bar | Vienna I, 1986–1988 | Photo: 1989

From the "Eternit anonymous" series | Upper Austria | Photo: 1992

Today's MuseumsQuartier, interim use before conversion | Vienna VII | Photo: 1996

Peter Cook, Colin Fournier | Kunsthaus | Graz, Styria, 2000–2003 | Photo: 2004

Josef Hoffmann | Sanatorium | Purkersdorf, Lower Austria, 1904 | Photo: 1982

Meili & Peter, Jürg Conzett Architekten | Mur bridge | Murau, Styria, 1993–1995 | Photo: 1996

Otto Wagner | Light rail bridge over the Vienna river | Vienna XII and XV, 1894–1898 | Photo: 1981

"Area B, Housing and Urban Renewal," now the North Railroad District | Vienna II | Photo: 1985

Walter M. Chramosta | Small power station | Jennersdorf an der Raab, Burgenland, 1989 | Photo: 1991

Johann Bernhard Fischer von Erlach, Joseph Emanuel Fischer von Erlach | Former court stables, today MuseumsQuartier, before conversion | Vienna VII, 1721–1723 | Photo: 1996

Johann Ferdinand Hetzendorf von Hohenberg | Schönbrunn Palace Park, Roman ruin | Vienna XIII, 1778 | Photo: 1986

Franz Schuster | Special kindergarten, donation from Switzerland | Vienna XV, 1948–1949 | Photo: 1992

Players   Canon Makers

Adolf Krischanitz, Oskar Putz (color concept) | Former Kunsthalle Karlsplatz | Vienna I, 1992–2002 | Photo: 1992

Hanno Schlögl, Daniel Süß | Gallery in the Taxispalais, conversion and extension | Innsbruck, Tyrol, 1997–1999 | Photo: 1999

Johann Georg Gsteu | Sculptors' lodgings | St. Margarethen, Burgenland, 1962–1968 | Photo: 2003

Josef Ignaz Gerl, Isidor Canevale | Altes AKH, 1st Surgery, interim use before conversion to university campus | Vienna IX, 1783–1784 | Photo: 1994

Harry Glück, Marija Kirchner, Wilfried Kirchner | Alt Erlaa housing estate, garden design | Vienna XXIII | Photo: 1989

Lukas Lang | Rinter tent, recycling plant | Vienna XXII, 1981–1982 | Photo: 1982

Granary in Simmering | Vienna XI | Photo: 1997

Freeway ventilation system for Arlberg 2 | Vorarlberg | Photo: 1991

Max Rieder | Glanegg duplex | Grödig, Salzburg, 1990–1992 | Photo: 1993

Oswald Haerdtl | Tanzcafé Volksgarten (today: Volksgarten Café and Restaurant) | Vienna I, 1947–1950 | Photo: 2003

F. H. von Hohenberg, Franziska Ullmann | Gloriette Café, interior | Vienna XIII, 1772–1775; 1996 | Photo: 1996

Lois Welzenbacher, Henke Schreieck Architekten | Parkhotel, former Turmhotel Seeber | Hall, Tyrol, 1930–1931; 2001–2003 | Photo: 2003

Viennese Werkbundsiedlung before renovation, unit by Adolf Loos | Vienna, 1930–1932 | Photo: 1981

Friedrich Kurrent | Maria Biljan-Bilger Exhibition Hall | Sommerein, Lower Austria, 1995–2004 | Photo: 2002

Initiators of a Brand: Vienna around 1900

arbeitsgruppe 4 (Wilhelm Holzbauer, Friedrich Kurrent, Johannes Spalt) | Exhibition poster, Architecture in Vienna around 1900, exhibition at Österreichisches Bauzentrum, Palais Liechtenstein, Vienna, 1964

<u>arbeitsgruppe 4 (Wilhelm Holzbauer, Friedrich Kurrent, Johannes Spalt)</u>
<u>Exhibition poster, Architecture in Vienna around 1900, exhibition at Österreichisches Bauzentrum, Palais Liechtenstein, Vienna, 1964</u>

The exhibition Architecture in Vienna around 1900, curated and designed by arbeitsgruppe 4 (Wilhelm Holzbauer, Friedrich Kurrent, Johannes Spalt), was a milestone in a city's rediscovery of its own history. For the first time, the building activity of Viennese modernism was comprehensively portrayed. The aim was to show the continuity between the generations, and to propose a new reading of Viennese modernism. In 1971, the exhibition travelled to Rome's Galleria Nazionale d'Arte Moderna, marking the beginning of the worldwide interest in the Vienna-around-1900 brand.

Hans Hollein | Proposal of temporary portico for Dream and Reality, Vienna 1870–1930 | Exhibition at the Künstlerhaus Wien, 1985 | Collage on whiteprint; water color and felt pen on paper | Archive Hans Hollein, Az W and MAK, Vienna

Hans Hollein
Proposal of temporary portico for Dream and Reality Vienna 1870–1930, exhibition at the Künstlerhaus Wien, 1985

Hans Hollein's 1985 exhibition entitled Dream and Reality, Vienna 1870–1930, commissioned by the Wien Museum and shown at Vienna's Künstlerhaus, signaled a shift in paradigm in the exhibition circuit. Attracting 622,000 visitors, the show was a blockbuster, and the brand "Viennese modernism" became an important economic factor. To this day, Hans Hollein's dramatization of several iconic reconstructions and models built expressly for the exhibition influences our perception of this era. In 1986, the exhibition was shown at the Centre Georges Pompidou in Paris and then at the Museum of Modern Art in New York.

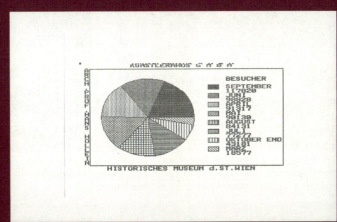

Attendance data | Computer print | Archive Hans Hollein, Az W and MAK, Vienna

Players Initiators of a Brand: Vienna around 1900 111

Installation, Vienna's Künstlerhaus | Three-dimensional reincarnation of Klimt's female figure from the faculty painting symbolizing medicine (originally designed for the ceiling of the University of Vienna's main ceremonial hall)

Reconstruction | Proposal for the Chicago Tribune Tower (1922)

Adolf Loos | Kärntnerbar (1908) | After the exhibition's run, the reconstruction by Hermann Czech was installed to replace Loos's original American Bar portal (address: Kärntner Durchgang 10), which was no longer in existence.

Architecture reconstruction: Otto Wagner | *Die Zeit* press agency (1902) | Portal reconstruction in original materials and dimensions, including aluminum facade by Adolf Krischanitz and Otto Kapfinger

All photos: Archive Hans Hollein, Az W and MAK, Vienna

Installation, Vienna's Künstlerhaus | An architectural motif employed at the Karl Marx Hof

Players   Initiators of a Brand: Vienna around 1900   112

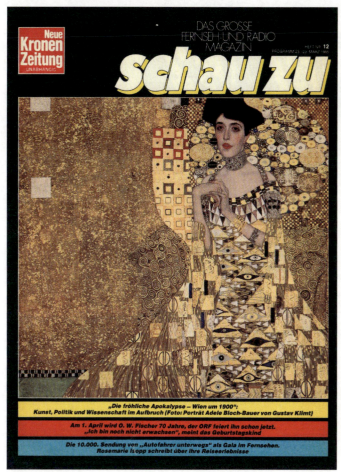

['The Joyful Apocalypse – Vienna around 1900': Art and Politics and Science at a Crossroads] | Cover of "schau zu" (a supplement to the *Kronenzeitung*), no. 12, March 1985

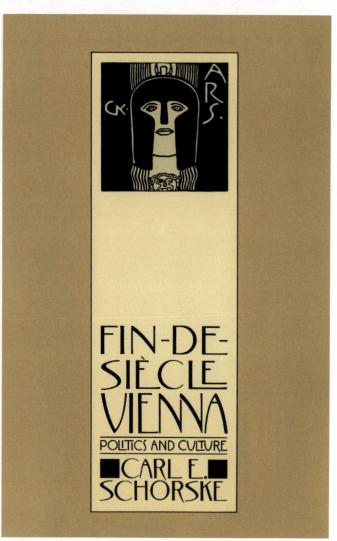

Carl E. Schorske | *Fin-de-Siècle Vienna. Politics and Culture*, New York, 1979 (German edition: *Wien. Geist und Gesellschaft im Fin de Siècle*, Frankfurt, 1980) | Cover

With his seminal book *Fin-de-Siècle Vienna. Politics and Culture*, the historian Carl E. Schorske not only paved the way for the rediscovery of the intellectual and cultural history of Vienna at the turn of the century, he also popularized the topic.

Stars are Born: Biennale Venice, 1980

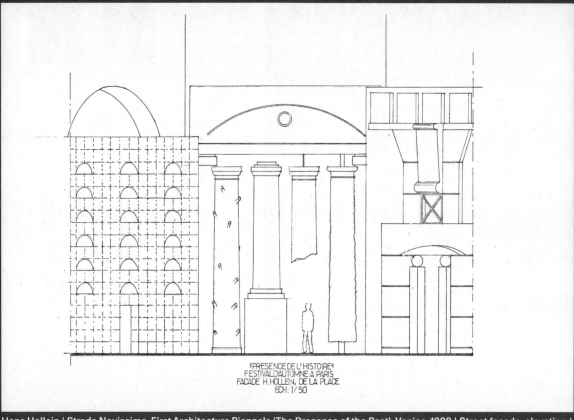

Hans Hollein | Strada Novissima, First Architecture Biennale (The Presence of the Past), Venice, 1980 | Street facade, elevation | Whiteprint | Archive Hans Hollein, Az W and MAK, Vienna

The Presence of the Past is the title Paolo Portoghesi gave to the first biennale in Venice dedicated solely to architecture. As its curator, he paved the way for postmodernism to make an impressive appearance. Twenty architects were invited to conceive a facade installation at the Corderie dell'Arsenale. Reflecting on how the dogmas of modernism might be overcome, Portoghesi asked the contributors to engage with historic cities and streetscapes. Hollein's facade – characterized by ironic stylistic flashbacks and his calling into question the column as load-bearing element – was one of the most convincing installations along the so-called Strada Novissima. In addition to enthroning postmodernism, this first purely architectural biennale also marked the birth of the now antiquated era of star architects. Hans Hollein was appointed commissioner of the alternating art and the architecture biennales on several occasions – a testimony to his cultural-political influence in Austria.

"The presence of the Past" is apparent in my contribution in a manifold way. It is an architecture of memories, memories, not only in the sense of architectural history, but memory of ones cultural heritage and of ones personal past – manifesting themselves in quotations, transformations and metaphors. My work of today incorporates – consciously – the presence of the past in terms of a continued (sometimes fragmentary) re-elaboration of earlier work and ideas. I am concerned as much with history as with my own history.

Almost as a countermove to what would suggest itself, I decided to do my facade in the "street" as a presence of the past as found in the "corderia" – the columns.

Both the facade – as applied sheet – and the column are a matter of concern in my work. I could have transplanted some of my storefronts right to the exhibition site both in terms of scale but also of intent – they are not just facades but built manifestos, incorporating in a nutshell an approach, an attitude. As I have done this so often (in real streets), I rather decided to continue (the past) on the idea of the columns (continuing the already existing columns). A column – as Loos has clearly understood – presents itself. It is a structural element which has become absolute architecture. Bernini in San Ambrogio, Loos in Chicago, my predilection for the garden and my concern with the – sometimes menacing – presence of the past in terms of archaeological fragments is my selection here. I would have many more "columns" to fill the more than 300 meters of the colonnades of the corderia of the Arsenale in Venice.

Hans Hollein
1980

Hans Hollein | Contribution for the catalog of the First Architecture Biennale (The Presence of the Past), Venice, 1980 | Typoscript, colored pencil | Archive Hans Hollein, Az W and MAK, Vienna

Participation and co-determination in housing | Eilfried Huth | Eschensiedlung model dwellings | Deutschlandsberg, Styria, 1972–1992

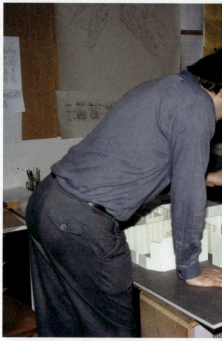

Participatory planning process in housing | Ottokar Uhl (with Franz Kuzmich, Renate Jesacher, Martin Wurnig) | B.R.O.T. housing | Geblergasse 78, Vienna XVII, 1985–1990

Protagonists

Self-organization and participation in cohousing | einszueins architektur (Katharina Bayer, Markus Zilker) | Wohnprojekt Wien housing | Krakauer Strasse 19, Vienna II, 2010–2013 | Photo: einszueins architektur

In the 1960s, in response to the monotonous, postwar apartment blocks, a participative planning movement came into existence. With significant personal commitment, Eilfried Huth and Ottokar Uhl developed a variety of participation models for the carefully considered interaction among professionals and laypeople.

Players Protagonists

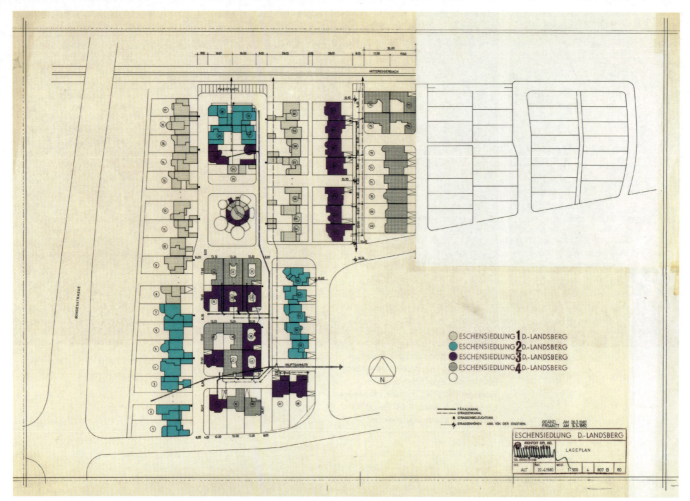

Eilfried Huth | Eschensiedlung model dwellings | Deutschlandsberg, Styria, 1972–1992 | Site plan with construction phases, 1980 | Ink on translucent paper, adhesive foil

Participation and co-determination in housing

Eilfried Huth
Eschensiedlung model dwellings
Deutschlandsberg, Styria, 1972–1992

This housing experiment consisting of user-defined units came into being over the course of fifteen years, within the framework of subsidized housing, structured in six construction phases – and produced a total of 110 dwellings. The point of departure for the Eschensiedlung was the popularity of the single-family house and the attempt to make it affordable to lower-income groups. Because residents themselves could carry out certain tasks on the construction site, it was possible to reduce the overall costs. Early concepts employing prefabricated components were therefore impracticable, and the team turned instead to conventional forms of construction such as sloped roofs and wood trusses. The future residents participated in

Construction work by future users

the planning process from the very beginning. Architect Eilfried Huth moderated and shaped the planning and implementation of the project by initiating lectures, discussions, and consultations. The site office became the marketplace for construction materials and the center of communication of the small self-organized groups, which joined forces as an advocacy group. The result is a novel rendition of semi-detached housing with strong neighborly support structures.

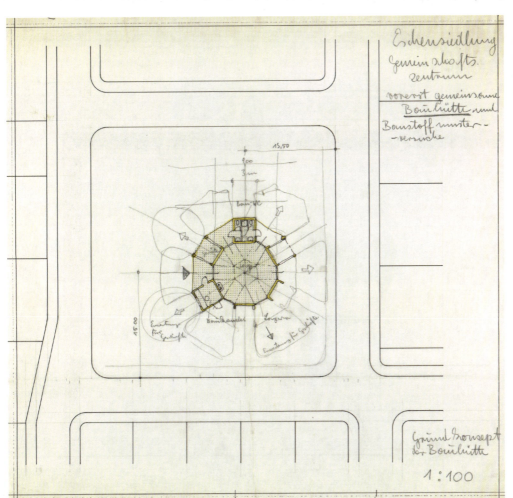

Concept for the construction-site office | Ink, pencil, and felt pen on translucent paper, adhesive foil

The community center was initially used as construction-site office and for testing the building material samples.

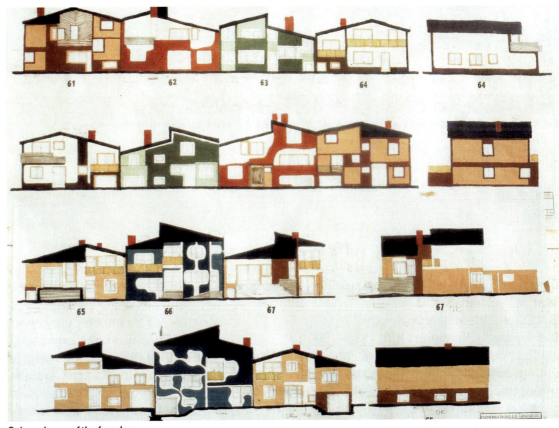

Color scheme of the facades

Players   Protagonists   119

Participatory planning process in housing

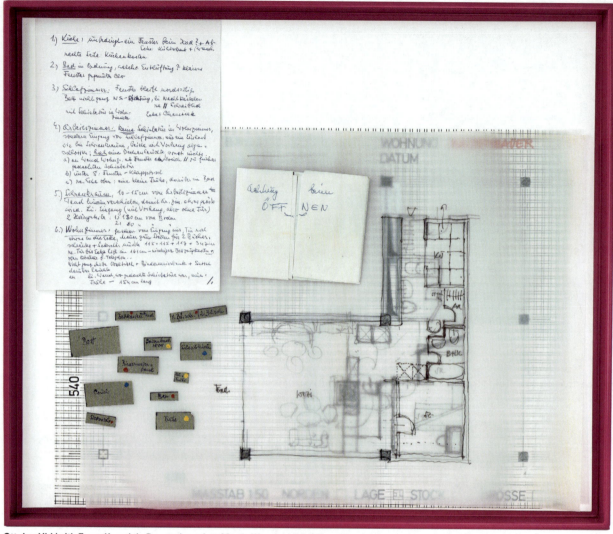

Ottokar Uhl (with Franz Kuzmich, Renate Jesacher, Martin Wurnig) | B.R.O.T. residential community | Geblergasse 78, Vienna XVII, 1985–1990

Ottokar Uhl (with Franz Kuzmich, Renate Jesacher, Martin Wurnig)
B.R.O.T. residential community
Geblergasse 78, Vienna XVII, 1985–1990

The housing is one of the first intergenerational initiatives to be erected in Austria. This participative project was made possible by B.R.O.T. (an acronym of Beten, Reden, Offen sein, Teilen [pray, discuss, be open, share]), for which the Hernals parish made a parcel of land available by providing a long-term land lease. Sixteen rental apartments and eight apartments for shorter stays were created. Uhl's participative approach is based on the open principles of prefabrication developed by N. John Habraken. All levels are organized in keeping with an underlying structure, allowing the users to shape their units according to their respective needs.

Lived participation, users
in architectural dialogue

Self-organization and participation in cohousing

einszueins architektur (Katharina Bayer, Markus Zilker) | Cooperative housing | Preliminary talks among the future residents | Krakauer Strasse 19, Vienna II, 2010–2013 | Photo: einszueins architektur

<u>einszueins architektur (Katharina Bayer, Markus Zilker)</u>
<u>Cooperative housing</u>
<u>Krakauer Strasse 19, Vienna II, 2010–2013</u>

In the development of new districts, the City of Vienna recognized the added value of co-commissioned projects, which were given the opportunity to apply for the respective lots. A building group is defined as a community of people who have similar interests, needs, wishes, and ideas about how neighborly structures could be achieved. Under the slogan "Living with us!" and as an alternative to anonymous housing types, this co-commissioned housing project with 39 units arose on the grounds of Vienna's Nordbahnhof. The residents of the intercultural, multigenerational endeavor, in which a non-profit organization fostering sustainable living rents apartments to its members, was involved in the entire planning process – from the allocation of apartments to planning their respective units and the shared spaces (700 m²). Each apartment has a unique floor plan, and this diversity is legible in the freely arranged balconies and windows. The crux of the project is achieving a self-managed community – based on innovative methods of organizations and decision-making (sociocracy) – coupled with the commitment to building and living sustainably. The architecture firm einszueins architektur, which has gained a reputation for collaborative housing and cooperative processes, has set up its office on the building's ground level.

Model | Wooden panel; wood, plastic

Individual unit | Working model | Cardboard, paper

Players Protagonists

Literature

Gender Firewall
pp. 86–88

Linda Nochlin, "Why Are There No Great Women Artists?," in: Vivian Gornick, Barbara Moran (eds.), *Woman in Sexist Society. Studies In Power And Powerlessness* (New York 1971), 344–366.

Patrick Werkner, Heinrich Gressel, *Ich bin keine Küche. Gegenwartsgeschichten aus dem Nachlass von Margarete Schütte-Lihotzky*, exh. cat. Universität für angewandte Kunst Wien (Vienna, 2008).

Despina Stratigakos, "What I Learned from Architect Barbie," in: *Places Journal,* June 2011, https://placesjournal.org/article/what-i-learned-from-architect-barbie/?cn-reloaded=1 (accessed July 2, 2022).

Ingrid Holzschuh, Sabine Plakolm-Forsthuber, Zentralvereinigung der ArchitektInnen Österreichs (eds.), *Pionierinnen der Wiener Architektur* (Basel 2022).

Ann-Kathrin Rossberg, Elisabeth Schmuttermeier, Christoph Thun-Hohenstein (eds.), *Die Frauen der Wiener Werkstätte / Women Artists of the Wiener Werkstätte*, exh. cat. MAK, 5/5–10/3/2021 (Basel 2021).

Archetypes
pp. 89–95

Günther Feuerstein, "Archetypen des Bauens," 2 vols. (dissertation, TU Wien 1966).

Frauenmuseum Hittisau, Raum für Geburt und Sinne, https://www.frauenmuseum.at/geburt-sinne (accessed July 2, 2022).

IG Geburtskultur a-z, Raum für Geburt und Sinne, https://geburtskultur.com/raum-fuer-geburt-und-sinne/ (accessed July 2, 2022).

Canon Makers
pp. 96–109

Architekturzentrum Wien (ed.), *Friedrich Achleitner 80* (*Hintergrund* 46/47) (Vienna 2010).

Architekturzentrum Wien (ed.), *Margherita Spiluttini. räumlich – spacious*, exh. cat. Architekturzentrum Wien, 6/12–9/24/2007 (Salzburg 2007).

Gabriele Hofer-Hagenauer, Gabriele Conrath-Scholl, *Margherita Spiluttini. Archiv der Räume. Archive of Spaces*, exh. cat. Landesgalerie Linz, 3/12–5/31/2015 (Linz 2015).

Initiators of a Brand: Vienna around 1900
pp. 110–113

Gabriele Kaiser, "Bilanzen mit Ausblick. Die Ausstellungen der arbeitsgruppe 4," in: Sonja Pisarik, Ute Waditschatka, Architekturzentrum Wien (eds.), *arbeitsgruppe 4. Wilhelm Holzbauer, Friedrich Kurrent, Johannes Spalt. 1950–1970,* exh. cat. Architekturzentrum Wien, 3/4–5/31/2010 (Salzburg/Vienna 2010), 142–160.

Museen der Stadt Wien (ed.), Traum und Wirklichkeit 1870–1930, exh. cat. Historisches Museum der Stadt Wien, 3/28–10/6/1985 (Vienna 1985).

Stars are Born: Biennale Venice, 1980
pp. 114–115

Gabriella Borsano, *The Presence of the Past. First International Exhibition of Architecture. The Corderia of the Arsenal*, exh. cat. La Biennale di Venezia 1980. Architectural Section, (London 1980).

Léa-Catherine Szacka, *Exhibiting the Postmodern: The 1980 Venice Architecture Biennale* (London 2016).

Protagonists
pp. 116–123

Gemeinschaft B.R.O.T., "20 Jahre Haus Hernals 1990–2010," Festschrift (Vienna 2010), https://brot-hernals.at/wp-content/uploads/2015/06/Festschrift-20-Jahre-Gemeinschaft-BROT.pdf (accessed July 2, 2022)

Kurt Freisitzer, Robert Koch, *Ottokar Uhl, Mitbestimmung im Wohnbau. Ein Handbuch* (Vienna 1987).

Bernhard Steger (ed.), *Themen der Architektur: z. B. Ottokar Uhl* (Vienna 2011).

Architekturzentrum Wien (ed.), *Ottokar Uhl*, exh. cat. Architekturzentrum Wien, 3/3/–6/13/2005 (Salzburg 2005).

Eilfried Huth, Doris Pollet, *Beteiligung, Mitbestimmung im Wohnbau. Wohnmodell Deutschlandsberg Eschensiedlung* (progress report 1972–1976, documentation of the study) (Graz 1977).

Andrea Jany, *Experiment Wohnbau. Die partizipative Architektur des "Modell Steiermark"* (Berlin 2019).

einszueins architektur, Wohnprojekt Wien, https://www.einszueins.at/project/wohnprojekt-wien/ (accessed July 2, 2022).

Wohnprojekt Wien, Verein für Nachhaltiges Leben, https://wohnprojekt.wien/ (accessed July 2, 2022).

Planet

How ca
we s

The Algae House (BIQ)	129
Rudrapur	132
Naturalization	**136**
Danube Island Vienna	137
Haus-Rucker-Co	140
Bodenfreiheit, Non-profit Association	142
"Moldiness Manifesto"	143
Gentle Urban Renewal	**144**
Planquadrat	144
LandLuft, Non-profit Association	146
Temporary Theater in Haag	147
Saving and Producing Energy	**148**
Residential Complex Purkersdorf I	148
Standard Solar I	150
Socially Sustainable	**152**
Rauch Workshop	152
VinziRast in the Countryside	154
Utopia–Dystopia	**156**

First the bad news. Construction is responsible for a large part of global resource consumption and contributes significantly to man-made climate change. The good news is that in a climate crisis, resourceful architecture has incredible leveraging power. In the twenty-first century, sustainability and climate equitability have become architecture's overarching themes. Back in the 1970s, the oil crisis and the Club of Rome reports sparked a search for alternatives. How can we repair the future and keep the planet and its inhabitants alive? The proposed solutions range from green technologies via low-emission materials to socially sustainable bottom-up initiatives that open up local scope for action. Others rediscover the existing building stock as an alternative to new construction or are devising plans to make faraway planets inhabitable.

The Algae House (BIQ)

SPLITTERWERK (Mark Blaschitz, Edith Hemmrich, Josef Roschitz)
The Algae House (BIQ)
Am Inselpark 17, Hamburg, Germany, 2011–2013

In 2013, SPLITTERWERK, a Graz-based architecture firm, was selected to implement one of four Smart Material Houses at Hamburg's Internationale Bauausstellung (IBA). The program focused on building envelopes of residential buildings that react dynamically to changing environmental conditions. This was the first application of a bioreactor facade utilizing algae for energy production. When carbon dioxide and nitrogen are added to the algae, bubbles form in the facade elements. The energy carrier heat, which is produced utilizing electricity and biogas, is made available to the building – or fed into the local network, or into the ground, where it is stored until it is needed. On the two shaded facades, the two dialogue balloons "Photosynthesis?" and "Cool!" tell of the cycle's sustainability.

To create algae biomass, carbon dioxide and sunlight are combined in vertical solar-conversion glass louvers (SolarLeaf) that contain a watery nutrient solution; at the same time, because the solar radiation warms the watery medium, a solar-thermal effect is achieved. Both energy media are directed via a closed loop into the building's energy management center, where a heat exchanger and algae separator extract the thermal energy. For demonstration purposes, in the exhibition a substitute liquid is used in place of the algae biomass.

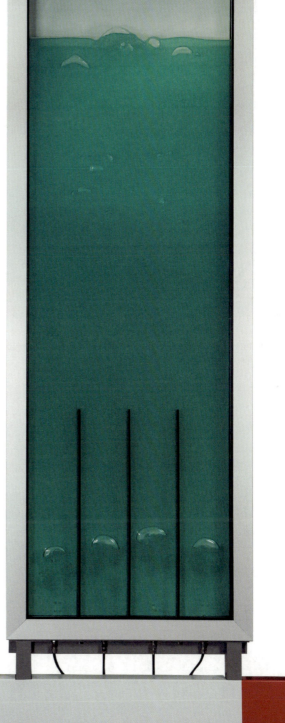

SPLITTERWERK (Mark Blaschitz, Edith Hemmrich, Josef Roschitz) | The Algae House (BIQ) | Am Inselpark 17, Hamburg, Germany, 2011–2013 | Colt SolarLeaf louver, bioreactor facade, 2022 | Product development: Arup, Colt International, Strategic Science Consult | The exhibit was kindly provided by Arup and Colt International.

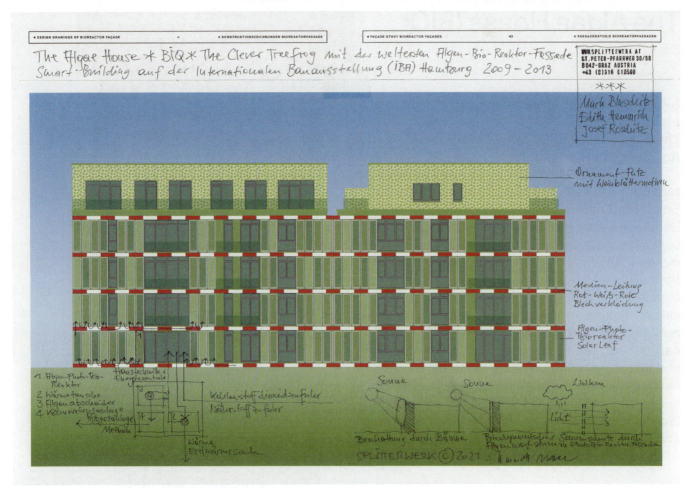

SPLITTERWERK (Mark Blaschitz, Edith Hemmrich, Josef Roschitz) | The Algae House (BIQ) | Am Inselpark 17, Hamburg, Germany, 2011–2013 | Bioreactor, elevation with handwritten notes and sketches | Pencil on color print

South elevation | Photo: Paul Ott

Planet

North elevation | Photo: Paul Ott

Rudrapur

1. METI school, 2004–2005
2. DESI vocational school for electrical training, 2008
3. HOMEmade residences, 2008
4. Anandaloy Therapy Center for People with Disabilities, 2019
5. Seamstresses, at work on the exhibited wall hanging at the Dipdii Textiles studio, located at the Anandaloy Therapy Center for People with Disabilities, 2021

Photos: Kurt Hoerbst (1, 3, 4), Naquib Hossain (2), Barbara Miranda (5)

As a nineteen-year-old, Anna Heringer spent a year in Bangladesh. Inspired by Dipshikha, an NGO, she learned that the most successful development strategy involves placing one's trust in available resources. In 2004, in her first project, the METI school in Rudrapur, she combined local materials such as bamboo and loam with the communication of new knowledge. This she achieved by including the local population from the very beginning in the planning and construction process. The next project she realized was the DESI education center, consisting of residences, a center for people with disabilities, and the Dipdii Textiles studio – these are all depicted in embroidery on the site plan. Dipdii Textiles creates jobs for women near their homes and in this way saves them from emigration or poor working conditions in urban textile factories. Following a tradition, worn-out saris and lungis are reworked as multi-layered, hand-sewn blankets. Since 2012, in Rudrapur the colorful fabric metamorphoses into bespoke items. A sustainable and durable rendition of "Made in Bangladesh".

Planet

Planet 133

Dipdii Textiles (Anna Heringer, Veronika Lena Lang) | Site plan with buildings designed by Anna Heringer in Rudrapur, Bangladesh | Wall hanging made of recycled saris and lungis, 2021 | Embroidered

Naturalization

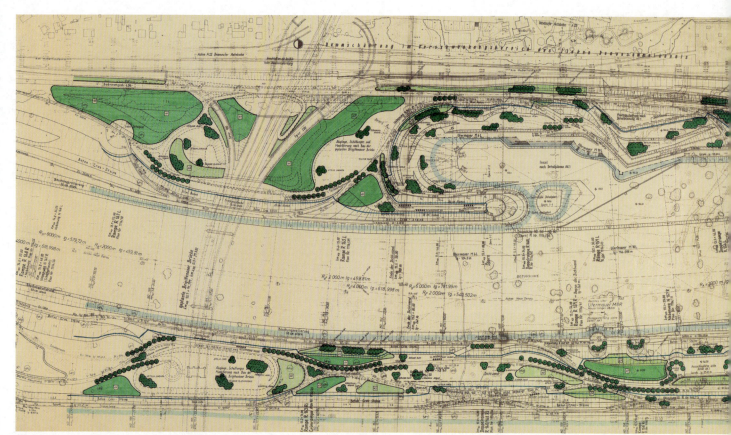

Marija Kirchner, Wilfried Kirchner | Danube Island Vienna, 1972–1987 | Vegetation patterns, topography, circulation system, planting | North central – Brigittenauer Bridge – Reichsbrücke | Design studies | Colored pencil on whiteprint

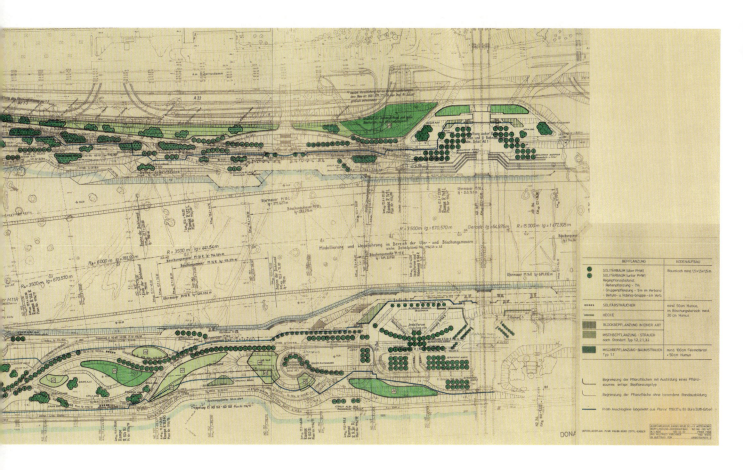

Danube Island Vienna

For the discipline of landscape planning, the construction of the Danube Island – the product of a gigantic flood protection project for Vienna – was an ecological milestone. The strip of green is over 20 kilometers long and, on average, 400 meters wide. It is home to biotopes, endemic plants, and natural riverbanks as habitat for flora and fauna. On top of that, it provides ample space for a variety of leisure activities. Vienna is indebted to landscape architects Marija and Wilfried Kirchner for turning what had initially been considered a hydrotechnological infrastructure project into a landscape in which spaces inhabited by nature and culture become intertwined.

Marija Kirchner, Wilfried Kirchner | Danube Island Vienna, 1972–1987 | Vegetation patterns, topography, circulation system, planting | North central – Floridsdorf Bridge | Design studies | Colored pencil on whiteprint

Haus-Rucker-Co (Laurids Ortner, Günter Zamp Kelp, Klaus Pinter, Manfred Ortner) | Undulating Meadow, 1974 | Collage | Photo, pencil, colored pencil on tracing paper

Haus-Rucker-Co

Haus-Rucker-Co's sketches dating from the 1970s reject a romanticized notion of bringing nature back into the city and reveal the increasing discrepancy between the city and the countryside. They show new forms of nature, which, as "Tree Towers" and "Undulating Meadow," not only make reference to the environmental threat we face, but also issue a plea for a new understanding of nature in urban space.

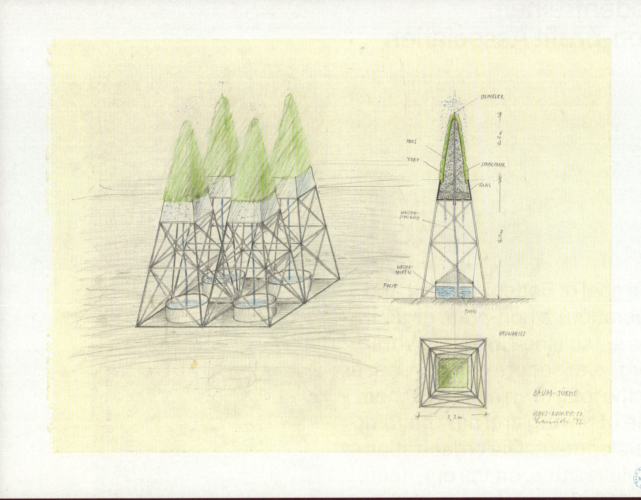

Haus-Rucker-Co (Laurids Ortner, Günter Zamp Kelp, Klaus Pinter, Manfred Ortner) | Tree Towers, 1972 | Pencil and colored pencil on paper

Bodenfreiheit, Non-profit Association

Bodenfreiheit [Land Liberation], non-profit association for the conservation of outdoor spaces | Boundary stone "Green zone written in stone" | Granite, worked, 2021 | Stonemason: Stefan Summer

The goal of Bodenfreiheit [Land Liberation], a non-profit organization established in 2011 in Vorarlberg, is to secure outdoor spaces for the long term and keep them free of paving and new building development. The organization achieves this, on the one hand, through the purchase (with the aid of supporters' donations) of small properties at strategic locations and readies them for uses such as community gardens or adventure playgrounds. On the other hand, it applies a specific version of the easement. To this end, the organization secures the title-guaranteed right to criss-cross a certain piece of property, and as a result, the site cannot be built upon. But why would farmers grant the organization the right to an easement? Because it alleviates the pressure often applied by the neighborhood or by investors to sell the property.

Bodenfreiheit [Land Liberation], non-profit association for the conservation of outdoor spaces
Boundary stone "Green zone written in stone"
   The first boundary stone securing the extents of the green zone was installed in 2019 in Ludesch, Vorarlberg. Depending on the location and significance of the land, as well as the duration of the way leave (ranging from 50 years to unlimited), the organization offers the owners financial compensation for their permission at a rate of about two to ten percent of the local price for agricultural land. In this way, Bodenfreiheit created an unconventional model to preserve open outdoor spaces.

"Moldiness Manifesto"

Television show *Wünsch Dir was* | Rheingoldhalle, Mainz, February 26, 1972 | ORF | Film stills

In 1958, as a response to the functionalism of the postwar era, Friedensreich Hundertwasser penned the "Moldiness manifesto against rationalism in architecture." In it he demanded a democratization of architecture and a fundamental realignment toward a way of building that occurs in close communion with nature and is characterized by asymmetry, organic forms, and polychromatism. On February 26, 1972, as a guest on the television show *Wünsch Dir was* [Make a Wish], Hundertwasser presented his ideas and several architectural models. On the whole, the audience viewed the concepts as a source of amusement. Just ten years later, with the implementation of the Hundertwasserhaus in Vienna, he drew attention to his most prominent concern: creating buildings that are sensitive to the needs of humans and nature.

Gentle Urban Renewal

Das Planquadrat | (1974–1976) | ORF | Film stills

Planquadrat

The modern city planning of the twentieth century sought to provide daylight, fresh air, and sun, but also plenty of room for cars. Therefore, practicing the ideology involves tearing down old buildings and large swathes of urban districts. In the 1970s, resistance to this practice mounted. It went hand in hand with the critique of an undemocratic city planning and the need to have one's voice heard and to have the opportunity to participate in the process.

The grounds of the Planquadrat in Vienna had consisted of several courtyards that were separated by walls and fences, and as a whole, amounted to a dreary "courtscape." The intention to tear down the buildings on Mühlgasse to make way for a wider thoroughfare prompted a community organizers' movement that ultimately achieved the revitalization of the existing urban fabric. To this day, Gartenhofverein, the non-profit organization established by the activists, looks after the green space (5,000 m²). Also unique to this venture was the active role played by state-run television, which produced documentaries about the project from the very beginning and presented them on prime-time television. The interaction between architects, residents, politics, and media led to an urban renewal model in which social criteria intersected with environmental protection.

Planet · Gentle Urban Renewal · 144

Das Planquadrat (1974–1976)

Between 1974 and 1976, the filmmakers put together a 20-episode TV series which was shown on ORF, Austria's public broadcasting service. It informed audiences about the concerns of the some 600 residents of the buildings surrounding an area made up of 34 small courtyards in Vienna's fourth district. The series spawned a lively public debate about urban maintenance and urban renewal.  The active inclusion of the population in the documentation was revolutionary. The film team occupied an apartment on site, repurposing it as a cutting room and meeting space. Thanks to the continuous attention garnered by the media coverage, an unusually high participation rate among the residents (72 percent) was attained. The cultural-anthropological approach applied intuitively by Elisabeth Guggenberger and Helmut Voitl sparked an initiative in which the residents became self-empowered.  The residents were ultimately able to convince the City of Vienna and the architects to implement their ideas. Through Gartenhofverein, a non-profit organization, the people living here continue to manage their immediate surroundings. To date, no other municipal project has been able to combine the revitalization of a central urban district with true participatory practice.

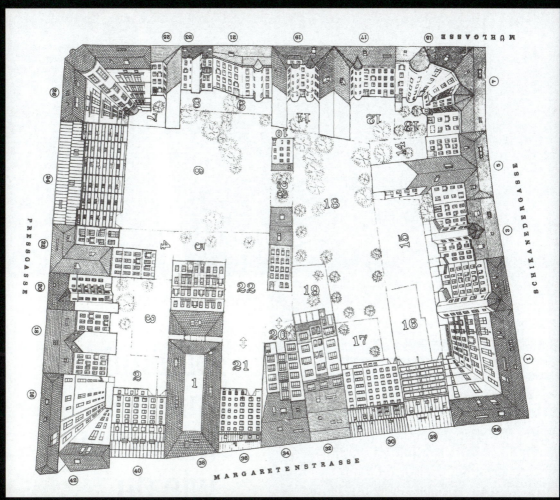

Barbara Langoth, Wolfgang Piller, Martin Schwanzer, Norbert Stangl | Planquadrat board game, 1975 | Gameboard

Planquadrat team (architecture): Irmtraud Goessler-Leirer, Timo Huber, Wilhelm Kainrath, Herbert Pirchner, Hugo Potyka (lead), Ilse Sanzenbecker, Rudolf Zabrana; initially also including Barbara Langoth, Wolfgang Piller, Martin Schwanzer, Norbert Stangl

The idea behind the game was to get the residents to share their aspirations for the project with the community organizers.

LandLuft, Non-profit Association

LandLuft
Baukulturgemeinde

A high standard of architecture can also contribute to climate protection, both in the city and the countryside. Rural exodus, aging population, abandoned properties, and sprawl are some of the greatest challenges to be addressed. Since 1999, LandLuft, a non-profit organization, has promoted architectural initiatives in the countryside and offered networking and continuing-education formats to mayors and city council members and engaged actively in consulting the municipalities. With its travelling exhibitions, its LandLuft Akademie (the organization's educational arm), lectures, and a community award, the organization draws attention to intelligent and sustainable architecture that is worthy of imitation. Measures to improve the quality of life and to respond to climate change include: development processes fostering better site selection, revitalization of town centers, and new mobility concepts.

LandLuft, non-profit organization fostering a high-quality built environment in rural areas | Community prize for regional building culture and "We are the ones who create a high-quality habitat!" tote bag | Plastic; printed fabric

Temporary Theater in Haag

nonconform (Roland Gruber, Dietmar Gulle, Peter Nageler), Justin & Partner (Hernan Trinanes) | Temporary theater | Hauptplatz, Haag, Lower Austria, 1999–2000 | Model | Wood

nonconform (Roland Gruber, Dietmar Gulle, Peter Nageler), Justin & Partner (Hernan Trinanes)
Temporary theater
Hauptplatz, Haag, Lower Austria, 1999–2000

The temporary bleachers for a summer stage, which can be set up each year, sparked a trend toward a more lively town center. With a population of about 5,000, Haag is a typical Lower Austrian small town. Symptomatic of the challenges facing rural communities, the commercial sector had moved from the center to the periphery. The process to reactivate the town center was initiated by establishing an annual theater festival. For more than ten years, architects, citizens, and decision-makers have worked together to implement measures that will revitalize the town center. The project's success has put Haag on the map as a model for other towns.

View of the bleachers | Photo: Dietmar Tollerian

Saving and Producing Energy

Residential Complex Purkersdorf I

Georg W. Reinberg, Jörg Riesenhuber
Residential complex Purkersdorf I
Wintergasse 53, Purkersdorf, Lower Austria,
1981–1984

Passive solar gains via winter gardens, hybrid construction method in wood and brick, cork insulation on the exterior with wood boarding, grass roofs, and on-site rainwater infiltration make the project – carried out by Alternatives Wohnen [Alternative Living], a non-profit organization – a pioneering contribution to ecological building in Austria. This particular type of development can be traced to the site's topography, and, on the other hand, the maximization of the solar yield. Here, energy conscious building is not solely a matter of technological solutions: by making an addition to an old villa it underscores the fundamental importance of the continued use of existing buildings.

Georg W. Reinberg, Jörg Riesenhuber | Residential complex Purkersdorf I | Wintergasse 53, Purkersdorf, Lower Austria, 1981–1984 | Winter garden, elevation | Photo: Margherita Spiluttini

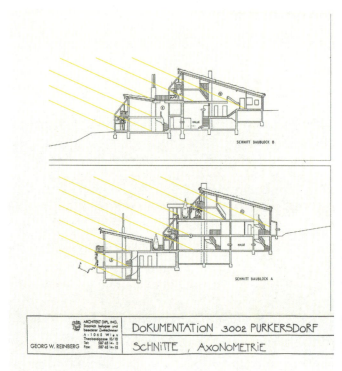

Documentation solar radiation | Sections, axonometry | Copy, ink on paper

Green roof

Invitation to the opening | Copy, ink on paper

Construction site, unrolling the green roof

Planet · Saving and Producing Energy

Driendl*Steixner (Georg Driendl, Gerhard Steixner) | Standard Solar I | Hauptstrasse 82 B, Langenrohr, Lower Austria, 1987–1989 | Elevation | Collage

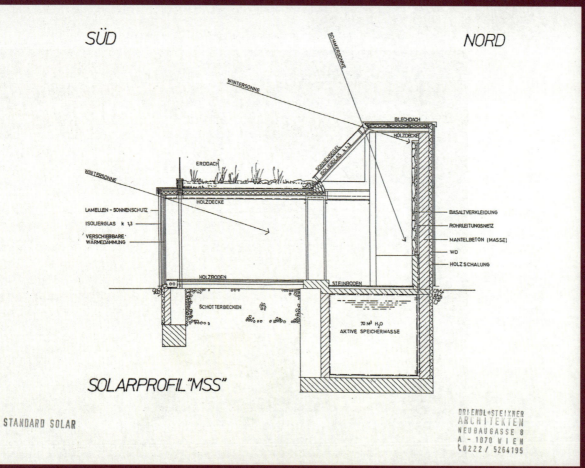

MMS solar profile, cross section | Plan copy

Planet · Saving and Producing Energy · 150

Standard Solar I

Driendl*Steixner (Georg Driendl, Gerhard Steixner)
Standard Solar I
Hauptstrasse 82 B, Langenrohr, Lower Austria, 1987–1989

The oil crisis of the 1970s triggered the awareness of energy-efficient building solutions. Georg Driendl and Gerhard Steixner began to develop their programmatic ideas for solar-energy-powered prefabricated homes. Like the American case-study houses, these make use of architectural and technological innovations. The most important aspect of these energy-efficient prototypes was the decision to employ a modular, hybrid construction method consisting of steel, wood, and glass, as well as the use of solar energy – and the combination turned out to be prescient from a building physics standpoint. Although the house never went into serial production, the architects applied these principles in several other projects.

1 Exterior
2 Interior
3 Entrance area
4 Exterior

Photos: Erwin Reichmann

Socially Sustainable

Rauch Workshop

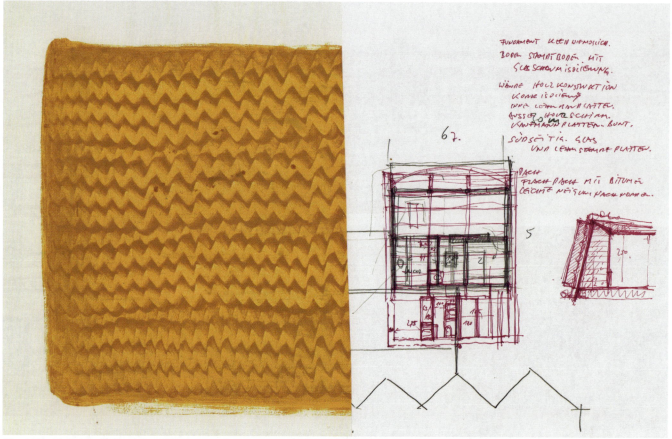

Martin Rauch, Robert Felber | Rauch Workshop | Quadernstrasse 7, Schlins, Vorarlberg, 1990–1994 | Loam texture, floor plan and sketch | Pencil, felt pen, and paint on paper

Martin Rauch, Robert Felber
Rauch Workshop
Quadernstrasse 7, Schlins, Vorarlberg, 1990–1994

This experimental building served Martin Rauch, a pioneer of rammed-earth construction, as a place to demonstrate the material. In what was still an era of purported "endless growth," the material was considered primitive and was not acknowledged by the construction industry. Yet, unparalleled among construction materials, loam fulfils a variety of ecological and biological requirements. It is locally sourced, completely recyclable, easy to process, thermally insulates and stores heat, does not release toxins, and naturally regulates humidity. In the meantime, Martin Rauch has realized countless international projects, and in a new production space, rammed-earth elements are also prefabricated. The completion of this early workshop marked the beginning of his mission, which even now encounters many obstacles.

The foundations and the basement walls were erected in reinforced concrete. Then a lightweight metal structure was mounted atop the walls. The former supports the grass-covered wood roof. Below the cantilevering canopy, on three sides, 55-centimeter-thick, four-meter high outer walls were erected in the rammed-earth technique. The earth excavated to create the basement was used as material. The fourth exterior wall was executed as lightweight wood and glass structure. Partially filled in with solar panels and Trombe walls, the facade is oriented toward the sun and interlocks – like a comb – with the adjoining covered work terrace.

Exterior

Loam workshop

Construction site
Photos: Lehm Ton Erde Baukunst GmbH

Planet   Socially Sustainable

VinziRast in the Countryside

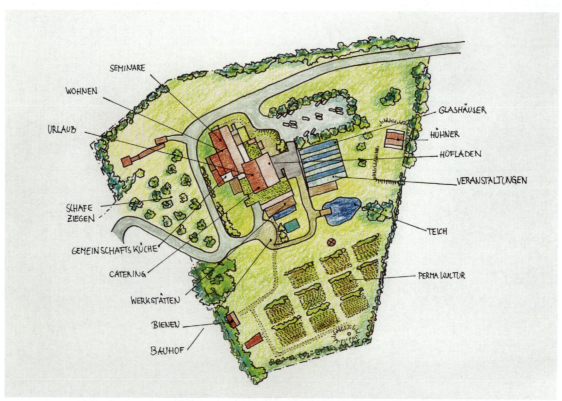

gaupenraub +/- (Alexander Hagner, Ulrike Schartner) | VinziRast in the Countryside | Mayerling 1, Alland, Lower Austria, 2019–2023 | Site plan | Photocopy, colored | Drawing: Ulrike Schartner

In the heart of the Vienna Woods, a community is being erected that offers a permanent place to live and work for people who have lacked a home. VinziRast in the Countryside is, however, much more than a socially-minded project. It is also a plea for taking a creative approach to the reuse of existing buildings. VinziRast – a non-profit organization – asked Alexander Hagner and Ulrike Schartner to make adaptations to the buildings and grounds of an empty former luxury hotel. This created the paradoxical situation in which the existing building does not need to be "ennobled," but also by means of "leftfield thinking," as the architects describe it, should become suited to fulfilling the program. The intention is to ultimately create a place where uprooted people – with all of their highly divergent needs – will feel at ease. This involved introducing agricultural uses and reinvigorating the notion of accommodation and community. Numerous volunteers pitched in. The use of upcycled materials makes the structures sustainable and gives them a distinctive appearance. The chicken coop's zebra pattern is, for example, attained by alternating old and new wood slats.

Community work in the future vegetable garden

The chicken coop under construction

The greenhouse was moved to Mayerling from a former nursery in St. Pölten.

The 100-year-old wood shed was dismantled in Kamptal by students of the Mödling technical high school and set up at VinziRast in the Countryside; converted to a coop, it now provides shelter to about 200 chickens.

Photos: gaubenraub +/−

Planet · Socially Sustainable · 155

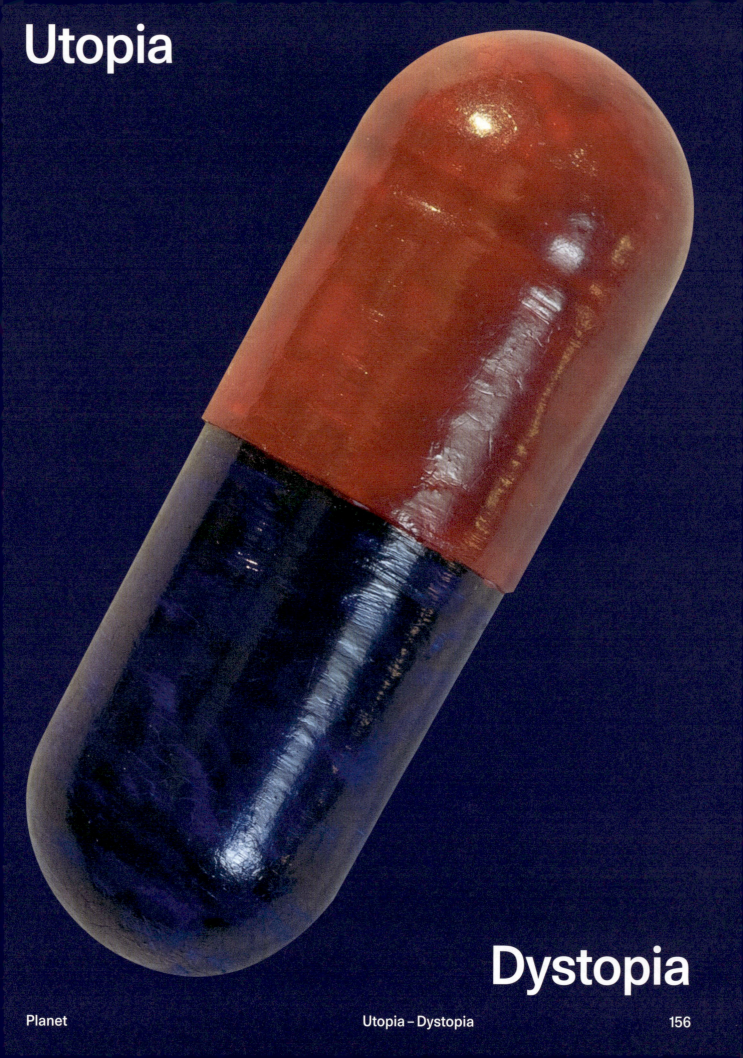

The year 1968 stands not only for space travel, student movement, sexual revolution, and pop-culture, but also for the early environmental debate. This is articulated both in utopian designs and in architectural visions for environments that are hostile to life. Architects grappled with big issues such as scarcity of resources, distribution battles, and the destruction of our natural basis of existence. To ensure survival, Haus-Rucker-Co und Coop Himmelb(l)au incorporated fresh-air receptacles in their projects. With his so-called architecture pill, Hans Hollein provided an escape from a possible threat. Raimund Abraham and Friedrich St. Florian promoted gigantic space structures in the air or buried in the earth – both solutions in response to doomsday scenarios. The technological advancements of the past decades had made these utopias practicable to a certain degree, as is demonstrated by the foldable habitat proposed by the architect group Liquifer. It ensures the survival of a two-person crew for a period of two weeks, both on Earth and in outer space. Inscribed on all of the projects is the awareness of the finite nature of resources and the potentially abrupt end to the utopias.

Hans Hollein | Architecture pill | Non-physical Environmental Control Kit, 1967 | Replica

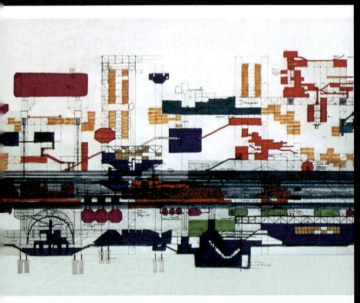 

Engelbert Zobl, Helmut C. Schulitz, Dale Dashiell | Mojave Desert Project,

With a gigantic trailer park in a three-dimensional lattice, Engelbert Zobl, Helmut C. Schulitz, and Dale Dashiell conquered the Mojave desert in order

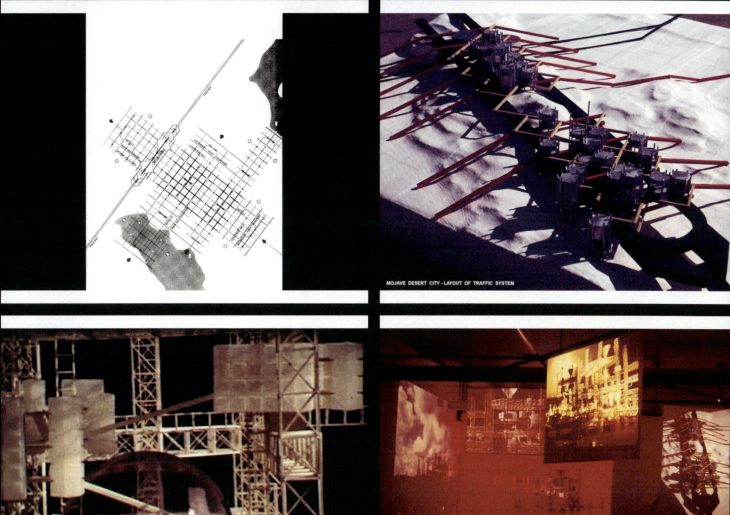

MOJAVE DESERT CITY - LAYOUT OF TRAFFIC SYSTEM

MOJAVE DESERT CITY - PRESENTATION

Friedrich St. Florian | Waiting rooms, imaginary architecture, 1968 | Collage | Paper and pencil on C-Print

Raimund Abraham | House with Two Horizons, 1976 | Exhibition panel for the Biennale di Venezia, 1976 | Photo mounted on wood fiberboard

Hans Hollein | Car Building, 2011 | Two-part sculpture for the exhibition Car Culture. Media of Mobility, ZKM Karlsruhe, 2011–2012 | Model | Plastic | Archive Hans Hollein, Az W and MAK, Vienna

The auto pile-up makes a plea for an adaptation to changed environmental conditions.

The bus shelters (a total of seven were designed by world-renowned architects) in Bregenzerwald make a plea for the urgent reduction of CO_2 in private transport.

Sou Fujimoto, Bechter Zaffignani | BUS:STOP, Krumbach, Vorarlberg, 2012–2014 | Bus stop in Bränden | Model | Wood

Coop Himmelb(l)au (Wolf D. Prix, Helmut Swiczinsky) | Frischzelle [Fresh Cell] – a vertical, bio-climatic park and recreational facility, 1971–1972 | Model photo

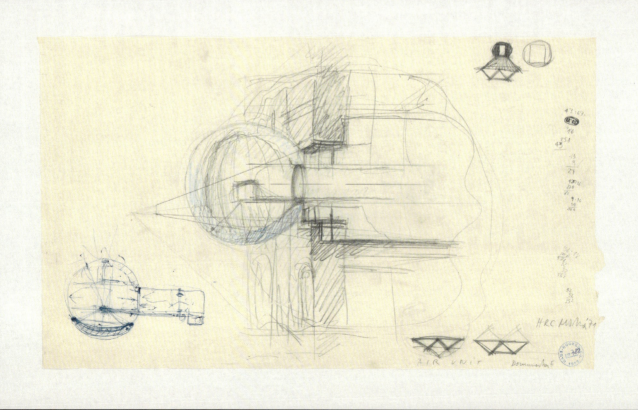

Haus-Rucker-Co (Laurids Ortner, Günter Zamp Kelp, Klaus Pinter, Manfred Ortner) | Air Unit, 1971, for Documenta 5 (Inquiry of Reality) | Sketch, 1972 | Ballpoint pen, pencil, and colored pencil on translucent paper

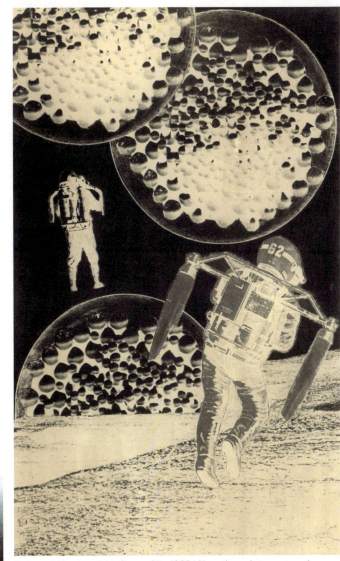

Raimund Abraham | Air Ocean City, 1966 | Negative print, montage | Whiteprint

Photos from: Executive Study. Self-Deployable Habitat for Extreme Environments (SHEE). Europe's first transportable space analogue habitat | Illkirch-Graffenstaden, 2016 | SHEE Consortium, visualization: SPIN

Barbara Imhof, LIQUIFER Systems Group | Self-deployable Habitat for Extreme Environments (SHEE), 2013–2015 | Model | Plastic (3D print)

Literature

pp. 128–135

Angelika Fitz, Elke Krasny, Architekturzentrum Wien (eds.), *Critical Care. Architecture and Urbanism for a Broken Planet*, exh. cat. Architekturzentrum Wien, 4/24–9/9/2019 (Cambridge, MA 2019).

Bernd Scherer, Jürgen Renn (eds.), *Das Anthropozän. Zum Stand der Dinge* (Berlin 2015).

Edith Hemmrich, Mark Blaschitz, Jan Wurm, *The Algae House: About the First Building with A Bioreactor Facade* (Sulgen 2014).

Anna Heringer, "School. Handmade in Bangladesh" (master's thesis, Kunstuniversität Linz 2004).

Tobias Hagleitner, *Ort – Beziehung – Funktion. Eine Dorfstudie in Bangladesh Rudrapur* (Linz 2003).

Naturalization
pp. 136–143

Matthias Osiecki, "Gelungene Vorreiter-Rolle" (Ö1 radio program on 8/4/2003), in: *nextroom*, https://www.nextroom.at/article.php?id=3557 (accessed June 3, 2022).

Leopold Redl, Hans Wösendorfer, *Die Donauinsel. Ein Beispiel politischer Planung in Wien* (Vienna 1980).

ZUG Zentrum für Umweltgeschichte, Universität für Bodenkultur Wien (eds.), *Wasser Stadt Wien. Eine Umweltgeschichte* (Vienna 2019).

Dieter Bogner, *Haus-Rucker-Co. Denkräume – Stadträume 1967–1992*, exh. cat. Kunsthalle Wien, 9/30–12/2/1992 (Klagenfurt 1992).

Haus-Rucker-Co, *Stadtgestaltung. Projekte 1970–76*, exh. cat. (Linz 1977).

Laurids Ortner, Manfred Ortner (eds.), *Haus-Rucker-Co. Drawings and Objects 1969–1989*, L.O.M.O. Archive, Roc Flomar Collection, 5 vols. (Cologne 2019).

Bodenfreiheit, Verein zur Erhaltung von Freiräumen, https://www.bodenfreiheit.at/ueber-uns.html (accessed June 3, 2022).

Friedensreich Hundertwasser, "Verschimmelungsmanifest gegen den Rationalismus in der Architektur (1958/1959/1964)," in: *Die Hundertwasser Gemeinnützige Privatstiftung*, https://hundertwasser.com/texte/mouldiness_manifesto_against_rationalism_in_architecture (accessed June 3, 2022).

Gentle Urban Renewal
pp. 144–147

Gartenhofverein Planquadrat, http://planquadrat.weebly.com/ (accessed June 3, 2022).

Wilhelm Kainrath, Hugo Potyka, Rudolf Zabrana, *Projekt Planquadrat 4. Versuch einer „sanften" Stadterneuerung* (Stuttgart 1980).

Helmut Voitl, Elisabeth Guggenberger, Peter Pirker, *Planquadrat. Ruhe, Grün und Sicherheit. Wohnen in der Stadt* (Vienna 1977).

Maya Habian, Tobias Gossow, *Die Ballade vom Planquadrat-Garten. Eine wahre Geschichte aus Wien. Ein Mitmach-Buch* (Vienna 2017).

LandLuft, Verein zur Förderung von Baukultur in ländlichen Räumen, http://www.landluft.at/ (accessed June 3, 2022).

Roland Gruber, Peter Nageler, Hernan Trinanes, "Temporäres Theater für die Stadt Haag," in: Walter Zschokke, Marcus Nitschke (eds.), *ORTE. Architektur in Niederösterreich*, vol. 2 (Basel 2007), 30–31.

nonconform, *Stadt Haag: eine Tribüne, die mehr kann*, https://www.nonconform.at/architektur/stadt-haag-die-wiederbelebung-eines-ortes-durch-eine-theaterbuehne/ (accessed June 3, 2022).

Saving and Producing Energy
pp. 148–151

Verein Initiative Gemeinsam Bauen & Wohnen, https://www.inigbw.org/wohnprojekte-plattform (accessed June 3, 2022).

Georg W. Reinberg, Matthias Boeckl (eds.), *Reinberg. Ökologische Architektur. Entwurf, Planung, Ausführung = Ecological Architecture. Design, Planning, Realization* (Vienna 2008).

Georg W. Reinberg, *Architektur für eine solare Zukunft = Architecture for a Solar Future* (Basel 2021).

Vera Purtscher, "Haus Standard Solar," in: *Architektur & Bauforum* 145, 1991, 10–16.

N. N., "Haus Magerl. Experiment mit Solarkraft," in: *Architektur & Wohnen* 6, 1991.

N. N., "Standard Solar, Das etwas andere Fertighaus," in: *Sparen Bauen Wohnen* 2, 1999.

Standard Solar I, in: nextroom, https://www.nextroom.at/building.php?id=2607# (accessed June 3, 2022).

Socially Sustainable
pp. 152–155

Lehm Ton Erde Baukunst, https://www.lehmtonerde.at/de/ (accessed June 3, 2022).

Otto Kapfinger, Marko Sauer (eds.), *Martin Rauch. Gebaute Erde. Gestalten & Konstruieren mit Stampflehm* (Munich 2017).

VinziRast am Land, https://www.vinzirast.at/projekte/vinzirast-am-land/ (accessed June 3, 2022).

Utopia–Dystopia
pp. 156–165

Architekturzentrum Wien (ed.), *The Austrian Phenomenon. Architektur Avantgarde Österreich 1956–1973*, exh. cat. (Basel 2009).

Engelbert Zobl, https://www.engelbert-zobl.com/mojave-desert-city/ (accessed June 3, 2022).

Peter Weibel, *Car Culture. Media of Mobility*, exh. cat. Zentrum für Kunst und Medientechnologie Karlsruhe, 6/18/2011–1/8/2012 (Karlsruhe 2011).

Adolf Bereuter, Arnold Hirschbühl, Verein Kultur Krumbach (eds.), *Bus:Stop Krumbach* (Krumbach 2014).

BUS:STOP Krumbach, Bränden, Sou Fujimoto, Bechter Zaffignani, 5/7/2014, in: nextroom, https://www.nextroom.at/building.php?id=36373 (accessed June 3, 2022).

Capital Who shapes the city

Capital   Hot Questions

The Great Transformation: from 1867 to the Present Day	172
Drawing Boundaries: from Major Power to Small State	173
The Pendulum Swings: Migration and Politics	175
The Growth of Cities	178
First Urban Expansion	179
The New Vienna 1919–1934	182
Gross-Wien, National Socialism 1938–1945	184
Vienna after 1945	186
The Construction of the Ringstrasse	188
Capitalist City	192
"State Capitalism" Coined by Lueger	193
Concrete Gold	195
Anti-capitalist City	196
Breitner's Housing Tax	196
Showing Solidarity	200
The Other	202
Emancipation and Antisemitism	202
Persecution, Forced Migration, and Murder of Austrian Architects	206
Traces of Flight	208
Places of Empowerment	212
No Adolf Loos without Lina?	216

Thomas Piketty | *Capital et Idéologie*, Paris 2019; *Capital and Ideology* | Cambridge, MA, 2019; German edition: Munich, 2020.

Karl Marx | *Capital* | First published in English in 1887; Original German edition: Hamburg, 1867.

Karl Polanyi | *The Great Transformation* | New York, 1944.

City, society, and economic interests are shaped interdependently. The rapid growth of cities during the nineteenth century was the expression of a structural transfiguration from an agrarian society toward an industrialized one. Production, flow of goods, and workforce became concentrated in metropolitan areas and triggered conflicts of interest. In the city and in architecture, these conflicts became palpable and graspable. With his book *Das Kapital* (1867), Karl Marx emerged as the fiercest critic of the capitalist mode of production. In Marx's view, the process in which capital is accumulated is responsible for the inequalities in the class-based society (blue-collar workers, entrepreneurs). In contrast, in his book *Capital and Ideology* (2020), Thomas Piketty asserts that social inequity cannot be traced exclusively to class struggle: ideology must also be taken into account.

In his theory, this includes institutional control mechanisms such as legal, tax, and education systems. In the eyes of the Viennese economist Karl Polanyi, each and every economic activity is embedded in social relationships. According to Polanyi, the unfettered and increasingly autonomous business sector sparked both of the catastrophic world wars. His book *The Great Transformation*, which was first published in 1944, is more valid than ever before and disproves Margaret Thatcher's neo-liberal assertion that "There is no such thing as society!"

"The economic system is, in effect, a mere function of social organization."

(Karl Polanyi, 1944)

The Great Transformation: from 1867 to the Present Day

1 <u>Austro-Hungarian Empire 1867–1918</u>
The Austro-Hungarian monarchy was a multi-national state. Established by the Austro-Hungarian Compromise, it existed from June 8, 1867 to October 31, 1918. In 1908, Austro-Hungary's territory extended 676,000 km², and in late 1910, with 51.4 million inhabitants, it had the third largest population in Europe.

Austria-Hungary, 1905
Template: *Library of General and Practical Knowledge for Military Candidates*, vol. I, 1905
Berlin, Vienna, 1905

2 <u>First Republic 1918–1938</u>
After losing the First World War, the multi-national state was dismantled. The borders established in 1919 by the peace treaty of Saint-Germain-en-Laye created new nation states. The former world power had become a small nation. Although the democratic, short-lived Republic of German-Austria had already been proclaimed on November 12, 1918, doubts about its fitness for survival and thoughts about an annexation to Germany were present from its inception. An annexation was forbidden in the 1919 peace treaty, and the fledgling country's name was changed to the Republic of Austria.

Successor States of the Austro-Hungarian Monarchy, 1919
Template: Friedrich Wilhelm Putzger, Egon Lendl, Wilhelm Wagner, *Historical World Atlas on General and Austrian History*, Vienna, 1974

Graphic adaptation: seite zwei

Drawing Boundaries: from Major Power to Small State

3 "Annexation" to Germany 1938–1945
On March 12, 1938, the German Wehrmacht entered Austria. Three days later, addressing a jubilant crowd on Heldenplatz, Adolf Hitler proclaimed the "Annexation" and Austria became part of the German Reich.

Political Overview of the German Reich, May 1939
Template: Architekturzentrum Wien, Collection

4 Second Republic 1945–1955 under Allied Occupation
The Moscow Declaration of 1943 set forth the intention to restore a free and independent Austria. For the following reasons, during the years of occupation, Austria had a special status: it was viewed not as having lost the war, but as having been liberated, and was perceived neither as an ally nor as an enemy, instead presenting itself as a victim of the National Socialist dictatorship. Austria was administered in four sectors, and Vienna – similar to Berlin – was also divided into four sectors, with the distinction that there was no territorial separation of East and West.

Allied Occupation of Austria, 1949
Template: *Austria: A Graphic Survey*, Vienna, 1949

Graphic adaptation: seite zwei

5 Austria's Neutrality 1955–
On May 15, 1955, Austria and the nations which had prevailed in World War II signed the Austrian State Treaty. Upon its ratification, Austria again became a sovereign state. On October 26, 1955, Austria's parliament enacted the Declaration of Neutrality.

Austria's Neutrality 1955–
Template: *Austria: A Graphic Survey, Vienna*, 1949 (adapted)

6 European Union
In 1989, the Iron Curtain ceased to exist. In 1995, Austria joined the European Union and two years later, the Schengen Agreement. An era began in which borders seemed to have lost their significance.

Map of EU Member States, 2011
Template: Lovell Johns, https://op.europa.eu/s/xcFu (December 2, 2021)

Graphic adaptation: seite zwei

The Pendulum Swings: Migration and Politics

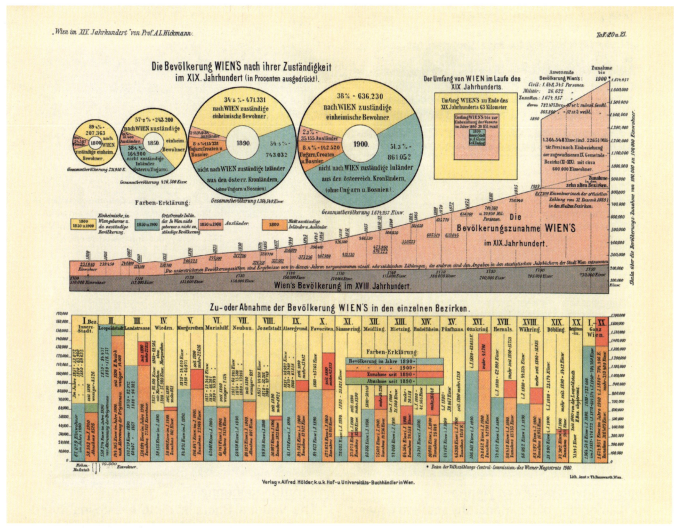

Anton Leo Hickmann | Vienna's Population according to Jurisdiction | In: Anton Leo Hickmann, *Historisch-statistische Tafeln aus den wichtigsten Gebieten der geistigen und materiellen Entwicklung der k. k. Reichshaupt- und Residenzstadt Wien im neunzehnten Jahrhundert* | Vienna, 1903

Vienna's Population according to Jurisdiction

Around 1900, migration within the imperial lands increased significantly. It was sparked by the liberalization of the employment market and the opportunity to move freely within the constitutional monarchy. At the time, with more than two million residents, Vienna was one of the world's largest cities and the center of a multi-ethnic nation. The government policies devised to control immigration were the *Heimatrecht* (literally: right to the homeland) and communal financial assistance. The Heimatrecht was obtained either at birth or by conferral. The latter was highly restrictive and corresponding tax payments were a prerequisite. In Vienna, around 1900, only 38 percent of the residents were in possession of the *Heimatrecht*. The conferral of the *Heimatrecht* was also employed as an instrument of forced assimilation. When a census was conducted, Viennese residents in possession of it were automatically registered as German-speaking.

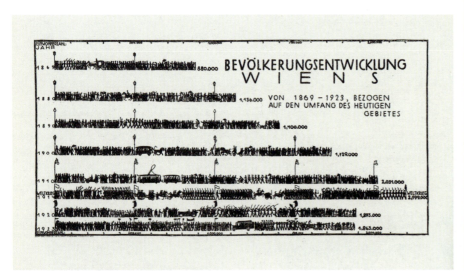
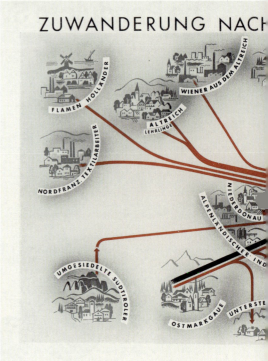

Otto Neurath | Population Development of Vienna |
In: *Österreichische Gemeinde-Zeitung*,
August 15, 1925 | Parlamentsbibliothek Wien

Walter Rafelsberger | Emigration to Vienna |
In: Walter Rafelsberger, *Grundlagen zum
Gauwirtschaftsplan von Wien* | Plan of Vienna,
1941 | Archiv der Universität Wien

Population development of Vienna

The dismantling of the monarchy sparked a major refugee crisis and turned persons who had been citizens into foreigners. The Treaty of Saint-Germain-en-Laye, negotiated in 1919, brought with it new rules for citizenship: the aim of the *Heimatberechtigung* (right to domicile) was to create, to the greatest possible extent, an ethnically pure German state. Partially responsible were the unification efforts with Germany, which were also supported by the Social Democrats. Toward the end of the First World War, between 25,000 and 34,000 Jewish refugees lived in Vienna; the law sought to stop them from gaining citizenship. In 1939, the Heimatrecht was repealed

Emigration to Vienna

The National Socialist dictatorship instituted unconscionable exclusion, forced migration, and annihilation of Jews and other "non-German" populations such as Roma and Sinti. In May 1938, the Nuremberg Laws were enacted in Austria. In 1938, there were about 206,000 Jewish residents; by the time war broke out, about 125,000 had fled. More than 65,000 Jews who had been deported from Austria died in the concentration and extermination camps.

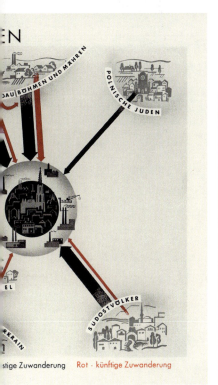
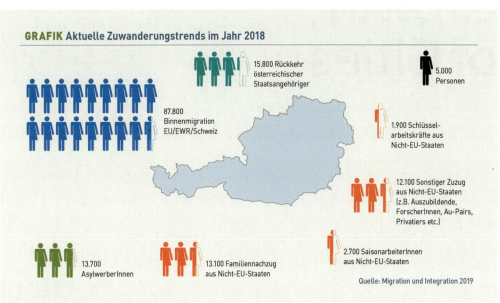

Current immigration trends as of 2018 | Demokratiezentrum Wien

Current immigration trends as of 2018

In 1995, Austria became a member of the European Union. In addition to migration to Austria from the member states, there was an increase in immigration from the neighboring countries and from eastern, central, and southeast Europe. In 2017, some 230,000 citizens of EU countries resided in Vienna – 44,000 of them from Germany; 41,000 from Poland; 29,000 from Romania; and 21,000 each from Hungary and Croatia. The refugee crisis sparked by the war in Syria caused the number of Syrian citizens in Austria to increase by about 14,000 in 2015 and 2016. During the same time period, the number of Afghan citizens increased by about 7,000. As of 2021, around 2.24 million people, or 25.4 percent of the total population, living in Austria have an immigrant background.

Capital | The Great Transformation

The Growth of Cities

Anton Leo Hickmann | First Urban Expansion: map of Vienna, 1850 | In: Anton Leo Hickmann, *Historisch-statistische Tafeln aus den wichtigsten Gebieten der geistigen und materiellen Entwicklung der k. k. Reichshaupt- und Residenzstadt Wien im neunzehnten Jahrhundert* | Vienna, 1903

Plan approved on September 1, 1859 for the expansion of the historic center | Wien Museum

First Urban Expansion 1850

Vienna's first urban expansion took place in 1850: the city center (district I) and the suburbs (districts II–IX) were incorporated into the city. On December 20, 1857, an imperial decree proclaimed the demolition of the fortification walls. Numerous magnificent buildings and palaces were created along the "via triumphalis," reflecting the prosperous bourgeoise's desire to put its wealth on display. At the same time, the ownership of the Glacis (the green space adjoining the bastions) was transferred from the military to the state, in other words, to a civil urban expansion fund, which, in turn, sold lots to private persons at a profit to finance the state's construction projects.

Development Plan of 1859

In 1858, an international city planning competition called for designs for the future layout of the Glacis. There were 58 submissions. Among those receiving prizes were Ludwig von Förster, Eduard van der Null and his partner August Sicard von Sicardsburg, and Friedrich August von Strache. Taking into account two subsequently submitted projects by Förster and the civil servant Moritz von Loehr, under the aegis of the Department of the Interior, a concept for the overall layout was devised and then approved by the emperor. In 1865, the first segment of the Ringstrasse was inaugurated; in 1885, the entire polyhedral, 4-kilometer-long boulevard (measuring up to 57 meters in width) was completed, as were the 38-meter-wide Franz-Josefs-Kai and the 26.5-meter-wide Lastenstrasse.

Otto Wagner | General Regulation Plan, 1892–1893, Overview of the concentric beltline roads with numbered nodes | Wiener Stadt- und Landesarchiv

Otto Wagner, General Regulation Plan 1892–1893

In 1892, an international competition called for "designs for a general plan to regulate the whole municipal area of Vienna." There was a tie for first prize – awarded to Josef Stübben of Cologne, Germany, and to Otto Wagner. Wagner proposed radial streets originating in the city center and concentric rings (also referred to as beltline roads). The public facilities were concentrated at the specified main nodes. The intention of this decentralized system was to enable the metropolis to grow "infinitely." The focus lay on extending the public transport offerings, developing higher-standard, proto-welfare facilities, and proposing a zoning concept. The modernization program envisioned by Wagner foresaw broad boulevards and new centers: its aim was to foster better communication in support of a cosmopolitan life. With the exception of the Stadtbahn (metropolitan railway), this program was only sporadically implemented.

The New Vienna 1919–1934

Erich Franz Leischner | The New Vienna | Map showing social housing, settlements, baths, and green spaces implemented by 1931 | 1931

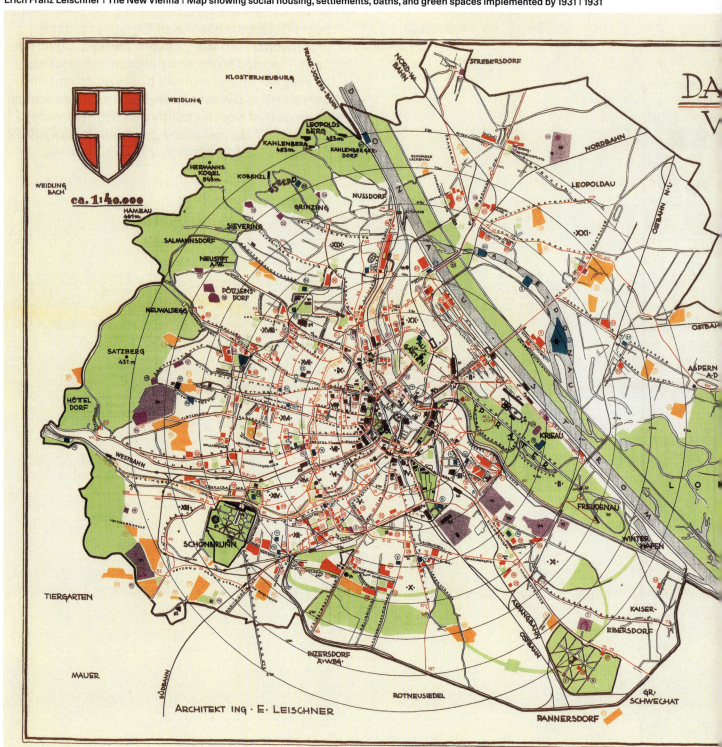

In 1919, Vienna became the first city with a population of more than 1,000,000 to have a Social Democratic government. In 1922, Vienna separated from Lower Austria and became an autonomous state. This was the beginning of the municipal social democratic experiment known as Red Vienna – an era marked above all by policies striving for a high standard of housing, welfare, and education. The large-scale building program, carried out largely by students of Otto Wagner, comprised not only housing and settlements, but also social amenities such as preschools, out-patient clinics, libraries, laundry facilities, lecture halls, theaters, and parks. The multi-story *Gemeindebauten* [communal housing] were usually erected as perimeter-block massing with spacious interior courtyards.

Gross-Wien, National Socialism 1938–1945

Major Settlement Areas of Greater Vienna, 1938–1941 | Overview of New Settlement Areas, 1941 | City map, colored

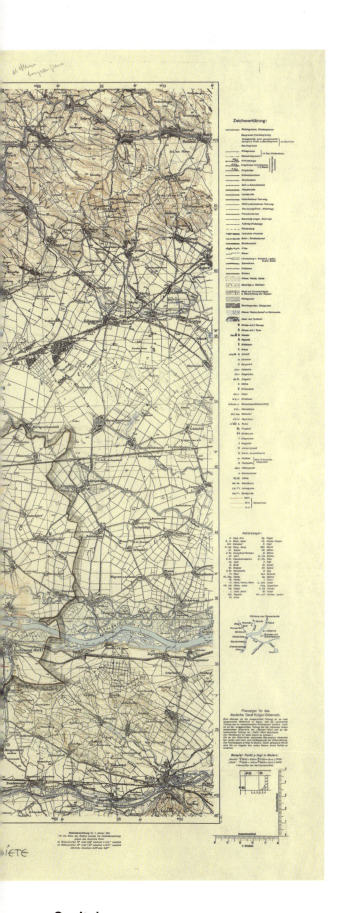

The spatial planning policies of the National Socialist regime were directly linked to its claim to political and economic predominance. Its leaders promoted rebuilding Europe to serve "German" interests and reducing independent nation states to colonialized "complementary space" for the Third Reich. "New guiding principles" were sought for Vienna as the second largest city of the Greater German Reich. The Danube and its environs, in particular, its ports, acquired greater significance: the plan was to transform Vienna into the "Hamburg of the east" and, at the same time, into a trade center with much-enlarged trade fair grounds – making the city a "gateway to the southeast."

The enlargement of the city's territory made it possible to reduce the density in the city proper, a measure closely connected to considerations regarding social and demographic policy. Ninety-seven surrounding localities were incorporated to create five new districts (Gross-Enzersdorf [XXII], Schwechat [XXIII], Mödling [XXIV], Liesing [XXV] and Klosterneuburg [XXVI]). With two million residents and a surface area that had increased fivefold (1,218 km²), Vienna became the largest city in the German Reich and the sixth largest in the world.

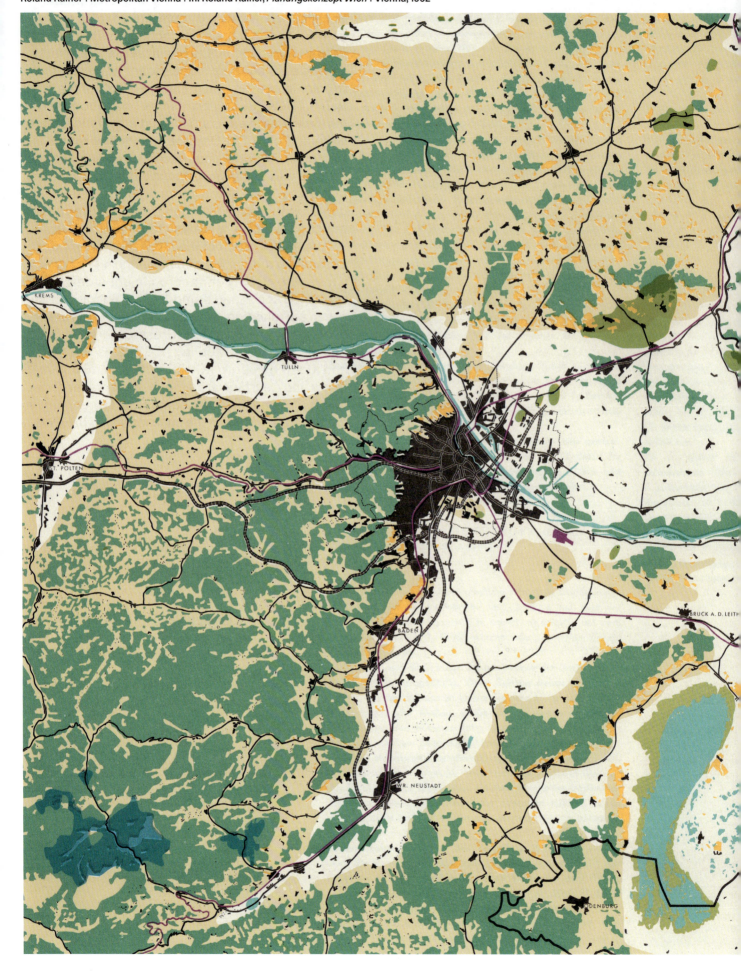

Vienna after 1945

After 1945, owing to the considerable damage wrought by the war, there was an opportunity to redefine the city's urban space. In 1961, Roland Rainer put forward a concept for Vienna's development for the next 30 to 50 years. Unlike the previous guiding principles, the crux of this concept was the flowing space of an urban landscape. In addition to taking pressure off the city proper by promoting dispersed neighborhoods at its edges, the concept's main proposals were to introduce new recreational areas and to coordinate traffic planning with the surrounding communities.

Outer Gate at the Imperial Castle (Peter Nobile, 1824) | Wien Museum |
Photo: August Stauda

The Construction of the Ringstrasse

Theophil von Hansen | Parliament | Dr. Karl Renner Ring 3, Vienna I,
1874–1883 | LEGO®-model, 2021 | Plastic | Model builder: Harald Gach

View from the roof of the Town Hall to Burggarten with Theseus Temple (Peter Nobile, 1820–1823), front right: the Parliament under construction | Wien Museum

Dr. Karl Renner Ring with Parliament, Town Hall and Imperial Court Theater (from left to right) under construction, in the background: towers of the Votivkirche | about 1881 | Wien Museum

Heinrich Ferstel | University of Vienna | Universitätsring 1, Vienna I, 1873–1884 | LEGO®-model, 2021 | Plastic | Model builder: Harald Gach

Heinrich Ferstel | Votivkirche | Rooseveltplatz, Vienna IX, 1856–1879 | LEGO®-model, 2021 | Plastic | Model builder: Harald Gach

Capital The Construction of the Ringstrasse

Opera intersection | Wien Museum

Friedrich Schmidt | Town Hall | Rathausplatz 1, Vienna I, 1872–1883 |
LEGO®-model, 2021 | Plastic | Model builder: Harald Gach

Capital The Construction of the Ringstrasse 190

Dr. Karl Renner Ring, Parliament and Town Hall under construction | Wien Museum | Photo: August Stauda

Dr. Karl Renner Ring, Parliament (foreground) and Town Hall under construction | about 1880 | Wien Museum | Photo: August Stauda

Gottfried Semper | Imperial Court Theatre | Universitätsring 2, Vienna I, 1874–1888 | LEGO®-model, 2021 | Plastic | Model builder: Harald Gach

August Sicard von Sicardsburg, Eduard van der Nüll | State Opera | Opernring 2, Vienna I, 1861–1869 | LEGO®-model, 2021 | Plastic | Model builder: Harald Gach

S. F. Hummel | "The New Light. On the Occasion of the Consecration of Vienna's Municipal Gas Works" | *Neuigkeits-Welt-Blatt*, November 1/2, 1899 | ÖNB

Lueger cleverly exploited the communalization of technical infrastructure to boost his own cult of personality. At the same time, Vienna followed a general modernization trend that was already taking place in other metropolises.

"State Capitalism" Coined by Lueger

Friedrich August Neuman | Gasometer Simmering | Guglgasse 6, Vienna III, 1896–1898 | Reconstruction of a facade segment | Wood, bronze

During the tenure of Mayor Karl Lueger (1897–1910), the city was modernized. One of the first projects to be implemented by the Christian Social Party made improvements to the energy infrastructure. After the contracts with the Imperial Continental Gas Association – a private British firm – had been terminated, a gas facility (1896–1899) was erected in Simmering; the four attendant gasometers have since been revamped and now serve new functions. The utilities were profit-oriented and akin to "state-run capitalism." Lueger's communalization concentrated economic and political power in the hands of one person and thereby facilitated cronyism at the expense of the general public. The *Kurienwahlrecht* (curial suffrage) tied voting rights to property ownership and level of education. Not until 1918 did women receive the right to vote.

REAL CITY OWNERSHIP.

How the City of Vienna Runs Certain Kinds of Business.

Under the somewhat despotic rule of its recently deceased burgomaster, Dr. Karl Lueger, Vienna has developed municipal ownership to a degree far beyond that of any other great capital, says the Vienna correspondent of the Chicago News. Before the advent of Dr. Lueger the old liberal administration had done nothing toward acquiring any of the semipublic enterprises, such as gas, electric lighting and street railways. To-day the municipality of Vienna owns and operates not only gas and electric light, plants and street railways but also such diversified undertakings as slaughter houses, a brewery, cemeteries, funeral undertaking and funeral insurance, life insurance and savings banks, besides several other minor enterprises, which employ together tens of thousands of workers.

Unfortunately, however, hardly any of these multifarious enterprises have fulfilled the hopes anticipated for them while several have resulted in heavy financial losses not always unaccompanied with scandal. The arbitrary manner, too, in which some of the larger undertakings were forcibly wrested from their original owners has left behind much bitterness of feeling toward the too aggressive municipal ownership party.

The first and most important undertaking acquired by Dr. Lueger was the street railway system, which formerly belonged to the Vienna Tramway company. To gain this property the burgomaster carried on a long and bitter fight with the stockholders who finally were forced to part with their interests at a loss of hundreds of thousands of dollars. This was in 1903.

Although the city has now invested $28,000,000 and greatly developed and improved the service for an average yearly return of about $500,000, this is considerably less than the city would have received without any investment at all, from the old company whose charter provided for payment to the municipality of 9.8 per cent of the gross earnings. This showing is the less satisfactory, too, as the traffic has increased enormously and the fares have been raised all around, much to the disgust of the taxpayers. It is also to be noted that the municipal tramways escape taxes of about $200,000 a year which the old company had to pay.

Following the taking over of the tramways came the erection of municipal electrical works at a cost of $12,000,000. Again after a disagreeable fight with the stockholders the city bought out two private companies for a total of $5,000,000. Last year the electrical works showed a clear profit of $1,000,000, but this was largely achieved by making the tramways pay a most exorbitant eprice for the power supplied. The original estimate for the power plant were exceeded by nearly $5,000,000 and the consumers have never received any reduction in price for electric light, as they would have done if the private companies had continued in business.

In municipalizing the gas works, Dr. Lueger once more trampled on the rights of the original owners, stockholders of an English corporation, absolutely refusing to take over any of their property at the expiration of their concession. Instead of enlarging and developing the existing plant of the English company, which was quite good and satisfactory, he involved the city in an immense outlay for entirely new work. Although the municipal gas plant showed a profit last year of $700,000 the consumers have gained nothing from the city's ownership. Gas for all purposes, lighting, heating and power, costs in Vienna, 3.2 cents a cubic meter (about 97 cents for 1,000 cubic feet), and is the dearest gas in all Europe with the exception of Paris.

Two years ago an English company which for many years has operated an omnibus line here with varying success went into bankruptcy. After long hagglings with the receivers, Dr. Lueger forced them to sell the whole property of the company to the city for $500,000, which was far below the actual value. Notwithstanding his sharp bargaining, the investment resulted last year in a loss of $88,000 which it is estimated will be increased this year to $100,000.

Another losing municipal investment of the Lueger regime is the public slaughter houses. It was thought that these would keep down the wholesale price of meat by providing a regular market, and also by competing with the butchers would give the public cheap meat. Neither of these expectations was fulfilled. The slaughter houses, built with funds provided by a Vienna bank, entailed a loss to the city of $188,000 last year, which will probably be considerably increased this year.

Certainly the most unfortunate venture of Dr. Lueger's administration has been the municipal brewery, which, besides costing the city a regular annual loss, has occasioned a good deal of scandal. It was started with a capital of $400,000, but the first owners lost heavily from the outset and were forced to give up the business. Then quite suddenly the city council came to the rescue, largely, it is said, in the interests of the owners of restaurants and "gasthauser," who hoped to get better terms of credit from a municipal brewery. Despite much public opposition the city bought the brewery and carried it on with a steady annual deficit.

Almost the newest incursion into the field of municipal ownership was Lueger's purchase of the two largest funeral undertaking businesses in the city, which, in fact, almost monopolized that trade. In the first year this project made a profit of $45,000, but much dissatisfaction exists because the tariff for the cheaper classes of funerals has not been reduced in accordance with the public demands.

TIMES AND MORALS.

When a modern boy defies home rule and laughs at ordinances, "moving" pictures are promptly blamed.

When the boy's father did the same thing they were charged to "dime novels."

There being neither moving pictures nor dime novels when the boy's grandfather was a lad, they laid all his naughtiness to infant depravity.

New times bring new morals.—Cleveland Plain Dealer.

The article questions the tremendous variety of the municipal enterprises during Karl Lueger's tenure.
"Real City Ownership" | *The Brooklyn Daily Eagle*, June 13, 1911

Concrete Gold

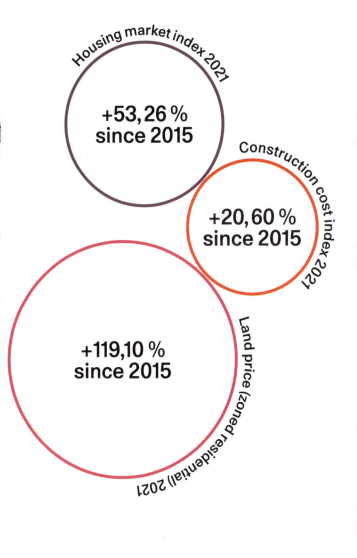

Housing market index 2021
+53,26 % since 2015

Construction cost index 2021
+20,60 % since 2015

Land price (zoned residential) 2021
+119,10 % since 2015

Comparison of housing market index, construction cost index, and land prices 2015 and 2021 | Source: Statistics Austria

Walter Fitz | Agricultural Soil Profile 2021 | Soil type: chernozem (black soil) on loess (Ziersdorf, Weinviertel, Lower Austria) | Soil, clay, plants, stone

Walter Fitz | Non-permeable Urban Ground, 2020 | Soil profile: asphalt, recycled material, sandy-silty sediments of the Rhine (Altach, Vorarlberg) | Stone, soil, brick, asphalt

From time immemorial, members of the bourgeoisie have wielded the ownership of land as an instrument of power. Monetary policy measures such as the low interest rates have in recent years been accompanied by increased investment in real estate. In Austria's cities and in tourist destinations, communes compete with international real estate fonds for a non-renewable commodity: land. The consequences are rising land and real estate prices, a higher cost of living, inequitable distribution of wealth, and ever more surfaces impervious to water.

"Breitner's taxes. That's why you should vote for the Social Democrats" 1927 | Graphic design: Victor Slama | Poster | Wienbibliothek im Rathaus, :urn:nbn:at:AT-WBR-113614

Anti-capitalist City

Breitner's Housing Tax

With its separation from Lower Austria in 1922, Vienna became fiscally autonomous. The new financial policies enacted by Social Democrat Hugo Breitner were founded on levying luxury, operating, traffic, property, and rental taxes. The housing tax – one type of rental tax – was earmarked, and its intention was to redistribute wealth by means of its progressive tax rates. By 1934, the City of Vienna had erected a total of 61,175 apartments in 348 apartment complexes, as well as 42 settlement groups containing 5,257 settlement houses. In 1934, a tenth of Vienna's population already resided in communal housing. To this day, these units, along with the ones completed after 1945, are owned by the City of Vienna. From outside Austria, these tax measures were seen as pioneering, but as far as domestic policy was concerned, the financial policies became a point of contention. In 1934, the polarizing aggressive rhetoric between the Social Democratic party and the Christian Social party led to civil war. On account of his Jewish ancestry, Hugo Breitner had to emigrate, and after 1945 he was not given the opportunity to return to Austria.

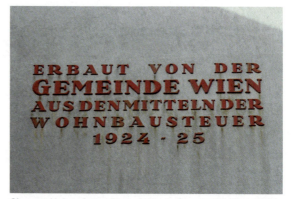

Clemens Holzmeister | Blathof | Linzer Strasse 128, Vienna XIV, 1924–1925 | "Erected with Resources from the Housing Construction Tax" | Photo from a series: Herbert Hrachowina, 2005–2013

Vienna finds Housing for its Workers

THE BUILDING TAX PROVIDES FUNDS FOR MODEL TENEMENTS

by

PAULA ARNOLD

VIENNA.

VIENNA is the only great city on earth (of more than a million inhabitants) which has a socialist majority in its administration. It was to be expected that this "red municipality" should do a good deal for that part of the population which was most in need of support and which had helped to bring them into office. That their work in this direction should be crowned with such signal success that today municipal and relief officers from the richest and most progressive cities of the world come to study the social and relief institutions of Vienna, has been something in the way of a surprise. For after all, the administration was taken over by the Social Democrats at a time —ten years ago exactly—when the town was broken by war and famine and when there seemed neither cash nor credit to be had either at home or abroad.

Their achievements, marvelous under the circumstances, are due partly to their excellent organization, partly to the great talents among them, especially to those of, doubtless, the best-hated man in Vienna, Dr. Hugo Breitner, finance secretary of the municipal board. He has for ten years been wringing blood out of stones with such ingenuity that Vienna the pauperised, the hopeless invalid whose immediate decease was prophesied on all sides, is today an extremely prosperous township with huge reserves, and all this in spite of unheard-of expenses, above all the building of houses for sixty thousand families, erected without the aid of credit, merely out of taxation moneys.

The taxes introduced by Breitner are of course such as to fall hardest on the well-to-do. They increase in geometrical progression in relation to income, and to expenditure. Thus for instance you have to pay a tax if you keep more than one servant. For the second servant it is only fifty Austrian shillings a year, but for each further one two hundred and fifty shillings more than for the last, so that you pay three hundred shillings for the third, five hundred and fifty for the fourth, nine hundred for the four together. The household hit hardest by this employed thirty-eight servants last year and accordingly paid a servants' tax of over $16,000 shillings—quite a tidy little sum!

THE TAX which interests us in this connection, however, is the so-called building tax, levied on all premises in Vienna and used exclusively for the purpose of building houses for workers. It is meted out according to the rent paid in 1914, and as it consists of two to three per cent only of the small rents (that is ten to one hundred shillings a year) for flats up to four rooms and kitchen, it is not much felt by the tenants of the working class. Upward of four rooms, however, it increases alarmingly, rising at last to dizzy heights, such as thirty and even, in extreme cases, almost forty per cent—with means paying a building tax of more than 30,000 shillings a year. Thus the 500,000 cheap lodgings, making eighty per cent. of all there are in Vienna, pay only twenty per cent. of the sum gained by the building tax. The 90 most expensive houses pay as much as the 350,000 cheapest.

With this "ill-gotten money," as those living in palatial mansions complain, the township has built excellent tenement houses. To understand what the new way of living means for workmen and minor employes one must see the places they lived in before, and live in still by the hundred thousands. There were simply no new rooms to be had for newly married couples and for people whose number of children had increased. Though they could and would gladly have paid for better lodgings, they had to go on living with their families in one room, to the detriment and sometimes to the destruction of family relations in consequence of the terrible crowding.

IN THE OLD TYPE of Vienna tenement house, not the slums but normal, even good flats of one or two rooms and kitchen, not even the water-tap is in the flat itself. It is to be reached only by a corridor, and is common to all the tenants living on the same floor. The kitchen in most cases gives on to the same corridor, being airless and dark in consequence, and many of the rooms look out on a narrow airshaft merely. The courts of these houses are small and squalid, not large enough to swing a cat in, and the children consequently sit on the stairs in bad weather and play in the roaring streets in good. The streets are full of danger, and the staircases full of abominable smells, combined of drain and kitchen odors. That many of these houses have no gas-supply, and most of them no electric current either, goes without saying. Also that they are ugly enough to give you the creeps.

Some of the new tenement houses (they are all built by competitive building and the very best architects compete)—are so beautiful that visitors from foreign countries sometimes believe you are jesting when you point them out and identify them. They look more like palaces or castles than like tenement houses, with their large open spaces, greensward and trees, the graceful balconies, terraces and pergolas, their fountains and statues. All of them are up to the latest demands of sanitation and hygiene. The rooms without exception are light and airy, giving onto the streets or the garden-like courts. The houses fill forty per cent of the lot, or less, generally only thirty, the rest being taken up by play-grounds, gardens, children's shallow bathing-pools with lawns for sun-baths adjoining, and the like. Houses built before the war take up eighty-five per cent of the lot, no wonder most of the rooms are dark and musty!

IN THE NEW HOUSES, always grouped together to form a little community of some hundred, sometimes some thousand inhabitants, there are tub baths and shower-baths, and laundries with the most modern contrivances such as had previously been unknown in Austria even in the best households. The housewife can manage the washing for a family of five in one morning, bringing it back into her flat ready ironed by noon. There are baby nurseries and infant schools, libraries and lecture halls, and what not.

The occupants take a great pride in their altered surroundings and the unwonted luxury of their rooms. They keep them extremely neat and clean and are proud to show them to visitors. No question but that the feeling of having a home to be proud of keeps many a family man away from the public houses today. The usual flat consists of one small anteroom, one living room and one bedroom, kitchen and pantry. There are smaller flats also for childless couples, and single rooms with kitchenette for single people. The largest flats, designed for families with more than one child, contain three rooms besides the kitchen. That is not too much, but considering that families who were well able to afford more have been forced to live six and seven in one room which was kitchen, living room, workshop and bedroom in one, it is an immense step forward.

NATURALLY there is a run on these flats, and as among the many thousand applicants for homes at the municipal Lodgings Office about 15,000 are marked "urgent," it is clear that the building program of the town is no more than a necessity.

For there is next to no private building

A MUNICIPALLY BUILT WORKERS' APARTMENT HOUSE IN VIENNA

activity in Vienna. This is owing to the Tenants Defense act passed soon after the war, a law which made rents so cheap (in fact nominal only) that it is not worth while to build, in spite of the pressing demand; building costs are so high that naturally the actual economic costs of rent would be those of pre-war times or more. Private builders would not cope with the competition of the old houses, where tenants pay next to nothing, a state of things amounting in fact to the expropriation of landlords, of which of course the Social Democrats are very proud. Private landlords would have little hope of letting new flats, except for a very few to well-to-do people.

Just at present, however, there is every likelihood of the Tenants Defense act being amended enough to compel the tenants of the better and larger flats to pay a justifiable rental. But as the majority of tenants (probably those living in flats smaller than four rooms) will still be exempt, there is not much hope for any great movement in housebuilding, especially as the most pressing demands will be met by the latest municipal buildings still in course of erection.

THE RENTS paid in the new tenement houses are, of course, higher than the merely nominal ones paid to private landlords. Still they are calculated to cover only running expenses not by any means to yield an interest on the money invested. The loss of interest is borne by the city itself.

Should some day the Tenants Defense act be abolished altogether, which is very unlikely indeed, still the policy of the municipality as regards building will not have been ill advised. In that case there would be great danger of unjustifiable demands on the part of the landlords, of rents jumping up to dizzy heights—but with the municipality itself as the most powerful landlord in the city, controlling housing for more than 60,000 families, such a danger is averted. The importance of this control, as regards both prices and the standard of buildings, is obvious.

☆ ☆

Continued from preceding page

The Indian

claimants will know exactly where they stand. Any program for the solution of the Indian problem, of course, will have to be approved by Congress. And it is apparent that any program will entail increased appropriations.

"We know there are lots of things in the Indian Service that are not as they should be," Edgar B. Merritt, Assistant Commissioner of Indian Affairs, told the Senate Committee. "There is much that we could do to improve the conditions of the Indians, but we have not the money."

And this is corroborated by the report of the Institute for Government Research, whose staff spent a year in its investigation.

"The work of the Government directed toward the education and advancement of the Indian himself, as distinguished from the control and conservation of his property, is largely ineffective," the report said. "The chief explanation of the deficiency in this work lies in the fact that the Government has not appropriated enough funds to permit the Indian Service to employ an adequate personnel properly qualified for the task before it."

PRESENT APPROPRIATIONS are roughly $15,000,000 a year, of which a little more than $2,000,000 comes from the tribal funds belonging to the Indians. Conceivably, the bureau says, for several years the additional amount required will be almost as much as the present appropriations. But in from five to ten years, it says, the amount will begin to decrease materially, and from that time on a gradual but progressive reduction should be possible as more and more Indians become self-supporting and as progress is made in getting the States and local governments to render the service necessary for Indians in return for taxes paid by the Indians.

SOCIALIST TAX POLICY ENVY OF VIENNA REGIME

Municipal Administration at Austrian Capital by Radicals Apparent Success.

VIENNA—The difference between the tax policy of a capitalist and a socialist administration is drastically illustrated by the amounts provided for the unemployed by the national government of Austria and the municipal government of the city of Vienna.

The finances of the Austrian government are in the hand of an expert of the league of nations who manages Austrian government accounts for foreign bankers that periodically loan money to the Seipel administration. The finances of Vienna are in the hands of a socialist expert who refuses to mortgage the city to foreign bankers.

The national government provided 52,000,000,000 crowns for the Austrian unemployed, the city government of Vienna 293,000,000,000 for the unemployed in the city. Vienna has about one-third of the total population of Austria.

Socialist Expert Rules.

The city government of Vienna, writes The Wiener Arbeiter Zeitung has neither a sanitation expert blessed by the pope nor an adviser or manager appointed by the league of nations. Yet the city has a practically balanced budget and one-third of its budget is devoted to productive investments, another third to the employment of maintenance of the jobless.

The city of Vienna never printed any paper money. Its ability to levy taxes is narrowly circumscribed by state and national laws. And most of its interfering taxation is subject to the int ring chicanery of the national secretary of the treasury.

Nevertheless the socialist expert of city finance goes right ahead doing things. While the Seipel administration manages the Austrian nation deeper and deeper into debt to foreign bankers, the socialist city expert of Vienna, Breitner, builds new homes, new hospitals, new parks and streets, provides for the unemployed created by the imbecile policies of the Seipel government and keeps the city out of debt without burdening the masses of the citizens with new or higher taxes.

Simplifies Tax System.

Breitner has not only kept taxation down for the mass of the citizens, but simplified the system of taxation. During the same period in which the Seipel government increased the external and internal revenue duties and added a sales tax to the former national taxation, the Breitner government of Vienna has simplified the municipal taxes to two kinds that must be paid by everybody: The housing tax and the water power tax. The other taxes that keep the city treasury filled are taxes on different resources of the rich.

The old party experts ask: How does Breitner do it? He certainly has taught the business classes something that they never learned under any old party administration. He taught them to pay their taxes regularly and fully without a chance at shirking, dodging or missing. And achieved this miracle while the national government is always running behind in its tax collections.

Breitner has arranged matters so that the money collected on the building and water power taxes always keeps circulating by increasing the buildings and making electric services cheaper by extending them.

Hit Wealthy Hardest.

Aside from good organization, the secret of Breitner's success as a tax financier consists in going after the money, where it is, not where it isn't. The national taxation fails, because it seeks to load the heaviest burdens on the poor, who simply reduce their expenditures in proportion as the cost of living rises and thereby defeat Seipel's tax plans.

Breitner goes after the wealthy and collects from them on luxuries, cars, incomes, surplus-profits, according to a graded system which preserves social justice while maintaining efficiency in business.

And in this way the city of Vienna is enabled to do something effective for the unemployed when the Seipel government first creates then neglects for the benefit of profiteers.

"Socialist Tax Policy Envy of Vienna Regime" | *The Oklahoma Leader*, June 12, 1923

The article highlights Hugo Breitner's Social Democratic financial policies for Vienna, because, unlike the capitalist position taken by the federal government, they respond constructively to the people's needs.

Black Chicago and Red Vienna

By Meyer Halushka

Chicago is the fourth largest and at least the fourth richest city in the world. It leads all cities in its grain trade, meat packing, mail order business and manufacture of furniture, dry goods and farm machinery. It is the terminal for 38 railroads. The per capita wealth of its inhabitants is $9,495. Surely a "City of Destiny," a city of promise and opportunity to all who live there?

Next year will mark the 100th birthday of republican and democratic rule in Chicago. Gang warfare and crime take heavy toll of life and property. Racketeers are still victimizing labor unions and small store keepers. School teachers have received only three months pay in the last ten months, and other city employes have been paid only up to January. A fraudulent tax assessment is ruthlessly bleeding the small home owner, while at least $16,000,000,000 of personal property of the rich is untaxed. Rotten politics steals or wastes most of the taxes that are collected.

At least 500,000 men are out of work. At least 150,000 families are in dire need, and only 9 cents a day is alloted each person for food, and nothing for rent. At least 100 square miles within the city can be described by no word less ugly than "slums." Want, fear and despair face the workers of Chicago.

Vienna, when the war ended, was in a complete state of financial collapse. Industry was at a standstill; the city treasury was empty; the Austrian krone was worthless. The treaties stripped Austria of nearly all her lands and wealth. The plight of the workers was desperate. Nine out of every ten lived in homes of only one room. Few homes had electricity, or even gas. Nine out of ten had no water supply; nineteen out of twenty had no toilets.

Vienna has had thirteen years of socialist rule. The first step of the "Reds" was to revise the tax program. In 1913 the per capita tax was $21.15; in 1931, it was only $23.33, but the system had been changed to collect taxes on the basis of ability to pay rather than of inability to dodge.

Today 60,000 municipal apartments have been provided for over 200,000 people. Every apartment is fireproof and noiseproof, and all have water, gas, electricity and toilet. Only half of the ground is taken up by the building, the rest is in parks and playgrounds. For these apartments— equal in beauty and comfort to many on Chicago's Gold Coast—the worker pays from $1 to $3 per room per month.

In addition, the city provides free medical care during pregnancy, a free layette for every baby, kindergartens which furnish free lunch, public playgrounds and swimming pools. Municipal ownership has taken the profit out of charges for transportation, gas, electricity, bakery and brewery goods, dental and medical care and funeral service. And the city's budget is balanced!

Rich Chicago, poor Vienna! Black Chicago, "red" Vienna!

Meyer Halushka | "Black Chicago and Red Vienna" | *The Lincoln Herald*, April 1, 1932

In his comparison of Chicago, which was, at the time, the world's fourth richest city, and Vienna, which was still recovering from World War I, and taking into account the latter's Social Democratic tax policies, the author comes to an exceedingly positive conclusion in favor of Red Vienna.

"sargfabrik. visions in space," 1989 | Poster printed on the occasion of the purchase of the Sargfabrik site | Graphic design: Baukünstlerkollektiv Wien

BKK-2 (Christoph Lammerhuber, Axel Linemayr, Evelyn Rudnicki, Franz Sumnitsch, Florian Wallnöfer, Johann Winter)
Sargfabrik – Residence on Matznergasse/Goldschlagstrasse 169, Vienna XIV
1993–1996

During the 1990s, on the grounds of a former casket factory, new standards were set in community-fostering, self-managed housing. Collective property forms the basis for a good shared living environment. A non-profit organization named Integrative Lebensgestaltung (literally: integrative design for living) is the owner and operator of the Sargfabrik. The members have contracts similar to those of cooperatives and pay a portion of the land and construction costs: if a resident moves out, the investment will be paid back (with interest); in addition, members contribute to paying back the housing loan. From the legal standpoint, the Sargfabrik is managed and administered as cohousing, and was therefore eligible for public subsidies for the numerous shared facilities. Moreover, an exemption made it possible to reduce the number of obligatory parking spaces. Instead of a subterranean parking garage there are, among other things, an events space and a bath house. The amenities are also open to the neighborhood residents. The access balconies and shared roof terrace are ideal counterparts to the 70 compact apartments.

Showing Solidarity

Site model | Wood, foam board, synthetic resin, cardboard

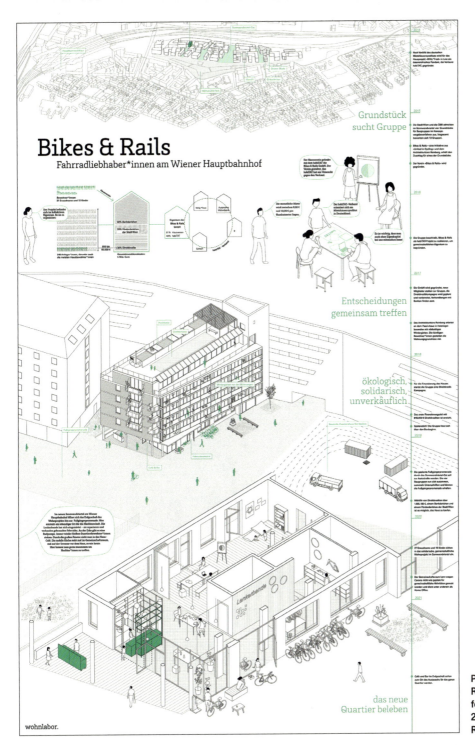

Picture story about the creation of Bikes and Rails, Bicycle Lovers at Vienna's Central Station, for the exhibition Let's Live Together, 2020–2021 | Graphic design: wohnlabor, Jomo Ruderer, Rebekka Hirschberg, Anna Jäger

Architekturbüro Reinberg
Bikes and Rails, cohousing
Emilie Flöge Weg 4, Vienna X, 2017–2020

With the aid of innovative financing and pursuing the long-term goal to keep housing out of the capital market, in the Sonnwendviertel district, affordable apartments were erected accessible, for example, to persons who cannot make up-front payments. For the financing, a model used by Germany's rental-apartment syndicate was employed. The property was bought by the company Hausbesitz: the residents' association holds 51 percent of the shares, while habiTAT holds 49 percent. Supporters of the project offset budget shortfalls by providing direct loans. In addition, the City of Vienna provided a promotional loan for the subsidized housing. The ecologically, economically, and socially sustainable project with 18 rental apartments and numerous shared facilities were executed in wood frame construction with passive-house technology. Energy is produced by the solar-energy system on the roof. Additional projects initiated by the syndicate are under construction. A portion of the revenue from the operation of buildings is directed to a solidarity fund for new projects.

The Other

Article 2: "All citizens are equal before the law."
(Staatsgrundgesetz [Basic Law] 1867)

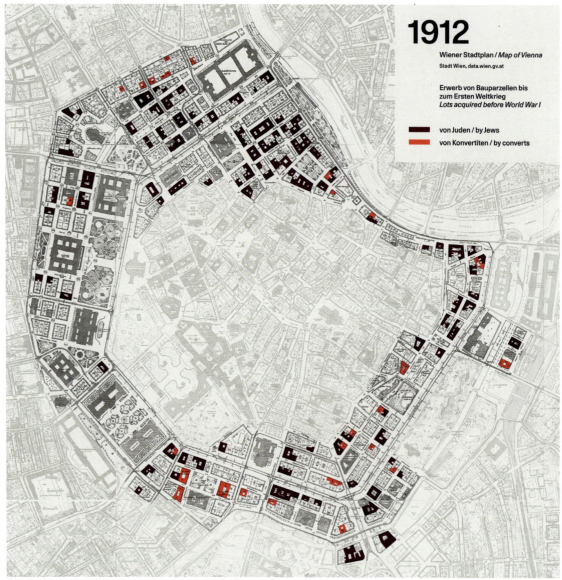

"1912 Map of Vienna. Building Plots Purchased by Jews and Converts," according to the research conducted by Georg Gaugusch Courtesy of Georg Gaugusch and Jüdisches Museum Wien

Emancipation and Antisemitism

In the era of liberalism, the Staatsgrundgesetz [Basic Law] of 1867 constituted a legal emancipation for Jews, who were, e.g., now allowed, for the first time without restrictions, to purchase land. Side by side with the aristocracy, an urban society made up of Jewish men and women, whose members – as patrons of the arts, artists, architects, scientists, and intellectuals – actively contributed to Vienna's transformation into a cosmopolitan city. The building boom accompanying the construction of the Ringstrasse and its surroundings illustrates the increasing self-confidence of Jewish clients, which in turn led to more business for many Jewish architects. The Jews' emancipation and will to become assimilated roused hostile sentiments among contemporaries, as is made clear by the reference to the Ringstrasse as the "Zion Street in New Jerusalem."

It is important to note that, contrary to the propaganda, the parcels were not acquired at inflated prices, but at the market price. Nor is it justifiable to claim that the buyers were engaging in real estate speculation because, as the column on ownership makes clear, the properties were seen as longer-term investments.

Purchaser	Category	Place of birth	Contract	Property (title number)	Ownership 1885 (1905; 1927)
Arthur Baron (1874–1944)	architect	Vienna	1907	III., Vordere Zollamtsstraße 11 (3358)	Dr. vet. med. Franz Hietel (1927)
Wilhelm Fraenkel (1844–1916)	architect	Oberglogau (Prussian Silesia, today: Poland)	18.08.1871	IX., Liechtensteinstraße 4 (356)	Nathaniel Freiherr von Rothschild
			1880	I., Rudolfsplatz 10 (1520)	Samuel and Regina Heit
			1881	I., Gölsdorfgasse 3 (1521)	Wilhelm Fraenkel
Jakob Gartner (1861–1921)	architect	Prerau (Moravia, today: Czech Republic)	1904	I., Stubenring 14 (1643)	Kary family and co-owner (1927)
			1905	I., Stubenring 2 (1655)	Adamkiewicz family (1927)
Friedrich Goldreich von Bronneck (1851–1932)	master builder	Hněkowitz (Bohemia, today: Czech Republic)	1882	I., Salzgries 12 (1513)	Alois Schumacher
Julius Goldschläger (1872–1940)	architect	Ismail (Romania, today: Ukraine)	1904	I., Stubenring 12 (1647)	Leo Brill (1927)
			1905	I., Biberstraße 9 (1685)	Imre Pirnitzer (1927)
			1905	IV., Brucknerstraße 4 (1271)	Andor and Alexander Teleki
Jacques Heller (1879–1934)	architect	Vienna	1907	III., Stelzhamergasse 4 (3360)	Emil Goldschmidt (1927)
Josef Heller & Co. (1854–1930)	construction firm	Teplitz (Bohemia, today: Czech Republic)	March 11, 1891	I., Kohlmessergasse 4 (638)	Antoinette Matzel (1905)
			June 17, 1891	I., Kohlmessergasse 6 (639)	Ignaz Steiner (1905)
			March 26, 1892	I., Wollzeile 34 (1470)	Karl Graf von Haugwitz (1927)
			March 26, 1892	I., Stubenbastei 4 (1586)	
			March 26, 1892	I., Stubenbastei 2 (1262)	
			March 30, 1896	I., Laurenzerberg 4 (884)	Anna Siller (1927)
			March 30, 1896	I., Dominikanerbastei 25 (883)	no longer exists (1905)
Heinrich Hellin (1850–1920), with Dionys Milch	master builder	Lemberg (Ukraine)	Nov. 22, 1880	I., Maria-Theresien-Straße 26 (720)	Mathilde Auspitz von Artenegg
			Sept. 21, 1881	I., Friedrich-Schmidt-Platz 2 (896)	Grave of Hermannswörth family (1927)
			May 22, 1906	III., Am Heumarkt 10 (3237)	Prague Society of the Iron Industry
			Sept. 19, 1860	I., Kärntner Ring 4 (568)	
			Sept. 19, 1860	I., Kärntner Ring 2 (566)	
			Jan. 21, 1862	I., Elisabethstraße 24 (238)	
			Oct. 21, 1862	I., Babenbergerstraße 1 (53)	
			Oct. 21, 1862	I., Elisabethstraße 26 (239)	
			Jan. 19, 1865	I., Parkring 2 (849)	
			Sept. 5, 1871	I., Maria-Theresien-Straße 10 (715)	Horace Ritter von Landau
Dionys Milch (1854–?), with Heinrich Hellin	architect	Kottesó outside Hlinik (Hungary)	Nov. 22, 1880	I., Maria-Theresien-Straße 26 (720)	see above [Heinrich Hellin]
			Sept. 21, 1881	I., Friedrich-Schmidt-Platz 2 (896)	
Alexander Neumann (1861–1947)	architect	Heinzendorf outside Bielitz (Silesia, today: Poland)	1900	I., Stubenring 22 (1629)	Leitenberger family and Riedl von Riedenstein family (1927)
Oskar Neumann (1870–1951)	architect	Friedek (Austrian Silesia, today: Czech Republic)	1905	IV., Schwarzenbergplatz 13 (1270)	Rosa Fischer (1927)
Samuel (1867–1943 dep.) and Wilhelm Schallinger (1875–?)	master builder	Brünn (Moravia, today: Czech Republic)	1905	IV., Lothringerstraße 4 (1275)	Generali Insurance
			1905	IV., Lothringerstraße 6 (1289)	
			1905	IV., Lothringerstraße 8 (1276)	
Adolf (1868–1934) and Viktor Schwadron (1865–1942)	construction firm	Draganowka near Tarnopol (Galicia, today: Ukraine)	1904	I., Franz-Josefs-Kai 3 (1704)	Adolf and Viktor Schwadron (1927)
Alois Schweinburg (1864–1939)	master builder	Vienna	1907	III., Gigergasse 6 (3359)	Austrian Treasury (1927)
Julie Stiassny, née Taussig (1848–1916), with her husband Wilhelm Stiassny	wife of architect	Stuhlweißenburg (Hungary)	April 16, 1882	I., Rathausstraße 13 (901)	Wilhelm and Julie Stiassny
Wilhelm Stiassny (1842–1910)	architect	Pressburg (Slovakia)	April 16, 1882	I., Rathausstraße 13 (901)	see above [Julie Stiassny]
Elias (Ely) Wasserstrom (1863–1937)	architect	Leipzig (Germany)	Aug. 16, 1905	I., Dominikanerbastei 22 (1679)	Sigmund Freud (1927)
			1908	I., Biberstraße 22 (1657)	Wagenberg family (1927)
Heinrich Weiner (1856–1941)	building contractor	Pirnitz (Moravia, today: Czech Republic)	1902	I., Biberstraße 4 (1637)	Ida Gallia (1927)
Donat Zifferer (1845–1909)	master builder	Bistritz am Hostein (Moravia, today: Czech Republic)	Oct. 1, 1877	I., Hohenstaufengasse 7 (961)	Witwen- und Waisen-Pensionsgesellschaft des juridischen Doktoren-Kollegiums [pension fund]
			April 2, 1879	I., Wipplingerstraße 30 (1441)	Janus-Versicherungsgesellschaft Viktor Kuffler [insurance agency]
			July 9, 1880	IX., Rooseveltplatz 6 (538)	Donat and Rosa Zifferer
			Aug. 8, 1881	I., Reichsratsstraße 17 (933)	Donat Zifferer
			Sept. 1, 1903	I., Dominikanerbastei 4 (1625)	Generali Insurance (1927)
Rosa Zifferer, née Schüler (1852–1911), with her husband Donat Zifferer	wife of master builder	Paderborn (Germany)	July 9, 1880	IX., Rooseveltplatz 6 (538)	see above [Donat Zifferer]

Table of plots purchased by Jewish architects, master builders, and construction firms on Vienna's Ringstrasse through 1914 | Courtesy of Georg Gaugusch and Jüdisches Museum Wien

VII. Rundgang über die Ringstraße.

Die Ringstraße — die Zionsstraße von Neu-Jerusalem — ist heute die prachtvollste Straße der Kaiserstadt. Die Paläste, welche dieselbe schmücken, sind fast durchgehends Eigenthum von Millionären des „auserwählten Volkes"; blos einige

wenige sind im Besitze von christlichen Eindringlingen, die man aber auch einen nach dem andern zu vertreiben sucht.

Die Ringstraße ist durchaus — ausgenommen wo sie abgestorben sind — mit Götterbäumen bepflanzt, die darum so heißen, weil sie rastlos himmelwärts streben und meistens nach kurzem irdischen Dasein in ein besseres Jenseits eingehen.

Die Ringstraße vom Burg- bis zum Kolowrat-Ring enthält, außer dem neuen Opernhaus, kein einziges öffentliches monumentales Gebäude, da man die Prachtbauten (Musikvereinsgebäude, Akademisches Gymnasium rc.) absichtlich in Seitengassen anlegte, um die Ringstraßenplätze möglichst theuer für einförmige Zinskasernen (siehe Palais Königswarter) zu verwerthen.

In: Franz Friedrich Masaidek, *Wien und die Wiener aus der Spottvogelperspektive. Wien's Sehens-, Merk- und Nichtswürdigkeiten* [Vienna and the Viennese from the Mockingbird Perspective. Vienna's Sights, Exceptionalness, and Unexceptionalness] | Vienna, 1873 | ÖNB

"The Ringstrasse – Zion Street of New Jerusalem – is now the imperial city's most magnificent street. The palaces which embellish it are almost exclusively the property of millionaires of 'the chosen people.'" The statements – accompanied by antisemitic caricatures – were made by Masaidek, who, together with Georg Ritter von Schönerer, was the founder of the anti-Jewish Deutsch-Nationaler Verband. The two of them paved the way for the antisemitism that soon thereafter was to become firmly established in Lueger's politics.

JEW-BAITING IN AUSTRIA.

Dr. Karl Lueger, Who Stands at the Head of the Anti-Semitic Party.

One of the strongest men in the public life of the Austro-Hungarian empire is Dr. Karl Lueger, burgomaster of Vienna, and the leader of the anti-Semitic party in Austria. He is a self made man, who rose from humble beginnings to be the leader of one of the most important political parties in the dual empire of Francis Joseph. Dr. Lueger began political life as an agitator pure and simple, and he addressed hundreds of meetings in support of the anti-Semitic program, denouncing the Jews as the origin of all evil in the world. The principles which he represents are strong in Austria to-day and have been responsible for many political broils in the Reichsrath. To an American it seems singular that in the 20th century Jew-baiting should exist in a country such as Austria. That it does exist is evidence that Austrian civilization has not progressed much since the middle ages, when Jews were accused of poisoning Christian wells and murdering Christian children. There was no justification for such charges then, nor is there any justification to-day for the anti-Semitic feeling of which Lueger is the chief mouthpiece.

DR. KARL LUEGER.

The antisemitism of the Christian Social Party under Karl Lueger's leadership was already notorious far beyond Austria's borders.

"Jew-Baiting in Austria" | *Semi-Weekly Ferndale Enterprise*, December 11, 1903

Otto Wagner
Project for the Künstlerhof, a rental apartment building, Vienna, 1917–1918

By 1938, Del-Ka (later renamed Delka), a shoe business that had been founded in 1907 by Jews, had already been "Aryanized" by the Creditanstalt. Ludwig Klauser, who had been its general manager, was deported to the concentration camp in Buchenwald; from there he managed to flee to the United States. While Mayor Karl Lueger was in office, his Christian Social Party increasingly instrumentalized hostile rhetoric against Jews for political purposes. As a private developer, Otto Wagner – architect and sympathizer with Lueger – profited from the mayor's cronyism. In 1917, in his final design for a mixed-use building (apartments and commerce), the wording on the facade included language hostile to Jews. In his diaries, Wagner also increasingly invoked negative stereotypes, which were directly related to his dissatisfaction with market mechanisms influencing the sale or construction of his buildings.

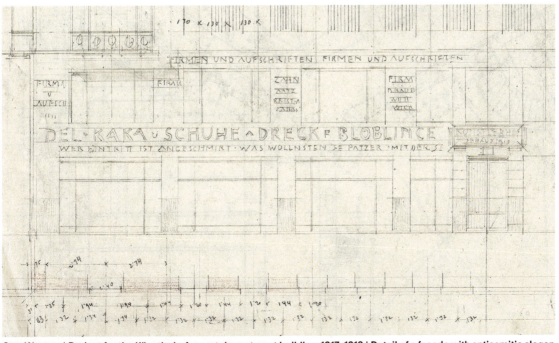

Otto Wagner | Project for the Künstlerhof, a rental apartment building, 1917–1918 | Detail of a facade with antisemitic slogan "DEL-KAKA Schuhe Dreck Wer Eintritt ist angeschmiert …" [Shitty shoes - anyone who enters is screwed…] | Kupferstichkabinett, Akademie der bildenden Künste Wien

Persecution, Forced Migration, and Murder of Austrian Architects

In the early 1930s, economic crises and increasing rates of unemployment led to a socio-political emergency. At schools and particularly at universities, riots directed toward Jews had already begun in the 1920s. In 1934, under the leadership of Engelbert Dollfuss, the Vaterländische Front (Fatherland Front) – a party with a corporative structure and invoking Catholic social ethics – became the only party tolerated by the authoritarian Ständestaat [corporative state]. During the era of Austrofascism, antisemitism was not officially sanctioned in the government's program, but was nevertheless subliminally widespread and hindered Jewish careers.

The murder and forced migration of thousands of Austrians in the wake of the "Annexation" of Austria to Germany in 1938 also had a devastating effect in architecture circles. A large share of the emigrants sought to rebuild their lives in the US, in Great Britain, and in South America. In forced exile, many of these men and women were not able to continue their careers.

The Az W commemorates the architects who were forced to emigrate from Austria or were persecuted or murdered by the National Socialist regime. We can only begin to imagine the vast gap this has left in Austria's cultural life.

The following list of persons is still far from complete:

Felix Augenfeld (1893 Vienna – 1984 New York, US): 1938 Great Britain, 1939 USA | Rudolf Baumfeld (1903 Vienna – 1988 Los Angeles, US): 1938 Czechia, 1940 Italy (internment), 1940 USA | Wilhelm Baumgarten (1885 Mährisch-Schönberg/Šumperk – 1959 Raleigh, US): 1940 USA | Josef Berger (1898 Vienna – 1989 London, GB): 1934 Haifa, 1937 London | Otto Breuer (1897 Vienna – 1938 Purkersdorf): 1938 seizure of his property, 1938 suicide | Ella Briggs, née Baumfeld (1880 Vienna – 1977 London, GB): 1936 Great Britain | Josef Franz Dex (1899 Linz – 1945 New York, US): 1941 USA | Friedl Dicker-Brandeis (1898 Vienna – 1944 Auschwitz, PL): 1934 arrest, 1936 emigration to Czechia, 1942 deportation to Theresienstadt, 1944 murdered at the Auschwitz concentration camp | Karl Dirnhuber (1889 Vienna – 1953 Birmingham, GB): 1939 London | Herbert Eichholzer (1903 Graz – 1943 Vienna): 1941 arrest, 1942 condemned to death, 1943 execution | Paul Engelmann (1891 Olmütz/Olomouc, Moravia – 1965 Tel Aviv-Jaffa, IL): 1934 Tel Aviv | Martin Eisler (1913 Vienna – 1977 São Paulo, BR): 1938 Argentina, 1953 São Paulo | Ernest Leslie Fooks, born Ernest Leslie Fuchs (1906 Pressburg/Bratislava, CZ – 1985 Melbourne, AU): 1938 Canada, 1939 Australia | Josef Frank (1885 Baden – 1967 Stockholm, SE): 1933 Sweden, 1941 USA, 1947 Sweden | Dora Gad (formerly: Goldberg), born Siegel (1912 Langenau/Câmpulung, RO – 2003 Tel Aviv, IL): 1936 Tel Aviv | Jacques Groag (1892 Olmütz/Olomouc, Moravia – 1962 London, GB): 1938 Czechia, Great Britain | Victor Gruen, born Viktor Grünbaum (1903 Vienna – 1980 Vienna): 1938 USA | Otto Rudolf Polak-Hellwig (1885 Vienna – 1958 Sydney, AU): 1939 Australia | Karl Hofmann (1890 Vienna – ?): 1938 Brno, then possibly Australia | Fritz Janeba (1905 Vienna – 1983 Vienna): 1939 Australia, 1962 Turkey, 1967 Austria | Arnold Karplus (1877 Wigstadtl/Vítkov, Silesia – 1943 New York, US): 1939 New York | Gerhard Karplus (1909 Vienna – 1995 ?): 1938 Czechia, Switzerland, Great Britain, USA | Leopold Kleiner (1897 ? – 1985 ?): 1938 USA | Julius Kornweitz (1911 Vienna – 1944 Mauthausen): 1939 France, Yugoslavia, Austria, 1941 arrest, 1944 murdered at the Mauthausen concentration camp | Heinrich Kulka (1900 Littau/Litovel, Moravia – 1971 Auckland, NZ): 1938 Czechia, Great Britain, New Zealand | Ernst Lichtblau (1883 Vienna – 1963 Vienna): 1939 USA, 1962 Austria | Anton Liebe (1905 Merano, IT – 1978 Vienna): 1938 Italy, 1941 Argentina, 1956 Austria | Walter Loos (1905 Vienna – 1974 Buenos Aires, AR): 1938 Great Britain, USA, 1940 Argentina | Viktor Lurje (1883 Vienna – 1944 Jaipur, IN): 1938 China | Fritz Michael Müller (1892 ? – ?): 1938 Brazil | Ernst Anton Plischke (1903 Klosterneuburg – 1992 Vienna): 1939 New Zealand, 1963 Austria | Leopold Ponzen (1892 Vienna – 1946 Shanghai, CN): 1938 Japan, Shanghai | Kurt Popper (1910 ? – 2008 ?): 1938 Australia | Alfred Preis (1911 Vienna – 1993 Honolulu, US): 1939 USA (Hawaii) | Fritz Reichl (1890 Baden – 1959 Los Angeles, US): 1938 Turkey, 1946 USA | Egon Riss (1901 Kunzendorf/Lipnik, Galicia – 1964 Colinton, GB): 1938 Great Britain (Scotland) | Helene Roth (1904 Göding/Hodonín, Moravia – 1995 Haifa, IL): 1933 Palestine | Franz Schacherl (1895 Vienna – 1943 Nova Lisboa, AO): 1938 France, 1939 Angola | Simon Schmiderer (1911 Saalfelden – 2001 Highland Beach, US): 1938 Netherlands, USA | Otto Schönthal (1878 Vienna – 1961 Vienna): 1938 Switzerland, Yugoslavia, 1945 Austria | Margarete Schütte-Lihotzky (1897 Vienna – 2000 Vienna): 1937 France, 1938 Turkey, 1940 Austria (arrest), 1945 release, 1946 Bulgaria, 1947 Vienna | Ernst Schwadron (1896 Vienna – 1971 New York, US): 1939 USA | Harry Seidler (1923 Vienna – 2006 Sydney, AU): 1938 Great Britain, Canada, USA, Australia | Stephan Simony (1903 ? – 1971 ?): 1938 Turkey, Austria | Franz Singer (1896 Vienna – 1954 Berlin, DE): 1934 Great Britain | Eugen Székely (1894 Budapest – 1962 Haifa, IL): 1935 Haifa | Hans Adolf Vetter (1897 Vienna – 1963 Pittsburgh, US): 1938 Great Britain, 1947 USA | Oskar Wlach (1881 Vienna – 1963 New York, US): 1938 Switzerland, Great Britain, USA | Margarete Zak, née Hofmann (1913 Vienna – ?): 1939 Great Britain, 1940 USA | Liane Zimbler, née Juliana Fischer (1892 Prerau/Přerov, Moravia – 1987 Los Angeles, US): 1938 USA

Traces of Flight

With the "Annexation" of Austria in March 1938, the emigration of Jews devolved into a mass exodus. Great Britain was one of the most important destinations for those who fled. Between the "Annexation" and the outbreak of World War II, Great Britain admitted 30,000 Austrians who had fled the Nazis; about 90 percent of them were Jews.

Leopold Ponzen
December 12, 1892, Vienna – October 10, 1946, Shanghai, China

Leopold Ponzen studied architecture – as did most of his Jewish colleagues – under Carl König at the Technische Hochschule Wien. He became a member of three Austrian organizations: the Ingenieur- und Architektenverein, the Zentralvereinigung der Architekten (associate member), and the Werkbund. In 1925, he worked as project architect in Oskar Strnad's office. Beginning in 1926, Ponzen worked on his own projects: In 1928, his design for a monument at Vienna's Central Cemetery (Gate I, Group 76B) commemorating Jewish soldiers was erected. In 1932, he took part in the competition Das wachsende Haus [The growing house]; Ponzen subsequently installed his design – in the form of a mock-up – at the construction fair on Vienna's trade-fair grounds.

From 1933, Ponzen worked on the Kahlenberg project, at first alone, and shortly thereafter with Erich Boltenstern. The jury awarded two first prizes: one of them to Carl Witzmann/Otto Niedermoser and the other to Leopold Ponzen/Erich Boltenstern. Because the financing was not yet secured, the project was put on hold. In October 1934, Richard Schmitz, Vienna's new mayor, initiated the implementation of the project, but in a much reduced version. The client's prejudice against Jews made it impossible for Ponzen to continue to work on the project, and the two architects ultimately withdrew from it. With a newly devised design, Boltenstern was awarded the commission a second time in 1935; Eugen Wachberger joined Boltenstern for the implementation of the project. Following the "Annexation" (1938), Ponzen emigrated via Japan to Shanghai, where some 18,000 persons found refuge from the National Socialist regime. Leopold Ponzen died of leukemia there on October 10, 1946.

A letter from a supporter of Leopold Ponzen dated July 26, 1938, is a touching testimony and at the same time exemplifies the efforts undertaken to make it possible for Jews to escape from Austria to Great Britain.

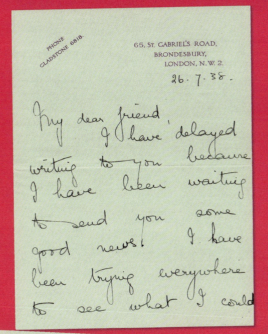

My dear friend,

I have delayed writing to you because I have been waiting to send you some good news. I have been trying everywhere to see what I could do to help you. Now I can tell you that if you want to come to London I will send you an invitation through the Home Office, which will enable you to get a visa at the British Consul and a permit to come to London on a "visit." When you are here, you need not worry, I have means of helping you.

Please let me know immediately if you would like to come and I will make arrangements as quickly as possible.

All best wishes to you dear friend. My son is getting better now, and I am also feeling a little better. Will write more next time.

Kindest regards and affectionate thoughts

Pauline.

Letter from Pauline (family name unknown) to Leopold Ponzen, July 26, 1938 | Ink on paper

| YEAR | PERSONAL PARTICULARS | ARCHITECTURAL WORK |||| PUBLISHED ||
| | | COMPETITIONS || PROJECTS | EXECUTED WORK | | |
		SUBJECT	AWARD			YEAR	IN PERIODICAL, BOOK, ETC.
1889	BORN						
1895-1900	PRIMARY SCHOOL						
1900-1908	SECONDARY SCHOOLS						
1908-14	UNIVERSITY VIENNA SCHOOL OF ARCHITECTURE						
1915-20	APPRENTICESHIP IN ARCH. OFF.						
1917	ARCHITECT'S DEGREE						
1919		HORTICULTURAL MARKET HALL IN VIENNA IV.	1st PRIZE				
1920		HOUSING SCHEME IN VIENNA XIII.	1st PRIZE				
		COMMUNITY CENTRE, PUBLIC SPORT GROUNDS, LIBRARY & HOUSING SCHEME FOR VIENNA XVI.	1st PRIZE			1932	WIENER ARCHITEKTEN
		SCHUBERT PARK FOR VIENNA XVIII.	1st PRIZE				
		RECONSTRUCTION SCHEME FOR WARDAMAGED TOWN KÖTSCHACH, CARYNTHIA, AUSTRIA	IIIrd PRIZE				
1921	ELECTION TO Z.V. (CENTRAL INSTITUTE OF AUSTRIAN ARCHITECTS)	SPA HOTEL IN TOBELBAD, STYRIA, AUSTRIA	COMMENDED				
				SMALLHOLDERS' SETTLEMENT IN PRIESTBAUM, LOWER AUSTRIA		1932	WIENER ARCHITEKTEN
				WORKERS' SETTLEMENT IN ASPANG, LOWER AUSTRIA			
				WORKERS' SETTLEMENT IN BLUMAU, LOWER AUSTRIA			
				YOUTH CENTRE, SCHEME I, LEOBEN, STYRIA, AUSTRIA		1922	SEPARAT BOOKLET
1922	COMMENCEMENT OF PRIVATE PRACTICE	CLINICS & MEDICAL SCHOOL OF UNIVERSITY VIENNA	COMMENDED				
		CREMATORIUM & GARDEN OF MEMORY VIENNA	COMMENDED	RECONSTRUCTION OF A RESIDENCE IN VIENNA XII.	RECONSTRUCTION OF A FLAT IN VIENNA XIII.	1922	DER ARCHITEKT
1922-24					YOUTH CENTRE SCHEME II. LEOBEN, STYRIA, AUSTRIA	1923 1932	BAU-UND WERKKUNST WIENER ARCHITEKTEN
		RIDING CLUB PALACE IN BARCELONA, SPAIN	1st PRIZE			1923	SPANISH PAPERS & BOOKS
1923	ELECTION TO GENOSSENSCHAFT BILDENDER KÜNSTLER (ASSOCIATION OF AUSTR. ARTISTS)	OFFICE BUILDING FOR COAL MINING LTD. LJUBLJANA S.H.S.	1st PRIZE			1923	JUGOSLAV PROF. PAPERS
				BANK FOR CORPORATION OF LJUBLJANA, S.H.S.			
				BLOCKS OF FLATS IN BELGRADE, S.H.S.			
				BLOCK OF FLATS & SHOPS IN AGRAM, S.H.S.			
1923-24					SCHUBERT PARK FOR CORPORATION OF VIENNA IN VIENNA XVIII.	1926 1932	BAU-UND WERKKUNST, WIENER ARCHITEKTEN MANY EUROPEAN PERIODICALS
					BLOCK OF FLATS FOR CORPORATION OF VIENNA IN VIENNA XVIII.		
1924				HOSPITAL FOR CORPORATION OF AGRAM, S.H.S.			
				BLOCK OF FLATS FOR CORPOR. OF LJUBLJANA, S.H.S.			
				MONASTERY EXTENSION OF ADMONT, STYRIA, AUSTRIA		1932	WIENER ARCHITEKTEN
				CHILDREN'S CONVALESCENCE HOME, LEOBEN, STYRIA, AUSTRIA			
1924-25					BLOCK OF WORKERS' FLATS FOR CORPORATION OF VIENNA IN VIENNA XVI.	1925 1932	STEIN-HOLZ-EISEN, WIENER ARCHITEKTEN
1925		BLOCKS OF FLATS IN BIELITZ, POLAND					
		BANKING OFFICES IN VIENNA I.					
		CONCRETE BRIDGE IN LOWER AUSTRIA					
		GARDEN OF MEMORY IN BERNDORF, LOWER AUSTRIA					
		CONCRETE BRIDGE IN LEOBEN, STYRIA, AUSTRIA				1932	WIENER ARCHITEKTEN
		SHOPS FOR CORPORATION OF BERNDORF, LOWER AUSTRIA					
		5 MAISONETTES IN WR.-NEUSTADT, LOWER AUSTRIA					
1925-26		TENNIS HALL IN VIENNA XVII.			BLOCK OF WORKERS' FLATS FOR CORPORATION OF VIENNA IN VIENNA XX.	1926 1932	BAU-UND WERKKUNST, WIENER ARCHITEKTEN
1926	DEGREE ZIVILARCHITECT						
1926-27					BLOCKS OF WORKERS' FLATS FOR CORPOR. OF VIENNA IN VIENNA III.	1928 1932	BAU-UND WERKKUNST, WIENER ARCHITEKTEN & OTHER EUROPEAN PAPERS
1927		GOVERNMENT BUILDING EISENSTADT, BURGENLAND, AUSTRIA	1st PRIZE			1927	MANY PAPERS & PERIODICALS
1927-31					BLOCKS OF WORKERS' FLATS, PUBLIC BATH & LAUNDRY, LIBRARY & NURSERY FOR CORPOR. OF VIENNA IN VIENNA XII.	1932	MODERNE BAUFORMEN, WIENER ARCHITEKTEN
					RECONSTR. & FURNISHING OF MANOR HOUSE DR. O.M. IN SMIRČIČ, C.S.R.	1932	WIENER ARCHITEKTEN
1928		MEDICAL ADMINISTRATION & INSURANCE BUILDING IN EISENSTADT, BURGENLAND, AUSTRIA	LIMITED COMPETITION	ELECTRIC POWER STATION FOR ALPINE MONTAN LTD. IN ZELTWEG, STYRIA, AUSTRIA		1932	WIENER ARCHITEKTEN
1928-31				8 RESIDENCES IN VIENNA & PROVINCES OF AUSTRIA	RECONSTR. & FURNISHING OF MANOR HOUSE STANZ, STYRIA	1930 1932	BAU-UND WERKKUNST, MODERNE BAUFORMEN, WIENER ARCHITEKTEN & OTHER EUROPEAN PERIODICALS
					HOUSE DENHUBER IN VIENNA XIII.		
1928-37				RECONSTRUCTION & FURNISHING OF MANY FLATS FOR VIENNA	RECONSTRUCTION & FURNISHING OF A RESIDENCE IN VIENNA XIII.	1930 1935	BAU-UND WERKKUNST, MODERNE BAUFORMEN
					RECONSTRUCTION OF TOWNHALL IN YBBS, LOWER AUSTRIA		
1929				2 SHOPFRONTS IN YBBS, LOWER AUSTRIA		1932	WIENER ARCHITEKTEN
				MOUNTAIN HOTEL BACHSTEIN, SCHEME I, STYRIA, AUSTRIA			
				WORKMEN'S CENTRE IN AMSTETTEN, LOWER AUSTRIA			
				HOUSING SCHEME FOR CORPOR. OF AMSTETTEN			
				BLOCKS OF FLATS IN VIENNA XII.			
1929-31				3 WEEKEND HOUSES ON THE DANUBE			
1929-37	ELECTED TO COMMITTEE OF Z.V.			GARDEN SCHEMES FOR HOUSES IN AUSTRIA			
1930-32				WEEKEND HOUSE IN YBBS, LOWER AUSTRIA	MODEL OF THAT WEEKEND HOUSE	1932	WIENER ARCHITEKTEN
				HOUSES FOR DR. M. IN MAUER NEAR VIENNA	RECONSTRUCTION & FURNISHING OF 4 FLATS IN VIENNA I.	1932	WIENER ARCHITEKTEN, PROFILE
1931	DEGREE OF DOCTOR OF ARCH.				PHOTO SHOP BENEDIK IN VIENNA I.	1932	WIENER ARCHITEKTEN
1931-37					RECONSTRUCTION & FURNISHING OF 4 SHOPS IN VIENNA I., III., VI. & XVIII.		
1932				SHOP FRONT FOR SHELL OIL LTD., VIENNA I.			
				PHOTO SHOP FRONT FOR VIENNA I.			
1933		"MONUMENT OF WORK" IN ASSOC. WITH SCULPTOR S.CHARWUX FOR VIENNA I.	IInd PRIZE		TIMBER HOUSE FOR DR. M. IN MAUER NEAR VIENNA	1934	PROFILE
					CIGARETTE PAPER FACTORY IN VIENNA XV.	1935	PROFILE
1934				ISOLATION HOSPITAL FOR WR. NEUSTADT, LOWER AUSTRIA			
					RECONSTRUCTION & FURNISHING OF A TAILOR'S SHOP IN VIENNA III.		
1935		EXHIBITION BUILDING FOR BRUXELLES, BELGIUM	—				
1935-36				RECONSTR. & EXTENSION OF "WIENER URANIA", VIENNA I.	RECONSTRUCTION & FURNISHING OF DEPARTMENT STORES GERNGROSS LTD. VIENNA VI.	1936	ÖSTERREICHISCHE KUNST
		ORIGINAL SUBJECT: "RECONSTR. OF WEST TERMINAL OF AUSTR. RAILWAYS." THIS THEME INCOMPLETE MODERNIZATION SPA WITH NEW SUBJECTS: CENTRAL RAILWAY STATION, PUBLIC PARKING ETC.	1st PRIZE HIGHLY COMMENDED			1936	MANY PROFESS. PAPERS
1936	PROPOSED FOR PROFESSOR'S CHAIR, DESIGN SCHOOL OF ARCHITECTURE, UNIVERSITY VIENNA			SHOP FRONT FOR "ZENTRAL BIBLIOTHEK" IN VIENNA I.			
				GARAGE & CYCLE SHED FOR STEEL WORKS IN TERNITZ, AUSTR.	6 HOUSES FOR STAFF OF SCHÖLLER-BLECKMANN STEEL WORKS LIMITED, TERNITZ, AUSTR.		
				DIRECTOR'S FLAT FOR SCHÖLLER-BLECKMANN STEEL WORKS LTD. IN WR.-NEUSTADT, AUSTRIA			
				HOUSES FOR WORKMEN OF STEEL WORKS IN TERNITZ			
				ADMINISTRATION BUILDING FOR STEEL WORKS TERNITZ			
				BUNGALOW FOR ING. SAUNDERS IN LOWER AUSTRIA			
				WORKMEN'S CENTRE FOR STEEL WORKS TERNITZ			
				WORK'S HOTEL FOR STEEL WORKS TERNITZ			
1937	ADDITIONAL Z.V. COMPETITIONS (OFFERED TO MEMBERS OF ASSOCIATION)			MOUNTAIN HOTEL BACHSTEIN SCHEME II., STYRIA, AUSTRIA	ADMINISTRATION BUILDING FOR STEEL WORKS TERNITZ		
				APPARTMENT HOUSE MADONNA DI CAMPIGLIO, TRENTO, ITALY	MODEL TO APPARTMENT HOUSE MAD. DI CAMPIGLIO		
					APPARTMENT HOUSE SCHEME II. IN MADONNA DI CAMPIGLIO, ITALY		
		TRADE'S FAIR FOR VIENNA	2nd PRIZE COMMENDED			1938	VIENNA PAPERS & BOOKS
1938-39				CANTEEN & RECREATION CENTRE FOR STAFF OF THE WORKS GERNGROSS LTD. IN VIENNA VI.			
				HOUSING SCHEME & TYPES OF HOUSES FOR STEEL WORKS IN TERNITZ, LOWER AUSTRIA			
				BLOCK OF FLATS FOR VIENNA XII.			
				STAFF FLATS & OFFICE FOR ALPINE MONTAN IN LEOBEN, AUSTR.			
				OFFICE BUILDING FOR ALPINE MONTAN IN VIENNA I.			
				ADMINISTRATION BUILDING FOR ALPINE MONTAN, VIENNA I.			
				FACTORY FOR KRUPP LTD. BERNDORF, LOWER AUSTRIA			
				2 SCHEMES FOR A TECHN. COLLEGE IN BERNDORF			

Karl Dirnhuber | Communal housing on Weimarer Strasse 1, Vienna XVIII, 1924–1925 | Portfolio | Black-and-white photos and drawing mounted on cardboard

Following the transition of power in Austria, Karl Dirnhuber's successful career in architecture was upended. Two portfolios bear witness to the architect's professional development from the start of his career to 1939. All works are meticulously listed in tables and documented in photographs and drawings. Standing in for the many testimonies of the persecuted and murdered architects of this era that have been lost to history, these portfolios illustrate the substantial cultural loss and the omissions in the historiography.

Karl Dirnhuber
October 7, 1889, Vienna – November 11, 1953, Birmingham, Great Britain

Karl Dirnhuber attended the Staatsgewerbeschule, a college-preparatory technical academy, in Vienna. He studied architecture from 1910 to 1915 at the Technische Hochschule Wien. To gain professional experience, he next spent a few years at Atelier Theiss & Jaksch. From 1919, he worked on his own projects and took part in numerous competitions. During the Red Vienna era, Dirnhuber designed outstanding apartment buildings for the city. He received wide acclaim for his repurposing of the Währing Cemetery into a park with adjoining monument grove (1924–1925). In 1931, he received his doctorate in technical sciences.

Following the National Socialists' seizure of power in Austria, in 1939 he and his wife Annie Stern – who had Jewish ancestry – were forced to emigrate. In Great Britain he initially received a work permit from the Cadbury family's Bournville Village Trust and later took up a position at the architecture firm Jack Cotton, Ballard and Blow, where he worked until his death. Beginning in 1946, he developed concepts to reshape Birmingham's urban infrastructure and amenities. Dirnhuber designed a central station, hotel complexes, shopping centers, squares with fountains and reflecting pools, parks, and a new cathedral. In the 1960s, Jack Cotton, Ballard and Blow built a portion of one of his designs posthumously, but did not mention Dirnhuber's contribution. Karl Dirnhuber died in 1953 in Birmingham.

Places of Empowerment

At the onset of the industrial and technological revolutions, a societal transformation set in which profoundly changed the way the roles attributed to the different genders are perceived. Many women joined the ranks of the sexual equality movement to fight for their political, social, and civil rights. As an alternative to public meeting places, which women were excluded from, they began to create their own spaces for self-organization. In Adele Bloch-Bauer's fin-de-siècle salon, members of the artistic and political elite interacted. The presence of *Danaë* in Maria Ast's boudoir pointed to a re-conception of how women view themselves. Adolf Loos designed the interior of the First Viennese Women's Club; the rooms provided a place to convene and to network – and became the point of departure for a socio-political (educational) campaign which is operational to this day.

In 1900, three hundred women were present at the inaugural meeting of the First Women's Club of Vienna in the club's original premises at Maximilianstrasse 2 (today Mahlerstrasse), Vienna I. In November of the same year, the premises furnished by Adolf Loos at Graben 29, Vienna I, were opened.

First Women's Club of Vienna (November 15, 1900 – July 31, 1902) | Graben 29, Vienna I | "Executive committee and board of the women's organization on opening day (billiard room)" | Based on a photo for the *Österreichische Blatt* | ÖNB

Capital   The Other   212

Josef Hoffmann | Villa Ast | Steinfeldgasse 2, Vienna XIX, 1909–1911 | Gustav Klimt's *Danaë* in the boudoir | In: *Moderne Bauformen. Monatshefte für Architektur und Raumkunst* 1, 1913

Reclamation of the female gaze challenges the male "privilege of seeing" and old gender hierarchies.

ZUR FRAUENCLUB-ERÖFFNUNG VON GRETE MEISEL-HESS, WIEN

Am 14. November lud der Wiener Frauenclub eine Gesellschaft von Künstlern und Journalisten zur Vorbesichtigung seiner geschmackvollen Räume. Obwohl man vorausgesetzt hatte, die äussere Ausstattung mit dem Geist, der diese Sache creirt hat, in Uebereinstimmung zu finden, war man überrascht: denn so viel Geschmack, so viel Distinction, so viel Zweckmässigkeit und so viel Behagen hatte man doch nicht erwartet. Dieses Intérieur ist beste Moderne . . . .

Der Salon mit den bequemen Divans und Fauteuils, in denen man versinkt wie in Apfelmus, mit den grossen, fragenden Blumenaugen auf allen Möbelstoffen — das Lesezimmer mit seiner imponirenden Reichhaltigkeit an Lectüre, die fast alle modernen Zeitschriften und eine grosse Anzahl Zeitungen umschliesst und deren treffliche, übersichtliche Anordnung noch besonders lobend hervorzuheben ist — ein Verdienst der Schriftstellerin Mizzi Franzos — das Billard-room mit den famosen Grotesken an den Wänden, — ein zerschnittenes Kinderbilderbuch von Nicolson!! — das Spielzimmer in seiner roth-grünen Freundlichkeit — alle diese Räume athmen anheimelnde Vornehmheit — zwei Begriffe, die sich selten vereint finden und die man in ihrer Zusammenwirkung getrost als untrügliches Criterium eines gelungenen Wohnungs-Ensembles gelten lassen darf. Die malerische corona des Abends bot aber ohne Zweifel der Speisesaal. Das Buffet in seinem »künstlerischen Aufbau« hätte einfach verdient, als Stillleben in die »Jugend« oder in die »Insel« aufgenommen zu werden. Wie wir erfahren, hat Frau Bertha Weiss, die Clubleiterin, all die guten und schönen Dinge, mit denen wir bewirthet wurden, in ihrer Privatküche anfertigen lassen und dem Club dadurch eine bedeutende Summe erspart.

Sonst war von »Stillleben« freilich nicht viel zu merken. Wenn die fröhlichen Geister, die mit dieser crémaillère im Frauenclub einzogen, wirklich die bleibenden sind, so werden alle Unholde der Langeweile und des Missbehagens, die sich etwa einnisten wollten, schon von selbst die Flucht ergreifen. Von den 230 geladenen Gästen waren beiläufig 200 erschienen und unterhielten sich in den vielen Plauderecken ganz vortrefflich. Frau Professor Jodl hielt mit der ihr eigenen Anmuth und Lieblichkeit die begrüssende Eröffnungsrede, welche mit viel Beifall aufgenommen wurde.

Mit der durch den Club gebotenen Annäherung der gesicherten Frau aus dem besitzenden Bürgerstande an die erwerbende gebildete Frau, für die die Annehmlichkeiten des neutralen Clublebens besonders geschaffen wurden, dürfte einem der wichtigsten Ziele der Frauenbewegung: dem Ausgleich der Classengegensätze, fördernd zugearbeitet werden.

— — — — Mit der Eröffnung des Frauenclubs hat die Wiener Frauenbewegung einen Erfolg zu verzeichnen. Der Club bietet allen gebildeten Frauen einen neutralen geselligen Vereinigungspunkt, eine Fülle von Lesematerial, Erfrischungen zu mässigen Preisen; in seinem Zukunftsprogramm plant er künstlerische Veranstaltungen, Discussionen, Ausflüge, Reisen etc.

Besondere Anerkennung verdienen die Firmen, die dem Frauenclub bei seiner Equipirung in liberalster Weise entgegenkamen. Architekt Adolf Loos hat das künstlerische Ensemble entworfen, das von der Firma Friedrich Otto Schmidt in glänzendster Weise durchgeführt wurde, wobei ihn die Firmen Allertshammer, Eugen Artin, Böck, Albin Denk, der Salon »Flora«, Knobloch's Nachfolger, Otto Maas, Novotny, Prag-Rudniker Korbwaarenfabrication, Ritter, F. Siemens und Wlassak und Hartwiger grossartig unterstützten. Durch dieses Zusammenspiel allererster Kräfte kam allein dieses auserlesen geschmackvolle Ensemble zustande. Wände, Plafonds, Vorhänge, Teppiche und Möbel, ein Accord in licht-fröhlicher Harmonie — die Beleuchtungskörper sind an sich Sehenswürdigkeiten — Alles weist die besten Principien des modernen Kunstgewerbes auf: Zweckmässigkeit des Gebrauchsgegenstandes, Aufrichtigkeit des Materials und neue Farbenfreudigkeit. Der Bilder- und Vasenschmuck wird von der Firma Artin in ganz eigenartig schöner und abwechslungsreicher Weise besorgt. Diese Kunstgegenstände sind nämlich verkäuflich und werden immer wieder durch neue ersetzt. Derzeit befinden sich im Frauenclub keramische Vasen der berühmten Münchner Künstlerfamilie Heyder, ferner Bilder von: Andri, Vogeler, Sigmundt etc.

Der Neid aller Hausfrauen aber ist der Küchen-Gasherd von Ingenieur Ritter. Wie ein Buddhist in Nirvanabetrachtungen verloren, kann man davor kauern und zusehen, wie viel »Stückeln« dieser Herd gleichzeitig zu spielen weiss. In 12 Minuten ist z. B. ein Entre-côte am Rost gebraten, fix und fertig, ohne die Misère des Kohlenheizens und Ofenputzens.

Es hat sich aber auch ein ganzer Stab tüchtiger Frauen zusammengethan, um diesen Club ins Leben zu rufen. Das Verdienst, diesen Stab von Frauen gewonnen zu haben, gebührt Frau Ritza Krisshaber, die die Hauptanregungen zur Frauenclub-Begründung gegeben hat. Mitfördernd hat eine ganze Reihe vortrefflicher Frauen ihr Bestes geleistet: die Präsidentin Frau Professor Jodl, die uns auch als vortreffliche Uebersetzerin der »Träume« von Oliv Schreiner bekannt ist, die Vicepräsidentin Marie Lang, Herausgeberin dieses Blattes, ferner Frau Brünauer, die durch ihre stramme Casseverwaltung der Sache ein finanzielles Rückgrat gibt, Frau Bertha Weiss als Clubleiterin, Fräulein Mizzi Franzos als Bibliothekarin, die Damen Helene Bruckner, Fensmark, Dr. Salka Goldmann, Fanny Markus, Daisy Minor, Clara Petrin, Dr. Gabr. v. Possanner, Else Zimmermann, als wacker Mitwirkende bei einer schönen Sache.

Wie alles Nothwendige wird sich auch die Frauenbewegung voll und ganz durchsetzen in all ihren ökonomischen künstlerischen und ethischen Erscheinungen. Wie bei jedem Entwicklungsprocess wird auch hier das Darwinsche Princip Recht behalten: das Tüchtige, Nützliche, Berechtigte, in harmonischer Auslese sich Ergebende wird sich behaupten, das Untaugliche, Unechte, Zufällige wird abfallen und zugrunde gehen. Solche Nebenschösslinge, solche parasitische Gebilde fehlen bei keinem Entwicklungsprocess und werden auch hier nicht fehlen. Sackgassen, die vom geraden Weg irreführen und eine Spanne Zeit lang aufhalten, verlocken bei jedem neuen Suchen.

Auf eine davon, die aber gerade bei diesem Club, der wirklich freiesten und schönsten Zielen dient, nicht in Frage kommt und von keiner Seite zu drohen scheint, in der ich aber schon des Oefteren Frauen, die es herzlich gut mit der rechten Sache meinen, verirrt gefunden habe, sei hier hingewiesen. Ich möchte davor warnen, in der modernen Frauenbewegung einen Standpunkt »wir Frauen — ihr Männer« zu fixiren. Auf die Verbesserung des socialen Zusammenlebens und des individuellen Für-sich-Lebens steuert die Frauenbewegung hin — alle natürlich denkenden Männer sind dabei ihre Bundesgenossen. Daher kein engherziges Frauen-Parteithum, in dem der Blick für die grossen Perspectiven verloren geht, keinen Chauvinismus in der Frauenbewegung!

Die Frauen sind keine Kaste und keine Classe, sondern sie bedeuten in ihrem Befreiungskampf gegen die grossen und die kleinen, die furchtbaren und die lächerlichen Gordonknoten der Unnatur, mit denen decadente Culturen sich aufputzen zu müssen glauben, eine imposante Massenvorwärtsbewegung der Menschheit.

SPLITTERWERK (Mark Blaschitz, Edith Hemmrich, Josef Roschitz, Nikolaos Zachariadis) | 1,000 Masterpieces series, 2007 | *Adele Bloch-Bauer I*, after Gustav Klimt | Color print on canvas

The portrait by Gustav Klimt is one of the most renowned works of Viennese modernism. In 2006, following a protracted legal battle with the Republic of Austria, the painting was returned to Maria Altmann – the lawful owner – and her co-heirs. Ronald Lauder purchased the painting shortly thereafter, and it is now on display at the Neue Galerie New York.

SPLITTERWERK's aim is to deconstruct the painting, which is part of their 1,000 Masterpieces series. The central theme is "dissolving" the painting's motif, which SPLITTERWERK achieves by introducing a seamless butterfly pattern. Depending on the observer's vantage point, the "masterpiece" or the ornamental abstraction comes into focus. The architects' engagement with ornament is computer generated; they are interested in the utilization of ornament's indwelling relations, symmetries, frequencies, intervals, and conditions. The results of their explorations could ultimately lead to a shift in paradigm.

No Adolf Loos without Lina?

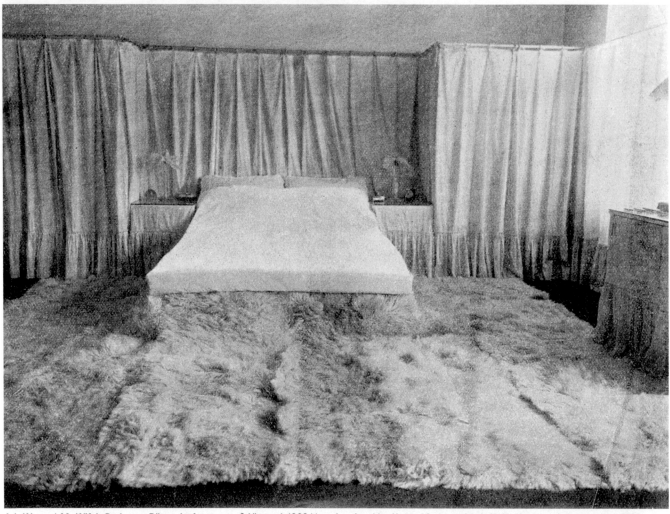

Adolf Loos | *My Wife's Bedroom*, Bösendorferstrasse 3, Vienna I, 1903 | Interior view | In: *Kunst. Monatszeitschrift für Kunst und alles Andere*, 1903

"Through you I now have an apartment – something I have always dreamed of, yet which on account of my frailty in money matters probably never would have been fulfilled. Through you I am in a much better position financially than two years ago, much has taken a turn for the good through your strength. [...] But concerning my viewpoints I also have so many reasons to be grateful to you. With respect to my profession: what had been incomplete, you have solidified or made whole."
(Letter from Adolf Loos to Lina Loos, 1904)

Adolf Loos is one of Austria's most renowned architects. His œuvre – and in particular, his pioneering conception of the *Raumplan* – is inscribed on the history of architecture. In light of his having been convicted of child abuse, it became necessary to critically reappraise the traditional narrative. The issue of the interdependency of Loos and his partners gives rise to another asymmetry calling the master narrative into question. The actress, comedian, and singer Lina Loos was married to Adolf Loos from 1902 to 1905. Beginning in 1904, she published feuilletons and essays in Vienna's daily newspapers. Lina Loos's contribution to Adolf Loos's development is multi-pronged. She supplied the funding for their shared apartment and thereby made it possible to implement the iconic work referred to as *My Wife's Bedroom*. At the same time, the fact that she was long classified as his muse obscured her creative accomplishments as client and protagonist of Viennese modernism. For instance, the reappearance of the materiality of her bedroom in Loos's work after their divorce alludes to her active role as client. In an essay entitled "Vandals" (1904), Lina Loos addressed her husband and recounted "crimes" in the treatment of cultural artefacts. Her "participation" in his essay "Ornament and Crime" – a text which was several years in the making – is a topic of feminist research.

"We will be adamant that women who bring furniture and an apartment into a marriage should have their ownership documented so that in case of divorce she is not simply shown the door."
(Lina Loos, "We Women," 1948)

Lina Loos's Bedroom | Sieveringer Strasse 107, Vienna XIX, 1906 | In: Adolf Opel, Lina Loos. | *Wie man wird, was man ist – Lebensgeschichten* | Vienna, 1994

Vandalen.
(Der Brief einer Dame.)

Frau Karoline Loos, die Gattin des bekannten Wiener Architekten und Schriftstellers Herrn Adolf Loos, hat nach einem Besuche in Eger an ihren Gatten aus Franzensbad einen Brief gerichtet, der es verdient, an die Oeffentlichkeit zu gelangen. Wir verdanken es der Liebenswürdigkeit des Herrn Adolf Loos, daß wir in der Lage sind, das interessante Schreiben unseren Lesern mitzuteilen. Es lautet:

Lieber Mann!

Heute Abends ist mir eine Zeitung in die Hand gefallen, die über Kulturvandalen schreibt. Ein Baum, den Shakespeare gepflanzt hatte, wurde gefällt. Ob in England oder bei uns alte historische Sachen ruiniert werden, es ist immer schrecklich. Aber die Engländer schreien doch wenigstens, so daß auch unsere Zeitungen darüber berichten. Doch um unsere Sachen kümmern sie sich nicht einmal. Sonst wäre es nicht möglich, daß ich im Laufe eines Nachmittags so viel Ruiniertes zu sehen bekommen hätte. Wenn es auch schade ist, einen Baum zu fällen, den ein großer Mensch gepflanzt hat, so ist er doch nur eine Erinnerung, eine Sache der Pietät; aber wert?! ... Wie viel wird bei uns zerstört, das Zeugnis geben könnte für eine einstige Kultur. Haben wir auch heute keine mehr — sollten wir doch die alten schönen Dinge in Ruhe lassen. Denn schön waren sie alle, wie doch alle Dinge schön sind, die einer festen, sicheren Kultur entsprießen. Aber nein! Wir müssen sie „verschönern", weil sie unseren gemeinen, ordinären Augen nicht mehr schön erscheinen, müssen den Stempel unserer unsicheren Parvenuezeit daraufdrücken.

Ich glaube, ich habe Dir noch gar nicht geschrieben, daß ich in Eger war. Also: ich war einen Nachmittag dort.

Warum ich diesen Brief überhaupt schreibe? Weil ich eine Wut hab' über die Menschen, die so blind sind, weil Du mich verstehst und weil ich hier niemanden habe, zu dem ich mich ausschimpfen könnte.

Weißt du, es gibt eine Kirche hier — die ist herrlich. Sie ist aus dem 12. Jahrhundert, riesig hoch — ich glaube 24 Meter. Acht dicke Säulen. Große, weite Bogen verbinden sie. Von Stil und so verstehe ich nichts, aber es ist eine Kirche, worin jeder Schritt hallt und wo einem ganz bang wird, wie es eben in einer richtigen Kirche sein muß.

Wenn du aber die Augen aufschlägst..., man sollte es nicht für möglich halten! Die Säulen — gemalte Ziegel, die Wände — gemalte Ziegel. Die Decke zeigt ein „modernes" stilisiertes Blumenmuster, unterbrochen durch Heiligenbilder. Soll man es glauben, daß es Menschen gibt, die Steinquadern wie Ziegel anmalen? Grellrote Ziegel, mit schönen weißen Streifen (Fugen) herum! Und um die ganze Kirchenwand ein drapierter Vorhang — gemalt natürlich.

Begreiflich wird das alles erst, wenn du beim Ausgange eine Gedenktafel findest: Renoviert 1891! und die Namen der beiden Architekten, denen es vorbehalten war, dieses Werk zu vollbringen ... Ganz ist ihnen ihr Werk nicht gelungen. Denn man kann, Gott sei Dank, den Stein durch den Anstrich durchfühlen. Bei einem neuen Baue hätten sie sicher Ziegel verwendet und dann wie Marmor gestrichen. Etwas muß doch geschehen! Nur nicht stehen bleiben!

Du kannst mir glauben, daß ich mit nichts weniger als andächtigen Gefühlen weggegangen bin. Ich glaube, wäre ich allein gewesen, ich hätte ..., ja, mitten in der Kirche!

* *

So gibt es hier noch altes gutes Zinngeschirr. Egerer Zinn. In einem kleinen, schmutzigen Geschäfte, unter guten und noch mehr schlechten alten Sachen, finde ich auch ein paar prächtige alte Zinnstücke. Hocherfreut über meinen Fund, kann ich mich nicht sattsehen an den schönen Formen. Ich bin ja furchtbar ungebildet und für die Egerer Bauern hatte ich gar kein Verständnis. Aber wenn ich mir so die Sachen ansehe, dann sehe ich auch plötzlich die Bauern. Wie kraftvoll die Formen sind! Und dann merkt man so die Freude der Leute an dem schönen Zinn. Ich kann mich vielleicht nicht gut ausdrücken, aber so sicher steht alles aus. Wie ich so herumstöbere, komme ich auch in einen Winkel, wo ein halbwüchsiges Bürschchen sitzt. Stöße von glatten, alten Zinntellern stehen dort. Sehnsuchten der Egerer Bauernfrauen — teilweise auch meine. Weißt du, was der macht? Er nimmt einen glatten Teller um den anderen und — graviert ihn. Schöne Bilder, Kränze, Heckenrosen — entsetzlich. Ich fahre natürlich gleich los, um zu retten, was noch zu retten ist: Was machen Sie da, sind Sie denn verrückt geworden?!! Doch der Meister, gekränkt, erklärt mir, daß alle diese Sachen graviert werden müssen. Die Karlsbader und Marienbader Kurgäste wollen sie schöner haben, sie sind zu einfach. So kann man sie doch nicht in den Salon stellen. Ja, haben denn diese Leute gar keine Empfindung mehr für den herrlichen verhaltenen Glanz einer ungetrübten Zinnfläche, die doch jeder Bauer noch besitzt! Manchesmal kommen ja Engländer, die wollen sie wieder glatt haben. Aber auf die kann man doch nicht warten.

Mir ist es heiß und kalt geworden und bin schnell hinausgegangen. Vielleicht wäre ich auch grob geworden. Aber dieses Bürschchen, das wahrscheinlich dazu von einer vom Staate geleiteten Fachschule ausgebildet wurde, sitzt noch dort, nimmt einen Teller, einen Krug um den anderen und alles, alles wird hin. Für ihn ist ja das nur Kleinigkeit. Der macht im Tage ein paar Dutzend Teller für seine Zeit mundgerecht. Aber wie lange die zu einem Teller gebraucht haben — einem glatten — Ja, wir sind Kerle!

* *

So kam ich also in Wallensteins Todeshaus. Im Sterbezimmer ist nur mehr der schöne alte Plafond vorhanden. Ich glaube, der hat es nur seiner kolossalen, kräftigen Konstitution zu verdanken, daß er noch lebt. Ihn umzubringen hätte zu viel gekostet. Die Wände — das ist schon billiger — sind schön blau gestrichen und patroniert. Das Sterbezimmer wird gleich als Museum ausgenützt. Alles ist ha zusammengetragen. Das ganze Haus wurde zum Stadthause adaptiert, wo Tauf- und Totenscheine ausgestellt werden, wo man Arrestanten und Vagabunden ein- und ausführt. Dazu ist es gerade gut genug, und wenn es nötig ist, werden auch ein paar alte Türen und Fenster nicht geschont.

Wäre nur Wallenstein darin ermordet worden — gut! Aber es ist auch ein Muster eines alten Patrizierhauses. Das letzte in der Stadt. Nur wer die großartigen Wandvertäfelungen des Stiegenhauses gesehen hat, kann sich vorstellen, wie sich die gemalten Streifen darüber ausnehmen. Dieses Holzgeländer, diese Stufen, da weiß man, da ist Wallenstein gegangen. Nicht wie im Burgtheater ist es, wo Wallenstein, wahrscheinlich seiner geschichtlichen Größe wegen, eine breite Treppe, einen Riesenvorhang und ein Zimmer, zehnmal so groß wie das wirkliche, zugewiesen bekommt. Und doch ist das kleine, niedere Zimmer so mächtig, so —. Man spürt: da haben große Menschen gelebt, hier konnten sich große Ereignisse abspielen.

* *

Ob das alles nicht weniger Verbrechen sind, als einen Baum fällen, den ein großer Dichter gepflanzt? Mein Gott! Auch ein von einem Dichter gepflanzter Baum ist eben nur ein Baum — nicht? Aber ein Zinnkrug ist etwas, was nicht wieder kommt. Wer es nicht versteht, dem kann ich es eben nicht sagen. Aber — wie sollte er denn wieder kommen, wenn wir ihn nicht einmal aufbewahren können.

Deine Frau
Karoline Loos.

VORTRAG
VERANSTALTET VOM AKAD. ARCHITEKTEN VEREIN.

ADOLF LOOS:
ORNAMENT UND VERBRECHEN.

FREITAG, DEN 21. FEBRUAR 1913, ½ 8ʰ ABENDS IM FESTSAAL DES ÖSTERR. ING. U. ARCH. VEREINES, I. ESCHENBACHGASSE 9. KARTEN ZU 5, 4, 3, 2, 1 K BEI KEHLENDORFER

**12. MÄRZ:
MISS LEVETUS: ALTENGL. KATHEDRALEN.
MITTE MÄRZ:
DR. HABERFELD: ÜBER ADOLF LOOS.**

DRUCK A. BERGER WIEN VIII/2

Literature

The Great Transformation: from 1867 to the Present Day
pp. 172–177

Rainer Bauböck, "'Nach Rasse und Sprache verschieden': Migrationspolitik in Österreich von der Monarchie bis heute" (IHS Political Science Series, Working Paper, 31), in: *IRIHS, Institutional Repository at IHS* Vienna, https://irihs.ihs.ac.at/id/eprint/899/1/pw_31.pdf (accessed May 26, 2022).

The Growth of Cities
pp. 178–187

Gottfried Pirhofer, Kurt Stimmer, *Pläne für Wien. Theorie und Praxis der Wiener Stadtplanung von 1945 bis 2005* (Vienna 2007), https://www.wien.gv.at/stadtentwicklung/studien/pdf/b008280a.pdf (accessed May 26, 2022).

Ingrid Holzschuh, Monika Platzer, Architekturzentrum Wien (eds.), *"Vienna. The Pearl of the Reich" – Planning for Hitler*, exh. cat. Architekturzentrum Wien, 3/19–8/17/2015 (Zurich 2015).

Roland Rainer, *Planungskonzept Wien* (Vienna 1962).

Eve Blau, *The Architecture of Red Vienna 1919–1934* (Cambridge, MA 1999).

Renate Schweitzer, "Der Generalregulierungsplan für Wien (1893–1920)," in: Österreichische Gesellschaft für Raumforschung und Raumplanung (ed.), *Berichte zur Raumforschung und Raumplanung*, vol. 14, 1970, 24–41.

Renate Banik-Schweitzer, "Urban Visions, Plans, and Projects 1890–1937," in: Eve Blau, Monika Platzer (eds.), *Shaping the Great City: Modern Architecture in Central Europe 1890–1937* (Munich/London 1999), 58–72.

The Construction of the Ringstrasse
pp. 188–191

Harald R. Stühlinger, Gerhard Murauer, *Vom Werden der Wiener Ringstraße* (Vienna 2015).

Capitalist City
pp. 192–195

John W. Boyer, *Political radicalism in late imperial Vienna: Origins of the Christian Social movement, 1848–1897* (Chicago 1995).

Karoline Mayer, Katharina Ritter, Angelika Fitz, Architekturzentrum Wien (eds.), *Boden für Alle*, exh. cat. Architekturzentrum Wien, 11/19/2020–5/3/2021 (Zurich 2020).

Anti-capitalist City
pp. 196–201

Hugo Breitner, "Die Finanzpolitik der Gemeinde Wien," excerpt of a campaign speech (Vienna n.d.).

Hugo Breitner, "Kapitalistische oder Sozialistische Steuerpolitik: Wer soll die Steuern zahlen? Die Armen oder die Reichen?" speech (Vienna 1926).

Sargfabrik, Verein für integrative Lebensgestaltung, https://sargfabrik.at/ (accessed May 26, 2022).

habiTAT, Verein zur Förderung selbstverwalteter und solidarischer Wohn- und Lebensformen, https://habitat.servus.at/ (accessed May 26, 2022).

Baugruppe Bikes and Rails, Verein zur Förderung gemeinschaftlichen Wohnens und nachhaltiger Mobilität, https://www.bikesandrails.org/wp/ (accessed May 26, 2022).

The Other
pp. 202–219

Gabriele Kohlbauer-Fritz (ed.), *Die Ringstraße. Ein jüdischer Boulevard*, exh. cat. Jüdisches Museum Wien, 3/25–10/4/2015 (Vienna 2015).

Gertrude Enderle-Burcel, Ilse Reiter-Zatloukal (eds.), *Antisemitismus in Österreich 1933–1938* (Vienna/Cologne/Weimar 2018).

Andreas Nierhaus, Alfred Pfoser (eds.), *Otto Wagner, Meine angebetete Louise! Das Tagebuch des Architekten 1915–1918* (Salzburg/Vienna 2019).

Werner Michael Schwarz, "Die Kunst der Bewegung. Otto Wagners Theorie und Politik der Großstadt," in: Andreas Nierhaus, Eva-Maria Orosz (eds.), *Otto Wagner 1841–1918*, exh. cat. Wien Museum, 3/15–10/7/2018 (Salzburg/Vienna 2018), 60–67.

Anthony Grenville, *Stimmen der Flucht. Österreichische Emigration nach Großbritannien ab 1938* (Vienna 2011).

Iris Meder, "Von Wien nach Shanghai. Der Architekt Leopold Ponzen," in: *David. Jüdische Kulturzeitschrift* 78, Sept. 2008, http://david.juden.at/2008/78/14_meder.htm (accessed May 26, 2022).

Inge Scheidl, "Karl Dirnhuber," in: *Az W, Architektenlexikon 1770–1945*, http://www.architektenlexikon.at/de/92.htm (accessed May 26, 2022).

Karl Dirnhuber (Wiener Architekten): Zivilarchitekt Dr.Ing. Karl Dirnhuber, zehn Jahre freischaffender Architekt 1921–1931. With a foreword by M. Eisler (Vienna/Leipzig 1932).

SPLITTERWERK, *The Label for Fine Arts and Engineering*, http://splitterwerk.at/database/main.php?mode=album&album=2006__1000_Masterpieces&dispsize=512&start=0 (accessed May 26, 2022).

Österreichische Nationalbibliothek, Ariadne, *Frauen in Bewegung 1848–1938, Erster Wiener Frauenklub*, https://fraueninbewegung.onb.ac.at/node/434 (accessed May 26, 2022).

Sara Ayres, "Staging the Female Look: A Viennese Context of Display for Klimt's *Danaë*," in: *Oxford Art Journal* 37, no. 3, Dec. 2014, 227–244.

Ana-Maria Simionovici, "The good wife: Lina Loos, Adolf Loos and the Making of an Idea" (dissertation, TU Wien 2015), https://publik.tuwien.ac.at/files/PubDat_243383.pdf (accessed May 26, 2022).

Dörte Kuhlmann, "Adolf Loos: Architekt und Urbanist (oder Adolf Loos und sein Schlafzimmer)," lecture, Andrassy Universität Budapest, 12/9/2015, unpublished manuscript.

Lisa Fischer, "Mit Frauen bauen. Das nützliche Beziehungsmuster eines antimodernen Ehemanns," in: Markus Kristan, Sylvia Mattl-Wurm, Gerhard Murauer (eds.), *Adolf Loos. Schriften, Briefe, Dokumente aus der Wienbibliothek im Rathaus* (Vienna 2018), 233–244.

Lisa Fischer, *Lina Loos oder Wenn die Muse sich selbst küßt* (Vienna/Cologne/Weimar 2007).

Adolf Opel, Herbert Schimek (eds.), *Lina Loos. Das Buch ohne Titel – erlebte Geschichten* (Vienna 2013).

Beatriz Colomina (ed.), *Das Andere: A Magazine for the Introduction of Occidental Culture to Austria – Written by Adolf Loos* (Zurich 2016).

Steinhaus	226
Plattner Residence	227
"Schwarzer Laubfrosch" [black greenback]	228
Raum Zita Kern	229
Berger Residence	230
Space House	231
Arrowhead House	232
Frauen-Werk-Stadt	233
Olof-Palme-Hof, Per-Albin-Hansson estate east	234
Kabelwerk housing estate	235
Lichtental rehabilitation proposal	236

Redevelopment of the Westbahn grounds	237
Stadt Ragnitz	238
"Wohnen Morgen" [housing for tomorrow]	239
Quartier Lichtental	240
"Am Hofgartel" garden settlement	241
Quadrangle Housing	242
M. Residence	243
SEG Apartment Tower	244
Wittmann Residence	245
Frontini Residence	246
"Softbag" Duplex	247
Heyrovsky Residence	248
BIG II	249
"Goldtruhe" stepped terrace housing settlement	250
"The Town Musicians of Bremen" housing estate	251
Terraced housing	252
Student dormitory	253
Gartenstadt Puchenau [garden city]	254
Karl-Marx-Hof	256
Pilotengasse housing estate	258

During the twentieth century, there was fierce debate about how new dwellings should be shaped. Housing is the site of everyday life. Who or what influences the ideals associated with "proper" contemporary living? Should we choose a single-family house, a row-house, a unit in a multi-family dwelling, or even in a high-rise? Where is the quality of life higher and where is it more ecologically sustainable? In the city, in the countryside, on the periphery? Ownership, rental, or communal solidarity? On account of its high rate of land consumption, the freestanding single-family house – Austria's most popular form of housing – is on its last legs.

    Models spanning a period of more than 100 years show how the places where we live become social rehearsal stages and fields of formal experimentation and continually create new links between the public and private realms.

Habitat How do we want to live?

Günther Domenig

Steinhaus

Paying homage to his grandmother, Günther Domenig designed this house for his own use: he viewed it as architecture that has metamorphosed into landscape. The building does not conform to traditionalist cliches, but instead enters into a dialogue with the terrain. It took more than two decades to complete this inhabitable sculpture. In addition to creating a place to live and hosting exhibitions and events, Domenig was interested in a manifestation of the art of building – celebrating the process of tweaking structural and functional parameters.

Günther Domenig | Steinhaus | Uferweg 31, 9552 Steindorf am Ossiacher See, Carinthia, 1982–2008 | Model | Corrugated cardboard, carton, metal, plastic

Helmut Richter, Heidulf Gerngross

Plattner Residence

An experimental single-family house à la Helmut Richter/Heidulf Gerngross is bound to yield "custom-tailored high-tech." The client and the architects formed an alliance – the former wanted a house "outside the norm" and the latter critiqued the status quo's attitude toward "building in the countryside." Prefabricated aluminum arches are joined to form a vault – the house's belly – and small structures latch on to it. The interior is akin to a spatial continuum, and, like the exterior, defies conventional expectations.

Helmut Richter, Heidulf Gerngross | Plattner Residence | Heiderosengasse 15, 2601 Sollenau, Lower Austria, 1978–1982 | Model | Plastic, metal

SPLITTERWERK

"Schwarzer Laubfrosch" [black greenback]

How does architecture respond to the fact that our buildings are riddled with digital media and the world no longer comes in through the windows, but through cables? Since the 1990s, the Graz-based architecture firm SPLITTERWERK has experimented with multi-incidence envelopes. Comparable to the windows that we open on our computer screens, here functions can be joined in a single space. In this conversion of a former fire station, this principle was put into practice for ten apartments. Each unit has a central space with its own specific colors and ornamental atmosphere. By utilizing foldable walls, the residents can transform it into a kitchen, bathroom, work space, living room, bedroom, or combinations thereof. A surface akin to a Venetian blind serves as exterior skin. With the aid of a vine trellis, the black gradually metamorphoses into a greenback.

SPLITTERWERK (Edith Hemmrich, Mark Blaschitz, Josef Roschitz) | "Schwarzer Laubfrosch" [black greenback] | 8271 Bad Waltersdorf No. 36, Styria, 1998–2004 | Model | Cardboard, paper, plastic

ARTEC Architekten

An addition for Zita Kern

A farmhouse in Marchfeld which arrived at its current state over several generations: the present owner is a farmer and literary scholar and wanted a study. ARTEC Architekten was obviously not interested in pursuing a similar formal vocabulary. The addition in lightweight wood construction with aluminum skin appears, at least at first glance, to perch like an alien on the old brick stable. At second glance the observer notices how the shiny surfaces reflect the sky's varying moods: then the addition seems every bit as natural as the existing building.

ARTEC Architekten (Bettina Götz, Richard Manahl) | An addition for Zita Kern | Poysdorf 1, 2281 Raasdorf, Lower Austria, 1997–1998 | Model | Cardboard, wood, metal, plastic

Habitat How do we want to live?

Josef Lackner

Berger Residence

This architecture does not adhere to the standard site-specific cliché of the Tyrolean chalet. A mimetic adaptation to local conditions was foreign to Lackner's position on contemporary architecture. Like the lining of an item of clothing, his buildings are adapted to the personal needs of his clients. With his design of Haus Berger, which included two shed roofs facing opposite directions, Josef Lackner responded to the family's desire for an open floor plan, an unimpeded view, and optimal privacy.

Josef Lackner | Berger Residence | Hinterinnweg 15, 6071 Aldrans, Tyrol, 1972–1973 | Model | Cardboard

Habitat — How do we want to live?

Friedrich Kiesler
Space House

The notion of an architectural structure that hovers above the ground is one of the central motifs in Friedrich Kiesler's work. After immigrating to New York in 1926, he dedicated himself to his ideas across all art genres. In 1933, the temporary 1:1 model of the Space House, a key work in Kiesler's lifelong theoretical and practical study of space, was installed inside the showroom of a New York furniture company. The self-supporting lens-shaped shell structure can be traced back to the concept of the so-called Space Stage (1924), with which the interdisciplinary and visionary artist had already left his mark on Vienna's theater architecture. The Space House – as a design for an affordable single-family dwelling – was never realized, but already during Kiesler's lifetime it – like most of his space models – pointed the way for many artists and architects.

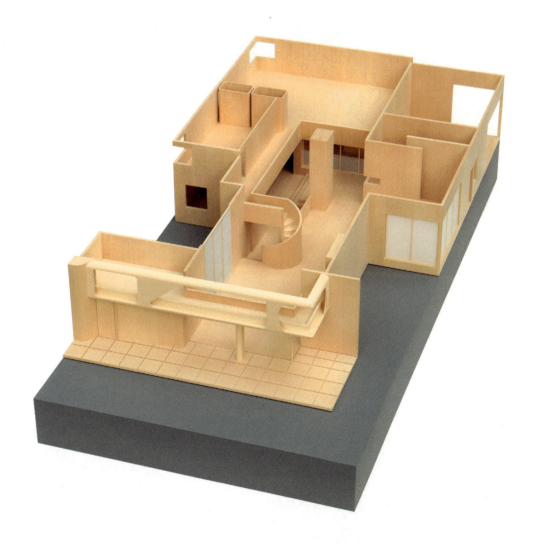

Friedrich Kiesler | Space House | New York, USA, 1933 | Cutaway model | Wood | Reconstruction: Adolph Stiller, Karl Schwarz, 1994

Raimund Abraham
Arrowhead House

In the early 1960s Raimund Abraham took his first tentative steps toward avant-garde architecture with the Pless Residence in Vienna, the house for the Salzburg-born photographer Josef Dapra, and the Dellacher Residence in Burgenland. After moving to the USA in 1964, he made a name for himself as a teacher and visionary. He went on to produce countless sketches and collages for utopian spaces, houses, and city models. Abraham saw the housing theme as an archetypal phenomenon. His house designs are characterized by his uncompromising attention to the interplay between geometry, arithmetic, and proportion. Among his final designs before his death in a 2010 car accident was the Arrowhead House, whose name is derived from its characteristic triangular form.

Raimund Abraham | Arrowhead House (for Todd and Jen Waltemath) | USA, 2008 | Model | Wood

Franziska Ullmann, Gisela Podreka, Elsa Prochazka, Liselotte Peretti

Frauen-Werk-Stadt

With 357 apartment units, the housing facility realized in the course of the Vienna expansion plan is to date the largest construction project in Europe planned exclusively by and for women. Since the outdoor spaces were an important assessment criterion for the competition, the architects were compelled to collaborate with a landscape architect (Maria Auböck). At the initiative of the Frauenbüro (Vienna Municipal Department 57, office of women's issues), key components of the design were to simplify household chores, promote contact with one's neighbors, and create a living environment in which residents could move about safely, even in the evening. At the same time, this model project sought to raise awareness about women architects and planners and increase their participation in the field of urban development, as the invited urban design competitions had until then been a strictly male domain.

Franziska Ullmann, Gisela Podreka, Elsa Prochazka, Liselotte Peretti | Frauen-Werk-Stadt | Donaufelder Strasse 95–97, Vienna XXI, 1994–1997 | Model | Wood

Carl Auböck, Wilhelm Kleyhons

Olof-Palme-Hof, Per-Albin-Hansson estate east

Located on the southern slope of the Laaerberg, the Olof-Palme-Hof (409 apartments) completes one of Vienna's largest settlement areas. It constitutes the final segment of the Per-Albin-Hansson estate, which was built in four stages: in 1951, the first phase, on the western part of the site, was the first major housing estate to be completed after the Second World War. While the first part was laid out as a garden city, the subsequent phases in the north and east took the form of nine to twelve story stepped-section buildings whose mantra was "urbanity through density." In combination with the cantilevering triangular loggias facing the green courtyards, the rhythmicized building massing, which brings to mind halved beehives, sought to produce intriguing contrasts and prevent monotony. The attempt to foster social relations solely by creating a mix of buildings and increasing density was ill-advised and in the 1980s led to a trend reversal.

Carl Auböck, Wilhelm Kleyhons | Olof-Palme-Hof, Per-Albin-Hansson estate east | Ada-Christen-Gasse 2, Vienna X, 1972–1976 | Site model, center on Favoritenstrasse | Wood, paint, cardboard, colored

Mascha & Seethaler, Schwalm-Theiss & Gressenbauer, Hermann & Valentiny, pool Architektur, Martin Wurnig, Branimir Kljajic, Werkstatt Wien, rainer pirker architeXture, the POOR BOYs ENTERPRISE

Kabelwerk housing estate

For nearly one hundred years, the Kabel- und Drahtwerke AG [cable and wire factory] was one of the most important businesses in Vienna's twelfth district. After its 1997 closure, the grounds were purchased by a consortium made up of eight property developers. rainer pirker architeXture and the POOR BOYS ENTERPRISE won the urban design competition held the following year. The site then served briefly as a cultural venue. In 2001, construction of the more than 950 apartments – providing homes to about 3,500 people – began. Thirty percent of the site's area is now used commercially and culturally. In 2004, this project received the Otto Wagner Prize for Urban Planning in recognition of the intensive planning and participatory processes. The award acknowledges the significance of outdoor spaces: a move away from architecture as an object occupying space toward space-shaping architecture.

Mascha & Seethaler, Schwalm-Theiss & Gressenbauer, Hermann & Valentiny, pool Architektur, Martin Wurnig, Branimir Kljajic, Werkstatt Wien, rainer pirker architeXture, the POOR BOYs ENTERPRISE | Kabelwerk housing estate | Oswaldgasse 33, Vienna XII, 1998–2005 | Site model | Wood, plastic, papier

arbeitsgruppe 4

Lichtental rehabilitation proposal

In 1958, at the initiative of Roland Rainer, Vienna's newly appointed commissioner of urban planning, arbeitsgruppe 4 was entrusted with the task of preparing a redevelopment concept for the Lichtental neighborhood (part of Vienna's ninth district). The section of the city bounded by three streets (Liechtenstein-, Alserbach-, and Althanstrasse) and a train station (the Franz Josefs Bahnhof) was to be restructured and its center shifted to the area around the Lichtental Church. The proposal adhered to principles embraced by the CIAM, the International Congresses of Modern Architecture, which had galvanized the architectural discussion after 1945. For the yet unfinished "Charte de l'Habitat," arbeitsgruppe 4 – part of the Austrian section of the CIAM along with the ABC group, Herbert Prader, Franz Fehringer, and Wilhelm Schütte – proposed a city divided into neighborhood groups with integrative community facilties. Among the planned public buildings were schools, kindergartens, an adult education center, post office, and large indoor market. A subsequent construction phase envisioned eight-story apartment buildings and intense urban greening of the entire zone. All in all, a completely new vision of the city embedded in a densely built-up area in the middle of urban Vienna.

arbeitsgruppe 4 | Lichtental rehabilitation proposal | Vienna IX, 1958–1959 | Urban design model | Wood

Atelier P + F

Redevelopment of the Westbahn grounds

Over the past few decades there have been countless plans to redevelop the "outback" behind the Westbahn Station separating the two fifteenth-district boroughs known as Rudolfsheim and Fünfhaus. Among them were practical proposals calling for such things as apartment buildings, schools, sports facilities, and green zones, but there was also a motion for a lake with its own lighthouse. So far nothing has managed to pass approval. Meanwhile, there is a growing awareness of the importance of the role of the grounds in maintaining a livable urban climate, as it, for now, forms part of the strip of open space in the west of Vienna.

The architects Prader and Fehringer, who created quite a stir in the 1960s and 1970s with their large-scale, visionary urban-development designs, took an interest in these grounds as early as 1975. The model shows a built-up area with alternating vertical and horizontal lines. What catches the eye are the semicircular tops of the towers. Since all long-distance trains began departing from Vienna Central Station in 2015, the Westbahn Station ceased to serve as an important terminal station in Vienna. What if – nearly fifty years after the initial studies of Prader and Fehringer – we could come up with a useful overall urban development plan that took infrastructural, cultural, architectural, and, above all, climatic criteria into account?

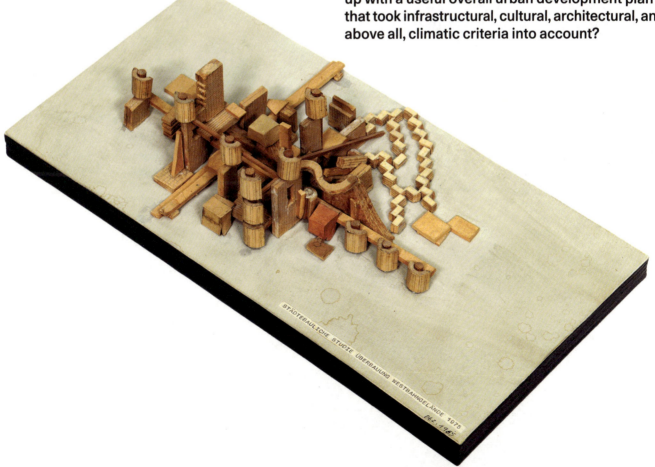

Atelier P + F (Herbert Prader, Franz Fehringer) | Redevelopment of the Westbahn grounds, Vienna, 1975 | Model | Wood, cardboard

Eilfried Huth, Günther Domenig

Stadt Ragnitz

Environmental degradation, population growth, sprawl – back in the 1960s, young architects had already begun to discuss these issues. Some of them responded by developing visionary projects. In 1966, Günther Domenig and Eilfried Huth were commissioned with a development study for a site outside Graz, in Ragnitztal. The design foresees a stacked housing estate with room units and supply ducts – a city of the future, which, despite its utopian appearance, was painstakingly dimensioned by a structural engineer and is definitely buildable. The project was published extensively internationally and in 1969 was awarded the Grand Prix of Cannes for Urbanism and Architecture.

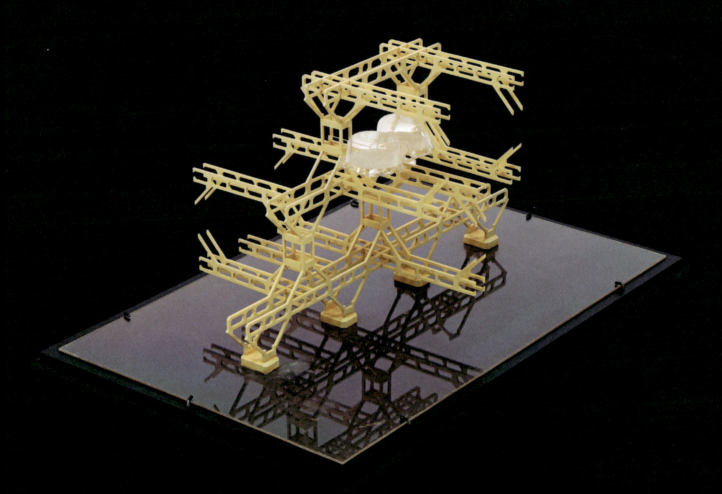

Eilfried Huth, Günther Domenig | Stadt Ragnitz, Graz, Styria, 1965–1969 | Detail model, 2002 | Plastic

Josef Lackner

"Wohnen Morgen" [housing for tomorrow]

Back in the 1970s, Austria had a federal ministry of construction and technology which supported efforts to reconceptualize dwelling by financing research into housing and by hosting architecture competitions on "Wohnen Morgen." For his proposal, Josef Lackner designed a linear megastructure of varying height – with a maximum of 8 stories – atop piloti. The floor plan solution foresaw a central living area with a higher ceiling which would have facilitated communication among the different levels and provided a spectacular view of Salzburg's landscape. The large loggia on the west side was to have been adjoined by two auxiliary spaces (for use as storage space, sauna, or hobby room). The ellipsoid underground parking space was to have been terraced and embedded in the landscape.

Josef Lackner | "Wohnen Morgen" [housing for tomorrow] | 5202 Neumarkt am Wallersee, Salzburg, 1975 | Site model | Wood, cardboard, foam board, colored

Atelier P + F
Quartier Lichtental

From 1928 to 1959, at the CIAM conferences (Congrès Internationaux d'Architecture Moderne) architects debated pioneering contemporary forms of building. In 1955, at the preparatory meeting prior to the conference in La Sarraz, the young Austrian architects Herbert Prader and Franz Fehringer were given the opportunity to present their project entitled "Lichtental residential district for 10,000 residents." An important component was the separation of circulation levels and living levels. The housing slab brings to mind Le Corbusier's famed Unité d'Habitation in Marseille. In addition to a pedestrian street, the perforated facades would also have accommodated play areas and quiet zones, as well as green spaces. With their CIAM design, Prader and Fehringer launched a debate about new urban structure which was taken up and further developed by the 1960s generation of visionary designers.

Atelier P + F (Herbert Prader, Franz Fehringer) | Quartier Lichtental | Vienna IX, 1945–1955 | Presentation model | Wood, paper

Geiswinkler & Geiswinkler

"Am Hofgartel" garden settlement

In this multi-story residential estate, by providing a combination of private and shared outdoor spaces, the architects managed to achieve the town planning qualities of a village green. The rowhouses stacked one upon the other have their own gardens or roof gardens, which are bordered by walls and therefore visually screened. The building massing, which tapers upward, supplies optimal shading and views – despite the relatively high density.

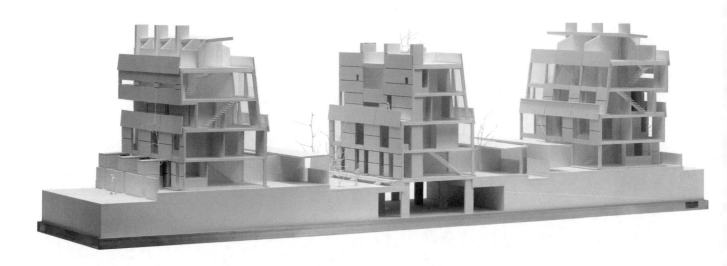

Geiswinkler & Geiswinkler (Kinayeh Geiswinkler-Aziz, Markus Geiswinkler) | "Am Hofgartel" garden settlement | Am Hofgartel 16, Vienna XI, 1998–2003 | Sectional model | Plastic

Carl Pruscha, Team Habitat

Quadrangle Housing

During the 1970s, Carl Pruscha documented the Kathmandu Valley in Nepal for UNESCO. His enthusiasm for anonymous architecture and his interest in high-density forms of dwelling had an influence on the design of Quadrangle Housing. With it he took his radical courtyard houses a step further than he had 20 years earlier in his design of the Traviatagasse residential estate. The Quadrangle concept proposes a reinforced-concrete L-shaped wall for each house; the rest of the work would, however, have been carried out in lightweight wood construction, in combination with extensive glazing. The low land-consumption rate, the prefabrication of the building components, as well as the technology were intended to hold unit prices to levels which are otherwise only attainable in multistory apartment buildings. A cluster consists of 13 to 27 units, and several such horizontal residential districts would yield entire residential neighborhoods.

Carl Pruscha, Team Habitat (Franz J. Loranzi, Julia Nuler, Andreas Pfusterer) | Quadrangle Housing | 2010 | Model | Cardboard, paper

Hermann Czech

M. Residence

This single-family home is at first glance unspectacular, but upon closer inspection, the unusual hybrid consisting of a gable roof and flat roof catches one's eye. The building seems as if two structures from different eras had met up in this neighborhood and somehow become attached. Inside, in contrast, the architect created a complex sequence of spaces in the tradition of Adolf Loos's Raumplan. At the house's core, four columns mark a square; from the stair and from spaces of varying heights positioned at different levels around it, numerous vistas through the building can be experienced.

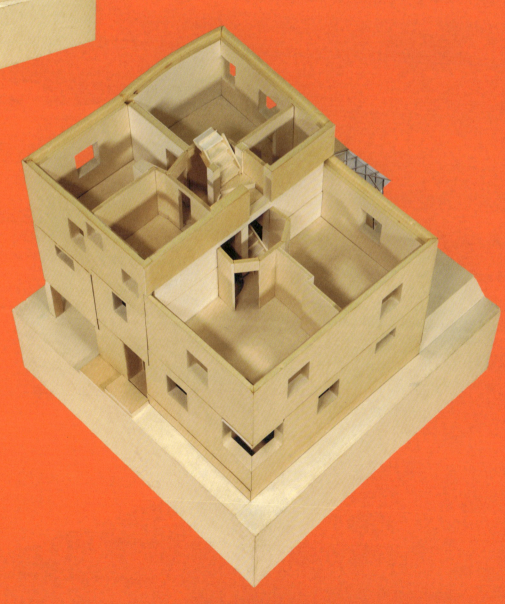

Hermann Czech | M. Residence | Kranichgasse 7, 2320 Schwechat, Lower Austria, 1977–1981 | Model, lower part of building (without attic level) | Wood

Coop Himmelb(l)au, Wolf D. Prix & Partner ZT GmbH

SEG Apartment Tower

One of the first buildings to be erected in the nascent Donau City, this residential tower by Coop Himmelb(l)au is named after its client. The high-rise was indeed one of the first to be built in several decades in all of Vienna, where the construction of tall buildings had halted. Its conception as energy-efficient building was also innovative. Two volumes are stacked one atop the other: where they intersect, a shared space – the sky lobby – is created. A climate facade cloaks and joins the two segments and provides soundproofing. The facade also supplies some of the apartments with glazed loggias, a green space not typically associated with high-rises. In combination with the mechanical equipment on the roof and the building's core, which was planned as thermal storage mass, the facade system cools the apartments in summer and heats them in winter. All of the apartments are lofts with open floor plans – free of load-bearing partition walls.

Coop Himmelb(l)au, Wolf D. Prix & Partner ZT GmbH | SEG Apartment Tower | Kratochwjlestrasse 12, Vienna XXII, 1994–1998 | Study model | Foam-core, plexiglass, styrofoam, cardboard, wood, metal | Model: Coop Himmelb(l)au

Johannes Spalt

Wittmann Residence

While still a pupil at the Staatsgewerbeschule (a precursor to today's technical high schools), Johannes Spalt studied airplane construction and other applications of lightweight construction. His encyclopedic collection of follies and pavilions situated in various cultural landscapes also indicates a focus of his architecture: combining a lightweight construction technique with a roof suspended above it. His realization of this concept in the residence for Franz and Hermine Wittmann, owners of a factory for upholstered furniture, is a remarkable accomplishment. In this design, a specific attitude about life has been transferred from the folly to the residence. Above the white stucco base is a continuous zone of ribbon windows: the roof, whose edges turn downward, appears to be suspended above the glass. The main living space is lined by a gallery, and not one of the adjoining spaces has walls that extend to the ceiling. Aside from the suspended roof, folding screens and paravents were also a recurring theme in Spalt's architectural vocabulary.

Johannes Spalt | Wittmann Residence | Kellergasse 6, 3492 Etsdorf am Kamp, Lower Austria, 1970–1975 | Model | Wood, metal, plexiglas

Bernard Rudofsky

Frontini Residence

Bernard Rudofsky was not an architect in the conventional sense of the word. He was first and foremost a critic and cultural theorist who not only wrote about architecture and design, but also about clothing, shoes, food, and bathing. In Rudofsky's design of the Frontini Residence, characteristics are manifest that reflect the ideals he pursued regarding dwelling and living. These include: insertion in the landscape, cues from the local building traditions, patios, and privacy for the residents.

Bernard Rudofsky | Frontini Residence | Rua Monte Alegre 957, São Paulo, Brazil, 1939–1941 | Wood, wire, paper | Model builder: Andrea Bocco

rainer pirker architeXture
"Softbag" Duplex

Beginning in the 1990s, digital tools facilitated "testing the limits" of the design process and offered favorable conditions for the development of new concepts such as the "Softbag." This design proposal foresees two separate dwelling units on a steep, narrow site; the units were to be separated by a foldable wall. Metal shelving at a distance of four meters to the primary load-bearing structure would provide stiffness to the soft outer membrane. In response to the clients' needs, the interior would expand by swelling outwardly, thereby changing the form of the building envelope. The design of the building would be determined by actions taken by its residents, not vice versa.

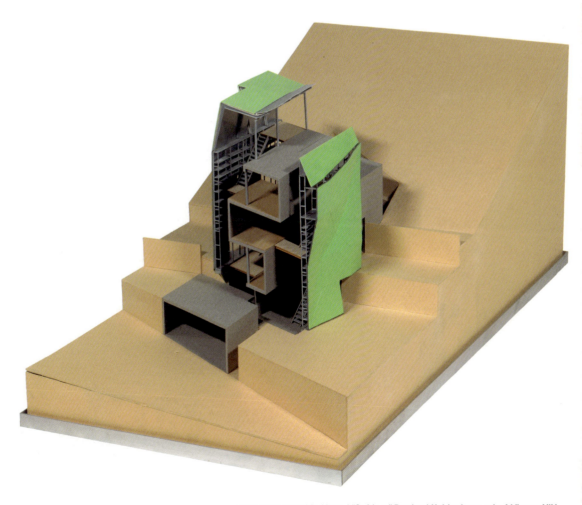

rainer pirker architeXture | "Softbag" Duplex | Kahlenbergerdorf, Vienna XIX, 1994 | Sectional model | Wood, cardboard, plastic

Lois Welzenbacher

Heyrovsky Residence

Lois Welzenbacher was one of Tyrol's early proponents of modern architecture. He was the only Austrian architect to take part in the canonizing International Style exhibition (1932) at the Museum of Modern Art in New York. His non-dogmatic stance and breadth of scope allowed him to incorporate local contexts in the modern formal vocabulary, as demonstrated in his design of the Heyrovsky Residence. His decision to implement a radial floor plan for a site on a hillside allowed him to emphasize the views of the landscape. The house does not possess a single right angle and is considered an outstanding example of organically inspired building in the Alps.

Lois Welzenbacher | Heyrovsky Residence | Thumersbach, Lohningstein, 5700 Zell am See, Salzburg, 1932 | Model with removable roof, 1987 | Cardboard, wood

Eilfried Huth

BIG II

"The industry forces us as a standard family to live in a standard home with standard furniture." (Eilfried Huth, 1996)

The question as to how we want to live is an issue that has concerned Eilfried Huth, a proponent of the Graz School and pioneer of participatory housing development, for many decades. In the Eschensiedlung, a seminal housing estate in Deutschlandsberg (1973–1975), he was able to realize his theoretical notions of self-determined housing by integrating the future residents into the project. Based on the principle of collective ownership, the Eschensiedlung also became a model for further measures taken toward ownership as part of the political program known as "Modell Steiermark." In contrast to standardized mass housing, the focus here was on the diversity of housing types with participatory involvement on the part of the residents. It proposed alternatives to the usual single-family houses, hoping to counteract the spread of urban sprawl into the landscape. With the project BIG (Beteiligung im Geschosswohnbau/ participation in multi-story housing), Huth wanted to achieve an even more marked reduction of land consumption in multi-story housing and at the same time offer apartments with well-articulated spaces.

Eilfried Huth | BIG II | Deutschlandsberg, Styria, 1978 | Competition model | Modelling clay on metal plate

Habitat

How do we want to live?

Hans Puchhammer, Gunther Wawrik

"Goldtruhe" stepped terrace housing settlement

The "Goldtruhe" stepped terrace housing settlement is among the first vertically densified residential buildings of this kind to be erected. Spread over four levels are a total of 152 apartment units – of which there are six different sizes with the floor area of each unit decreasing with each successive level. All apartments have generous terraces. The cantilevered concrete bands with flower troughs provide visual privacy. The appearance of the prize-winning facility that won the Austrian Bauherrenpreis in 1969 has since been changed: when it was renovated, sections were painted pastel colors. The terrace house is currently experiencing a renaissance among residents and architects alike, because this building type is able to embrace both nature and urban densification.

Hans Puchhammer, Gunther Wawrik | "Goldtruhe" stepped terrace housing settlement | Alfons-Petzold-Gasse, 2345 Brunn am Gebirge, Lower Austria, 1965–1966 | Site model | Wood

ARTEC Architekten

"The Town Musicians of Bremen" housing estate

In Vienna, communal housing and social housing policy have a 100-year-old tradition. Sixty percent of Vienna's residents live in subsidized apartments or communal housing. The commission for this apartment building on Tokiostrasse was awarded based on a limited competition hosted by the wohnfonds wien, a non-profit venture whose aim is to make the highest possible standard of affordable rental housing available to the public. What does the famous story by the Brothers Grimm – "The Town Musicians of Bremen" – have to do with architecture? Inspired by the successful performance of the donkey, dog, cat, and rooster, the architects stack four different housing typologies (atrium house, maisonette apartment, rowhouse, allotment garden house). This process yields a megaform – evidence of an urban stance involving large-scale interventions – which combines density and community with individualization and private outdoor spaces.

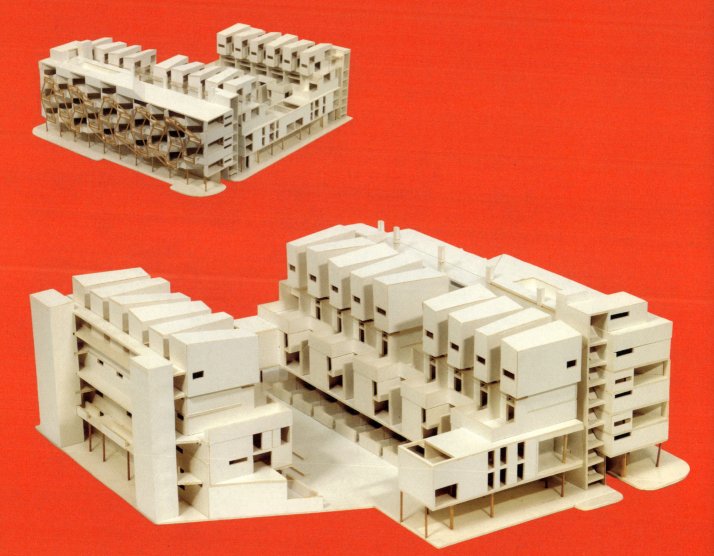

ARTEC Architekten (Bettina Götz, Richard Manahl) | "The town musicians of Bremen" housing estate | Tokiostrasse 6, Vienna XXII, 2006–2010 | Model | Cardboard, wood

Habitat — How do we want to live?

Florian Haydn, Georg Böhm, Mirko Pogoreutz

Terraced housing

In 2005, the City of Vienna initiated Yo.V.A. – Young Viennese Architects, a competition to promote the city's young talent. Architects aged 45 and younger who had realized at least one project in Vienna were eligible to participate. Florian Haydn, Georg Böhm, and Mirko Pogoreutz submitted a design of a terraced structure. This typology has been considered an innovative urban form of living in Vienna since Adolf Loos's early designs (Loos was an advocate of the peripheral *Siedlung*), which date back to 1923. It holds the promise of living close to nature, and consumes a relatively small amount of land – and also gives architects formal opportunities to reinterpret the existing city.

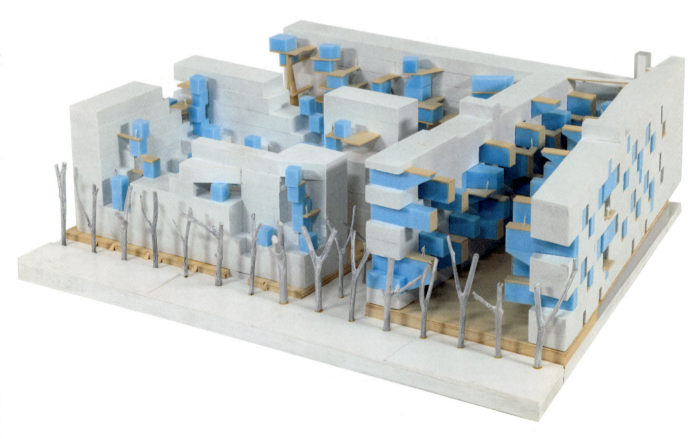

Florian Haydn, Georg Böhm, Mirko Pogoreutz | Terraced housing | Buchengasse, Vienna XI, 2005 | Presentation model | Plastic, foam board, wood

Anton Schweighofer
Student dormitory

Anton Schweighofer's radical version of a student dormitory unceremoniously tosses multiple conventions overboard. The building stands on a corner plot next to a park and is encased in a shell of construction wire mesh, behind which lies a circulation zone of outdoor walkways. Inside the structure, the architect allots the students small units with a floor space of only 2.30 x 2.80 meters (but with high ceilings affording 3 meters of headroom). Each unit has one window that opens to the outside and one facing the shared spaces. Built of acoustic blocks whose outer sides have been left untreated, these units are arranged irregularly throughout the building and are furnished minimally with tables, chairs, cabinets, and bunk beds. The individual rooms are grouped together in small clusters around a shared kitchen, bathroom unit, and spacious open areas – a special form of housing that emphasizes community.

Anton Schweighofer | Student dormitory | Van-der-Null-Gasse 26–28, Vienna X, 1992–1995 | Models | Foam board, styrofoam, paper

Roland Rainer

Gartenstadt Puchenau [garden city]

During the 1960s and 1970s, innovative projects inspired by the Siedler movement were realized throughout Austria in the form of low-slung housing estates. In developments of this sort, determining the smallest possible plot size is crucial, as are efficient circulation systems (consisting of narrow, water-permeable footpaths and underground parking garages), and harnessing solar energy for heating and the provision of hot water. Moreover, such estates offer private outdoor spaces and garden courtyards. As Austria's most important proponent of courtyard housing, Roland Rainer implemented all of these measures near Linz in the Gartenstadt Puchenau. The settlement has a total of nearly 1,000 apartments as well as important infrastructure buildings, such as day-care center, preschool, grade school and middle school, church, doctors' offices, shops, and playgrounds.

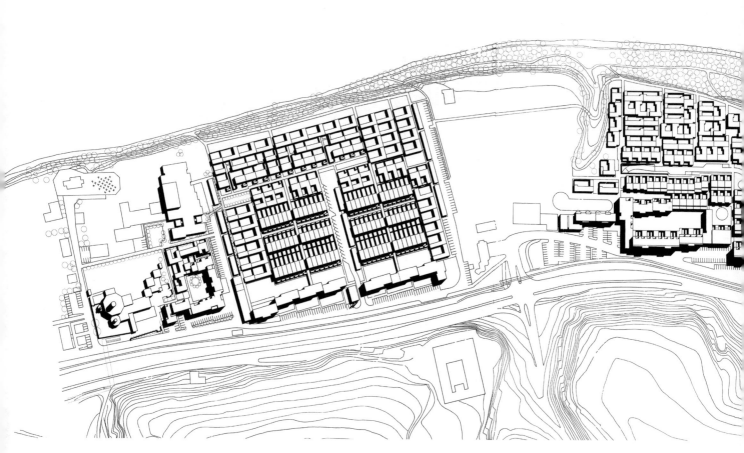

Roland Rainer | Gartenstadt Puchenau [garden city] | Gartenstrasse/Golfplatzgasse, 4048 Puchenau, Upper Austria, 1963–1968 (first phase), 1978–1995 (second phase), 1998–2000 (third phase) | Site plan Puchenau I–III (variant) | Whiteprint on translucent paper

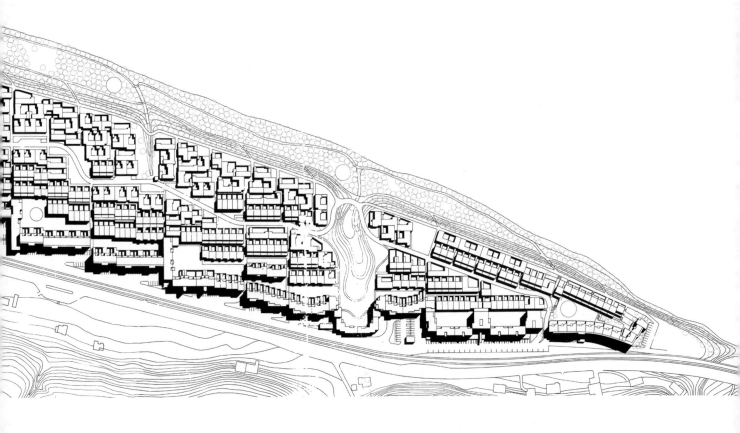

Karl Ehn

Karl-Marx-Hof

In 1923, the Social Democratic Workers' Party initiated an ambitious housing construction program. Its aim was to significantly improve the living conditions of the residents, providing more access to "light, air, and sun." With a length of about 1,050 meters, this apartment building is the world's longest and, at the same time, an icon of Austrian (architectural) history. It exemplifies the so-called superblock, a building type which was favored in Vienna between 1924 and 1934. In addition to the 1,382 apartments for about 5,000 residents, there are generously dimensioned outdoor spaces and numerous shared facilities, including laundry rooms, bathing facilities, pre-schools, a children's health clinic, youth center, library, dental clinic, outpatient clinic, pharmacy, post office, several doctors' offices, cafés, offices for political organizations, and 25 shops.

Karl Ehn | Karl-Marx-Hof | Heiligenstädter Strasse 82–92, Vienna XIX, 1926–1930 | Model | Wood, paper, lichen moss; foam board | Model builder: Christian Kronaus

Adolf Krischanitz, Otto Steidle, Herzog & de Meuron

Pilotengasse housing estate

A trio of firms – Adolf Krischanitz (AT), Otto Steidle (D) and Herzog & de Meuron (CH) – designed a "housing implant" that stands out from the pack. The aim of the distribution of more than 200 rowhouses and the crisscrossing network of footpaths was to underscore the flatness of the site. Outwardly they convey uniformity, inwardly they offer typological variety. The linear segment of the site designed by Adolf Krischanitz consists of a series subdivided in groups of five units. Each of the buildings is rotated 90 degrees to the estate's linear structure, which is partially responsible for the irregular arrangement of the openings in the facade. The color concept is the work of Oskar Putz and Helmut Federle.

Adolf Krischanitz, Otto Steidle, Herzog & de Meuron | Pilotengasse housing estate | Pilotengasse, Vienna XXII, 1987–1992 | Model of Krischanitz's linear segment, including rowhouses and transverse buildings | Plastic

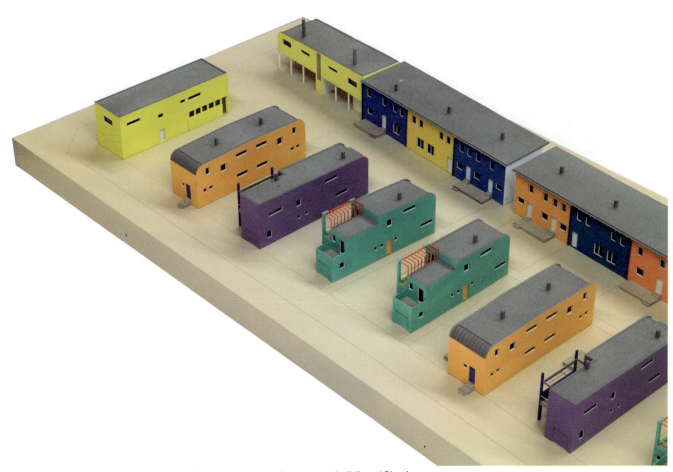

Model of Krischanitz's linear segment, including rowhouses and transverse buildings | Plastic

Comm...

From Cradle to Grave	262
Full Recovery	266
Children's Town	274
Education Initiatives	282
Child Friendly	292

Who p... for

on Good
rovides
us?

From Cradle to Grave

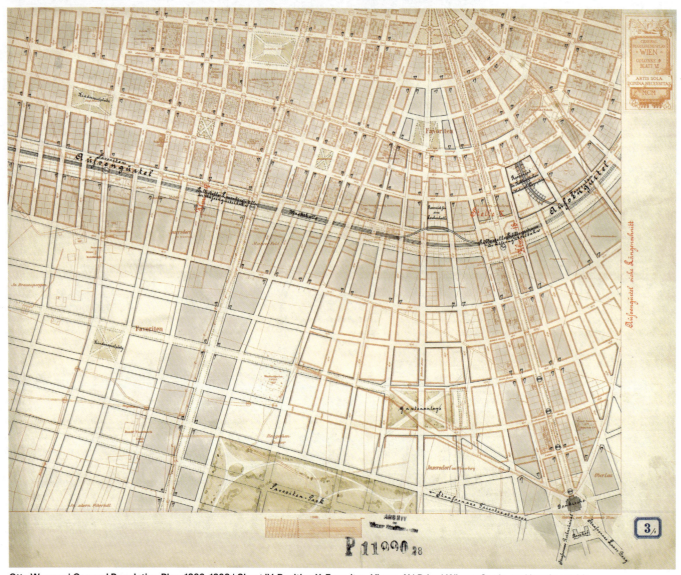

Otto Wagner | General Regulation Plan, 1892–1893 | Sheet IV, Position X, Favoriten, Vienna X | Print | Wiener Stadt- und Landesarchiv

With his proposal to locate morgues at strategic points along Vienna's Stadtbahn (metropolitan railway), Otto Wagner devised a plan to transport corpses hygienically from the urban neighborhoods to the burial sites.

Close on the heels of the nineteenth-century growth of cities and outbreaks of typhus, tuberculosis, and cholera, a series of innovations in urban hygiene were introduced. Otto Wagner's General Regulation Plan envisioned a city amenable to all of life's needs. His proposal for the disposition of human remains was one of the many ideas intended to bring about a healthy city. Following the inauguration of Vienna's first crematorium in 1922, the general public gradually came to accept cremation as the more hygienic and less costly option. Vienna, which was governed by the Social Democrats, had introduced this measure despite the opposition of the Catholic church. Other cities with Social Democratic majorities followed this example (Steyr 1927, Linz 1929, Salzburg 1931, Graz 1932).

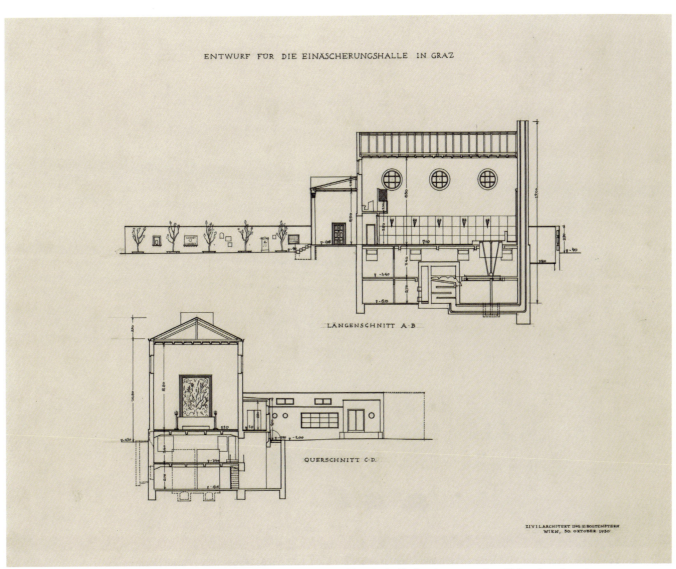

Erich Boltenstern | Crematorium | Alte Poststrasse 345, Graz, Styria, 1930–1932 | Longitudinal and cross sections | Ink on translucent paper

At the same time, the need to erect a public health care system – which had been the realm of private and sectarian initiatives – became apparent. Red Vienna made children the symbol of the "modern-day person" – and the focus of a massive campaign implementing new social and health policies. The design of the preschool by Erich Franz Leischner (1927–1929) reflects not just the significance of the program, but also symbolizes the belief in a reciprocity between architecture and way of living.

Julius Tandler | [Foster Care Facility, City of Vienna] | Brochure, 1925 | Cover

Erich Franz Leischner | Sandleiten Kindergarten | Rosenackerstrasse 5, Vienna XVI, 1927–1929 | Model, 1999 | Plastic, foam board | Model builder: Patrick Klammer

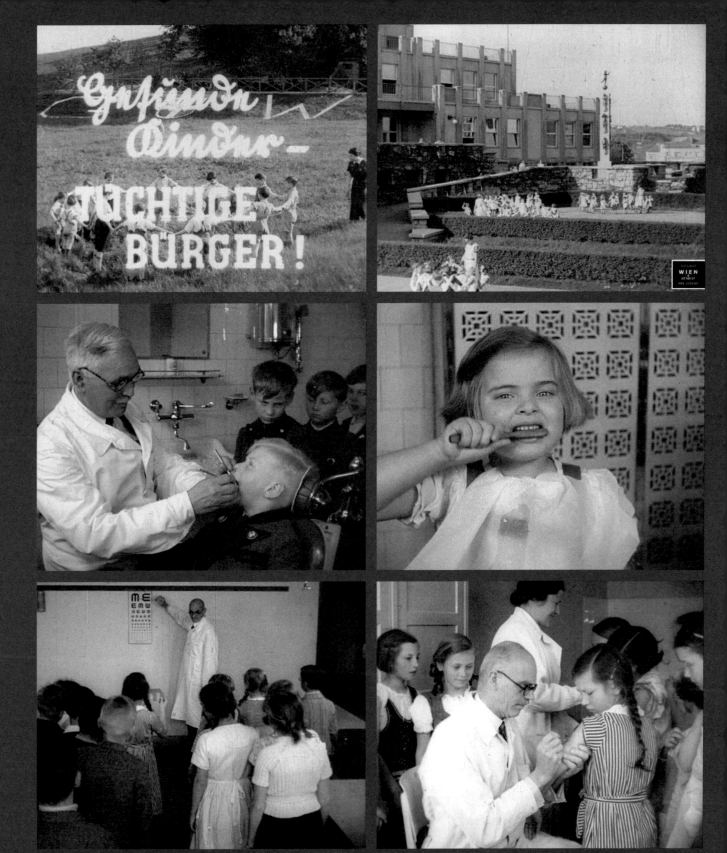

[Healthy Children – Competent Citizens], 1937 | A film about youth welfare of the City of Vienna | Film, 35 mm | Wiener Stadt- und Landesarchiv, Filmarchiv der media wien | Film stills

All of the public health achievements depicted here originated during the Red Vienna era, and as the film clearly shows, unlike the Social Democrats' school policies, these health policies stayed in place during the Austrofascist reign.

Full Recovery

Otto Wagner | Rental apartment house on Döblergasse | Neustiftgasse/Döblergasse 2, Vienna VII, 1909–1911 | Perspective with street sweeper | Lithography with tinted plate | Wien Museum

Architects and urbanists took on dirt and chaos. The garbage dump and the street cleaner represent a quest for "greatest possible cleanliness" and a cityscape in accordance with hygienic and artistic needs of a modern metropolis. Engineering accomplishments such as the water supply at Steinhof, the creation of shared laundry facilities in municipal housing, and public lavatories are evidence of the recognition of the significance of measures in support of public health.

    Advances were also made in the private sphere's standard of hygiene. Wagner's design of his own bathroom – which included a glass bathtub – was a pivotal work in the development of private bathrooms;

its influence was long-lasting, extending, for instance, to Helmut Richter's design of the Sares Residence's bathroom.

After 1945, the belief in the reciprocity between urban form and a healthy way of living was still in circulation. In the film *Operation Wien*, a link was created between medical and urbanistic knowledge. In an effort to avert a breakdown, an "open heart" intervention was performed on Vienna's traffic system.

Perspectival view of the building(s) planned by Wagner for the area where the Wienzeile begins, 1909; a photograph served as a template for the drawing; the photo is placed underneath the drawing to illustrate the point.

Otto Wagner | Drawing | Wien Museum | Photo: private collection | In: Andreas Nierhaus, *Ein Architekt als Medienstratege. Otto Wagner und die Fotografie* (Beiträge zur Geschichte der Fotografie in Österreich, vol. 19), Salzburg, 2020 | Courtesy of Photoinstitut Bonartes, Vienna

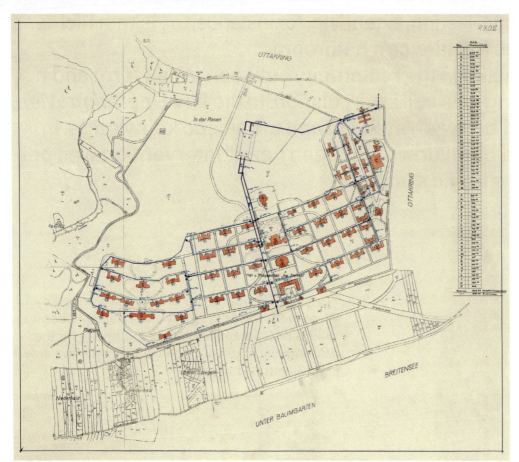

Otto Wagner | Am Steinhof psychiatric hospital (later: sanatorium for lung patients | Baumgartner Höhe 1, Vienna XIV, 1905–1907 | Wiener Stadt- und Landesarchiv

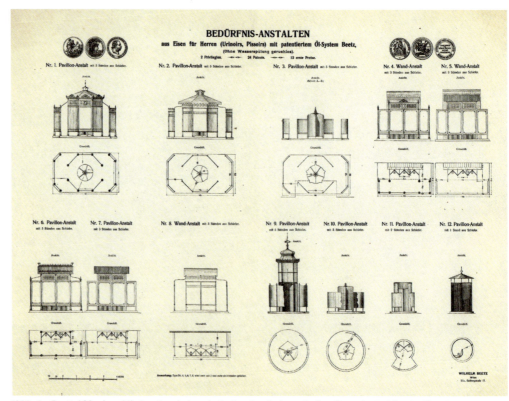

Wilhelm Beetz | Men's public lavatory in iron (urinals, pissoirs) employing the patented Beetz oil system, about 1900 | Matrix for a folder

This trash can belongs to a series of urban implements designed by Luigi Blau. He sought to go beyond a conception of these items as functional objects, but rather to communicate the importance of fostering aesthetics in the public realm. Between 1994 and 2002, 4,700 trash cans were installed in Vienna.

Luigi Blau | Urban furniture for Vienna | Trash can, 1989 | Steel sheet | Courtesy of Luigi Blau

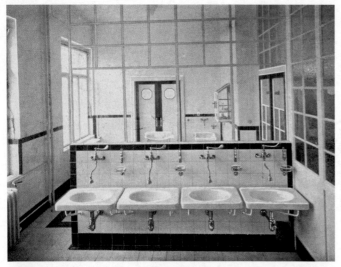

from left to right:

Josef Joachim Mayer I Brigitta Hospital I Stromstrasse 34, Vienna XX, 1924–1926 I Washroom with anesthesia I In: *Das Entbindungsheim der Stadt Wien, "Brigittaspital" im 20. Bez., Stromstrasse*, Vienna, 1926

Otto Wagner I Am Steinhof psychiatric hospital (later: sanatorium for lung patients) I Baumgartner Höhe 1, Vienna XIV, 1905–1907 I Pharmacy I Wiener Stadt- und Landesarchiv

Heinrich Schmid, Hermann Aichinger I Fuchsenfeldhof I Längenfeldgasse 68, Vienna XII, 1922–1925 I Central laundry I In: Heinrich Schmid, Hermann Aichinger, *Die Bauten der Gemeinde Wien am Fuchsenfeld* (Neue Werkkunst), Berlin, 1927

Otto Wagner I The architect's own flat I Köstlergasse 3, Vienna VI, 1898 I Bathroom I Wien Museum

Otto Nadel, Karl Schmalhofer I Amalienbad (public bath and spa) I Reumannplatz 23, Vienna X, 1923–1926 I Control device for all showers in the health spa I In: *Das Amalienbad der Gemeinde Wien im X. Bezirk. Reumannplatz*, Vienna, 1926

Common Good — Full Recovery

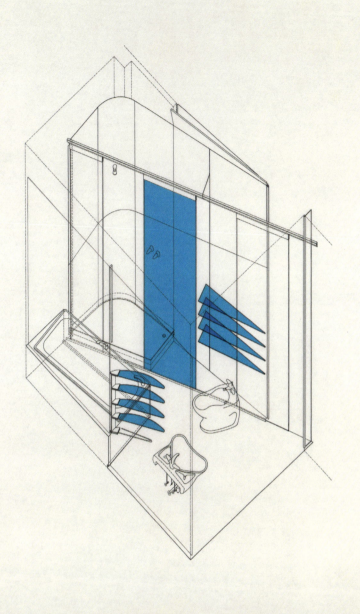

Helmut Richter | Bathroom, Sares Residence | Weyrgasse 8, Vienna III,
1983–1984 | Design, axonometry | Ink and adhesive foil on translucent paper

Operation Wien (film document IX) | A film on the city of Vienna's traffic problems, commissioned by Stadtbaudirektion Wien, 1957 | Film, 35 mm | Wiener Stadt- und Landesarchiv, Filmarchiv der media wien | Film stills

Paul Vogler, Erich Kühn | [Medicine and Urbanism. A Handbook for Urban Health], Munich/Vienna, 1957 | Cover

During the twentieth century, biology and medicine mutated into a guiding principle of sorts for city planning. The term organism designates a living unit, which – carried over to the city – is made up of arteries, cells, and organs, which, in turn, assume certain functions within the organism.

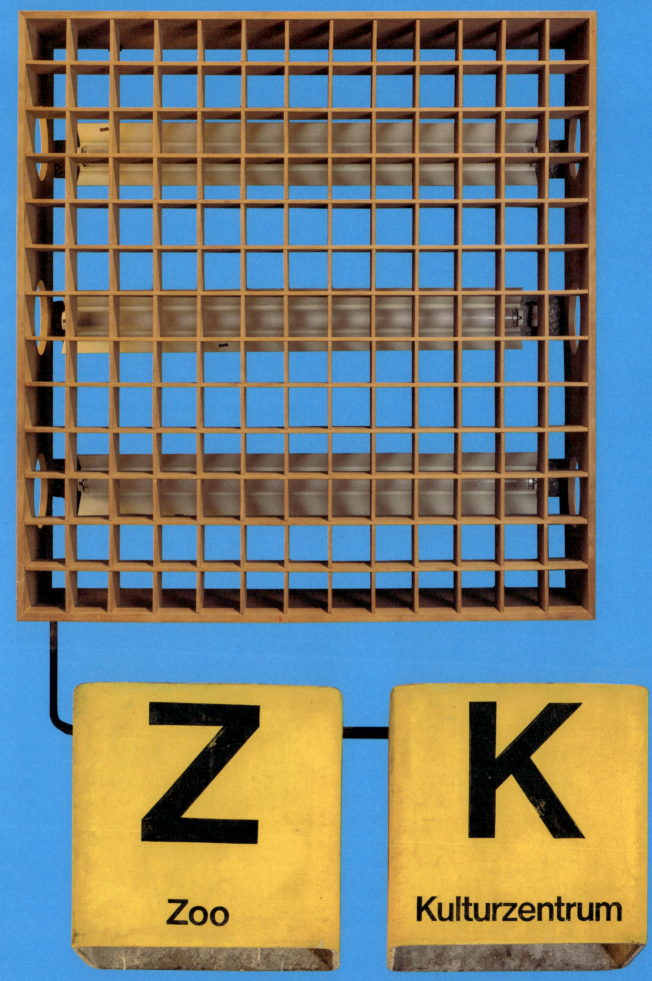

Acoustic ceiling panel, theater auditorium, designed by Anton Schweighofer | Wood

Signage system, designed by Anton Schweighofer | Fiber cement, lacquer, silkscreen

Chair 66, designed by Alvar Aalto | Birchwood, lacquer (partial) | Production: Artek

Swinging door, access to pool, designed by Anton Schweighofer | Solid wood, coated, lacquer

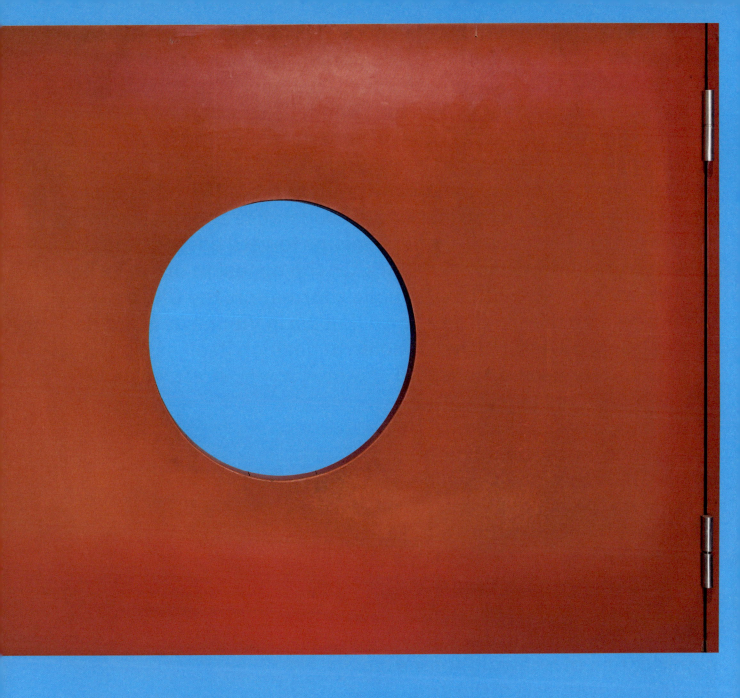
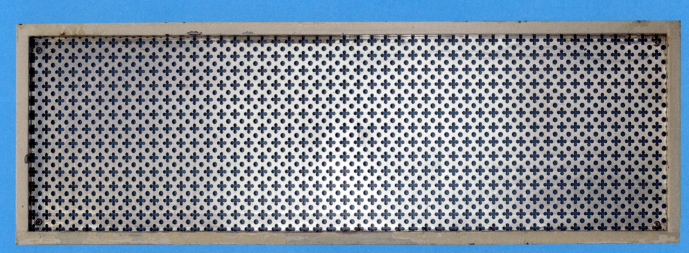

Ventilation grille, private room | Steel frame, lacquer, stainless-steel perforated sheet

In the late eighteenth century, childhood was recognized as a discrete phase of life. This called for the development and tailoring of specific spaces and building typologies such as schools, pre-schools, playgrounds, and orphanages. With the twentieth-century efforts to reform education serving as point of departure, children became the bearers of hope for a new and better future.

Coming on the heels of the social movements of 1968, reforms of youth welfare proposed taking a more cooperative approach, moving away from the use of control mechanisms toward advising and supporting children and teenagers. On the occasion of the fiftieth anniversary of the Austrian Republic's formation, the City of Vienna held up the Children's Town [known in Vienna as Stadt des Kindes], built by Anton Schweighofer, to position itself as a "city with a social consciousness." On a large site, it had been built to accommodate 300 children. The news that a partial demolition of the Children's Town – which was not on the national registry – was imminent prompted the Az W to salvage examples of the compound's bespoke furnishings. This step was taken owing to the architectural-historical significance of Schweighofer's quest for a synthesis of the arts. It also allowed Az W to preserve custom-made objects used on a daily basis – with the attendant wear and tear.

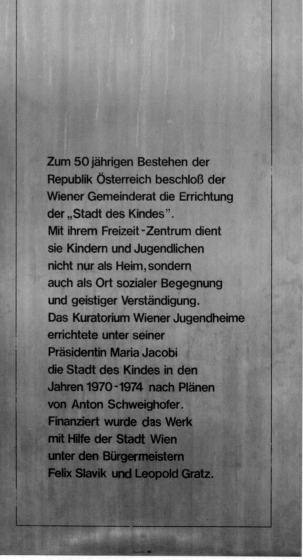

Dedication plaque | Stainless steel

Anton Schweighofer | Children's Town | Mühlbergstrasse 7, Vienna XIV, 1969–1974 | Reenactment following a design by Robert Rüf, Sammlungs-Lab #2 Stadt des Kindes: The Collapse of a Utopia, Az W, April 17, 2018 – May 28, 2018

Aerial photo | ca. 1975

Series of sketches | Felt pen on tracing paper

Schweighofer consciously employed means of scenographic representation to make the social and spatial interaction perceptible to one and all. The Children's Town comes into being before our eyes as a living urban organism. The focus is placed on the integrative form of human cohabitation and emotional security.

Education Initiatives

In 1774, during Empress Maria Theresia's reign, school attendance became obligatory; since then the government has been responsible for the construction of schools. As a consequence, spaces for education – past and present – are always also ideologically imprinted means of control. They also express societal change. Following World War II, efforts to modernize the education system gained steam, resulting in the establishment of several new schools. The aim was to democratize Austria's education system, and the corresponding processes were manifest in the production of space.

Theiss & Jaksch (Siegfried Theiss, Hans Jaksch) | Grade school and middle school | Schäffergasse 3–5, Vienna IV, 1949–1951 | Perspective | Pencil on translucent paper

Main stairway

Theiss & Jaksch (Siegfried Theiss, Hans Jaksch)
Grade school and middle school
Schäffergasse, Vienna IV, 1949–1951

For the design of the first post-1945 school in Vienna's central zone, two architects were commissioned whose formal vocabulary harked back to New Objectivity, establishing a continuity to the modernism of the 1920s and 1930s. The fact that architects who had worked for the National Socialist regime were selected indicates that the widely cited Stunde Null was a fabrication.

The classroom became the social setting for a new "community for living, working, and educating." In the wake of the authoritarian educational systems of Austrofascism and National Socialism, the aim was to foster a democratic coexistence. The well-lit, generously scaled stairway became emblematic of a progressive, modern, "healthy" pedagogy.

Robert Kramreiter | Minor Seminary of the Archdiocese Vienna | Sachsenbrunn 52, Kirchberg am Wechsel, Lower Austria, 1956–1963 | Model | Photo: H. Madensky

Washroom | Gym with wall bars | Cafeteria | Church interior | Departure of the pupils | Photos: Gerd Preser

Robert Kramreiter
Minor Seminary of the Archdiocese Vienna
Kirchberg am Wechsel, Lower Austria, 1956–1963

Robert Kramreiter – a student of Peter Behrens – was rooted in the liturgical movement and had built churches since the interwar period. In 1956, he received a commission from Cardinal Franz König to design a minor seminary. The new building was a symbol of the Catholic Church's educational initiative within the context of a predominantly Christian nation. Gerd Preser's photographic documentation focuses on the users and creates a symbiosis with the moderate modernism of the built environment. As of 1984, 30 percent of the school's graduates had elected to study theology. In 1992, the minor seminary was converted into a co-educational, college-preparatory secondary school.

Common Good — Education Initiatives

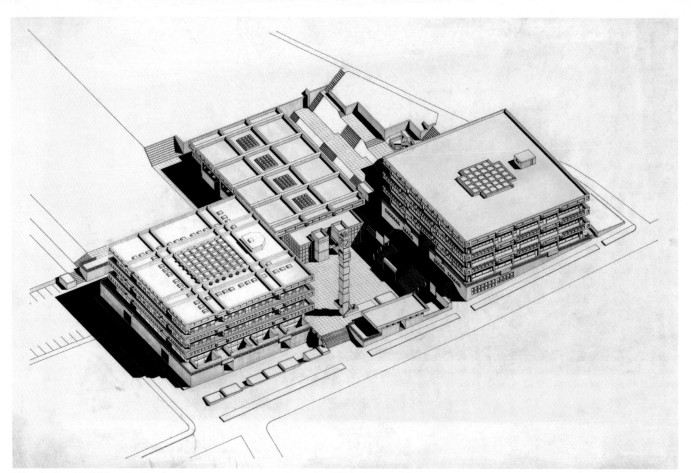

Viktor Hufnagl | Middle school and college preparatory secondary school | Friedhofweg 33, Weiz, Styria, 1965–1968 and 1976–1978 | Entire complex, axonometry | Pencil and ink on translucent paper

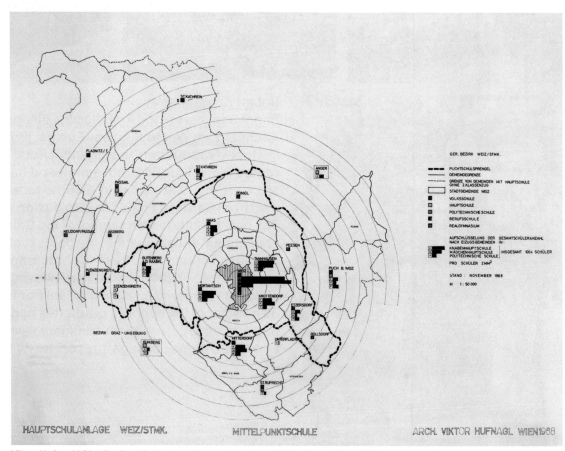

Viktor Hufnagl | Distribution of schools in the municipality of Weiz, Styria | Plan, 1968 | Pencil and ink on translucent paper

Viktor Hufnagl
Middle school and college preparatory secondary school
Friedhofweg 33, Weiz, Styria, 1965–1968 and 1976–1978

Societal and economical processes of growth occurred in association with the Schulorganisationsgesetz [school administration law] of 1962, which led to profound changes in Austria's education sector. Guided by the quest for "equal opportunities," the law sought to raise the general level of education. To that end, the length of compulsory attendance was extended to nine years. The asymmetries between urban and rural settings were to be balanced out through the establishment of new schools. At the same time, the subject matter in middle schools and in the lower grades of college-preparatory secondary schools was harmonized. The distinction between the two mid-level school types has remained in force to this day.

Originally planned to accommodate two middle schools, the school complex constitutes a decisive shift in the development of Austria's school construction. The commission for a school in Weiz provided Viktor Hufnagl the opportunity to implement an atrium school, in other words, a school in which the standard and specially equipped classrooms are arranged around a central space. What sets the design apart from other schools is the transformation of the rarely used corridors into a central, multipurpose hall "that becomes an open house for an entire city." The construction method provides a further advantage: a modular framework with cantilevering waffle slabs and a small number of columns affords considerable leeway in the subdivision of space.

Viktor Hufnagl | Middle school and college preparatory secondary school | Friedhofweg 33, Weiz, Styria, 1965–1968 and 1976–1978 | Middle school, assembly hall | Photo: Martha Deltios

Josef Lackner
School of the Ursulines
Fürstenweg 86, Innsbruck, Tyrol, 1971–1980

During the 1960s, the Ursuline sisters moved out of the old convents in the historic centers of Vienna, Salzburg, and Innsbruck and built new boarding schools and convents on the cities' periphery. The school designed by Josef Lackner – who had studied architecture at Holzmeister's master class – provided many young girls from the countryside access to higher education. The school's expansive ground-level space opens to the surroundings and contains a sunken double gym – which can be surveyed from above – as well as a swimming pool, while the upper level accommodates inward-facing classrooms: Lackner created spaces in which young people can experiment with their perception. The finely tuned synthesis of materiality, structure, and color concept is carried over to the neighboring dormitory.

Josef Lackner | School of the Ursulines | Fürstenweg 86, Innsbruck, Tyrol, 1971–1980 | Sectional model with removable roof | Wood, plastic, felt

Helmut Richter
Middle school
Kinkplatz 21, Vienna XIV, 1992–1994

A pioneering conception both in terms of architecture and building technology, this school building was completed in 1994 within the framework of the Schulbauprogramm 2000 [New School Initiative 2000] initiated by Hannes Swoboda, then Vienna's lead councilor for city planning. The fall of the Iron Curtain was followed by a period of growth and internationalization, as well as an education campaign to bring about a contemporary "digital-age school." With its spatial program, Richter's school broke through the conventions of school construction and made reference to global examples of high-tech architecture.

Facing south along an east–west main axis, like huge dragonfly wings, are two wedge-shaped volumes sheathed in glass. The smaller one contains the entrance hall, the larger one, the gymnasium. Toward the north, three slender wings holding the classrooms as well as the shared facilities and special zones latch on to the spine-like main axis. Richter proposed a photovoltaic system to be situated atop the two glazed roofs. Although it would have produced electricity and provided shade to the halls below, it was not implemented. The school is presently not in use. A new use is being sought for the building.

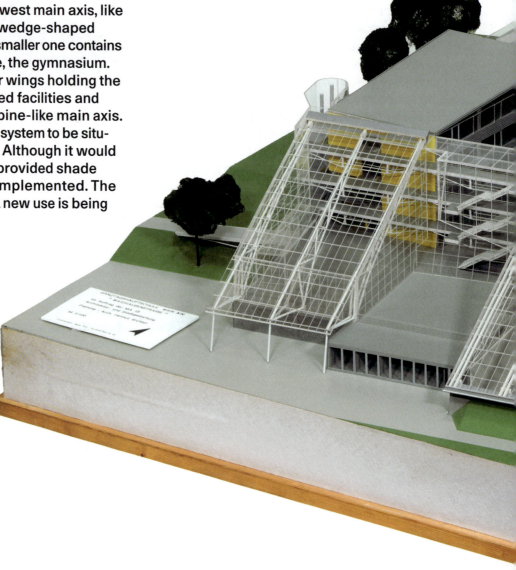

Helmut Richter I Middle school I Kinkplatz 21, Vienna XIV, 1992–1994 I Model I Wood and plastic

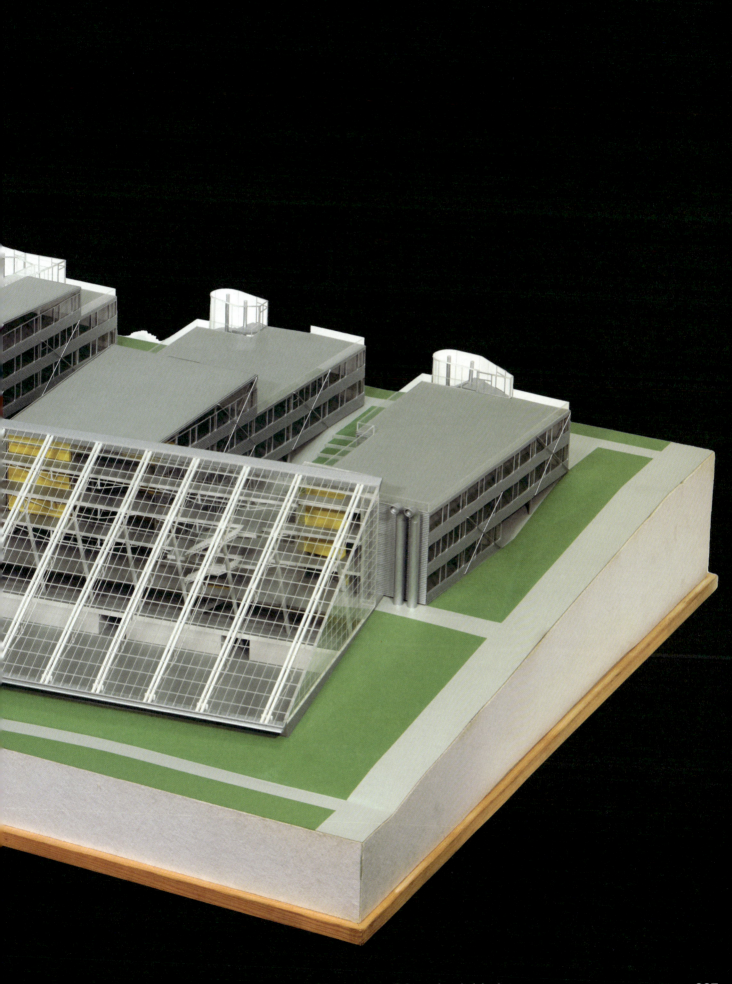

PPAG Architects (Anna Popelka, Georg Poduschka, Ali Seghatoleslami, Lilli Pschill)
Sonnwendviertel education campus
Gudrunstrasse 108, Vienna X, 2011–2014

This new school campus – consisting of preschool, elementary school and Neue Mittelschule (a reformed, more egalitarian version of the middle school) – is located in the city-expansion zone adjoining Vienna's central station. With their prototypical education building consisting of four units (clusters), the architects seek to rethink and animate the school in the broader scope. In each cluster, classrooms and a project space (also referred to as a team space) are arranged around a market square. Outdoor classrooms adjoin the pavilions. Space flows amply between the clusters, creating a series of squares and promenades. In sum, the interwoven spaces allow a fluid transition between learning and free time.

The Manta tables, which were developed specifically for this project, allow different configurations for group learning and are intended to help dismantle hierarchical structures. Table and desk surfaces positioned at standard heights enable the children – regardless of their height – to sit next to each other at the same level as their instructors. Chairs with adjustable footrests guarantee ergonomically correct posture. The teachers, who move from table to table, no longer have to kneel to communicate with the children: everyone's eyes are aligned.

PPAG Architects (Anna Popelka, Georg Poduschka, Ali Seghatoleslami, Lilli Pschill) | Sonnwendviertel education campus | Gudrunstrasse 108, Vienna X, 2011–2014 | Model of a cluster | Wood, plastic

PPAG Architects (Anna Popelka, Georg Poduschka, Ali Seghatoleslami, Lilli Pschill) | Sonnwendviertel education campus | Gudrunstrasse 108, Vienna X, 2011–2014 | Massing model and table models | Plastic

Eilfried Huth, Günther Domenig
Proposal for an extension to the
University of Vienna, 1973

Austria's first federal science agency was set up in 1970 – during the era in which Bruno Kreisky was chancellor. Hertha Firnberg headed the agency from its inception until 1983. The elimination of tuition fees, which took effect in 1972, helped improve, among other things, gender equality. Accordingly, the enrollment at the Universität Wien rose from 19,000 (37 percent women) in 1970/71 to 40,000 (50 percent women) by 1980/81, and enrollment doubled again, to 85,000 students (56 percent women), by 1990/91. In association with tuition-free access to university, the Universitätsorganisationsgesetz [university administration law], which was enacted in 1975, gave a stronger voice to all persons involved. On account of the rising numbers of students, the universities required more space. Eilfried Huth and Günther Domenig's proposal for an extension to the Universität Wien envisioned a topographical transformation. On the grounds of the former general hospital, the ring-shaped arrangement of interlocking towers, a structure informed by organic shapes, envisions the university as a democratic, pedagogic system that is part of the city fabric.

Georg Friedler, Paul Kolm | [Planning Universities in the Dialectic of Reform and Revolution Taking the University of Vienna as an Example], Union of Democratic Students, Vienna, 1968 | Cover

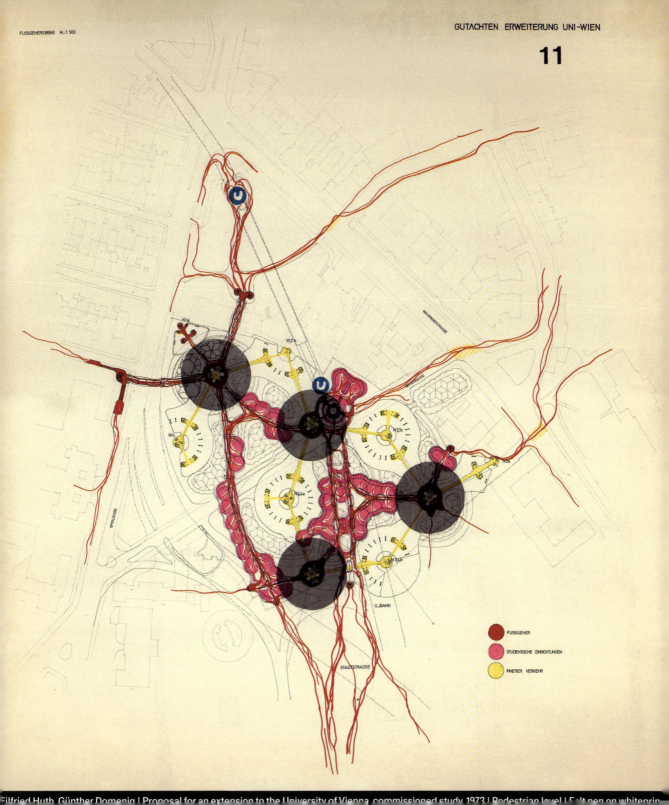

Child Friendly

Oskar Payer | Artistic toys | Rocking elephant | Pencil and colored pencil on translucent paper

Shop sign "Artistic Toys" | Ink and stickers on translucent paper

During the Red Vienna era, Montessori pedagogy, which focuses on children and their interests, began to gain traction in the city. Architects such as Franz Schuster, Friedl Dicker, Franz Singer, and Margarete Schütte-Lihotzky made strides in the development of children's furniture and toys. In the spirit of continuity with furniture designs of the past, Johannes Spalt designed *Zusammenbaumöbel* [self-assembled furniture] (1964, 1966). Central themes were the learning process and the users' social behavior. The furniture – made of fiberboard or plywood – was to be put together manually or with the aid of a hammer, by one or more persons. Neither Spalt's furniture nor the toys designed by Oskar Payer went into serial production.

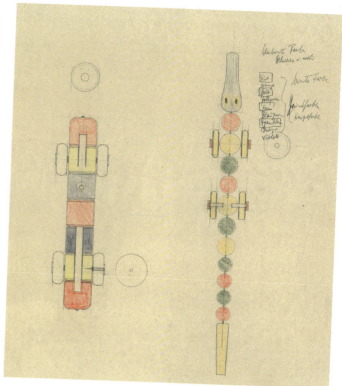

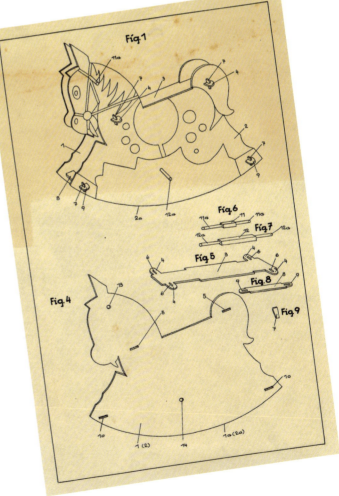

Oskar Payer | Artistic toys | Crocodile pull toy | Pencil and colored pencil on paper

Construction drawing of a rocking horse | Ink on translucent paper

Johannes Spalt | Children's furniture, 1964 |
Ladder-board | Hardboard, white and red lacquer | Production: Urban Warmuth
Chair | Plywood, hardboard, red lacquer | Production: Urban Warmuth

Design 1986 | Car-rocker | Hardboard, blue and red lacquer | Production: Urban Warmuth

Literature

From Cradle to Grave
pp. 262–265

Alfred Angerer, "Hygieia verführt Otto Wagner, Beispiele einer hygienisch motivierten Moderne" (master's thesis, TU Graz 2015).

Gerhard Melinz, "Armutspolitik und Sozialversicherungsstaat: Entwicklungsmuster in Österreich (1860 bis zur Gegenwart)," in: *Österreich in Geschichte und Literatur* 47, 2003, 136–161.

Norbert Fischer, "Zur Geschichte von Feuerbestattung und Krematoriumsbau mit besonderem Hinblick auf Wien und Österreich," in: Ewald Volgger, Florian Wegscheider (eds.), *Urne wie Sarg? Zur Unterscheidung zwischen Erd- und Feuerbestattung* (Regensburg 2018), 9–23.

Gudrun Wolfgruber, *Von der Fürsorge zur Sozialarbeit. Wiener Jugendwohlfahrt im 20. Jahrhundert* (Schriftenreihe zur Geschichte der Sozialarbeit und Sozialarbeitsforschung, vol. 5, Vienna 2013).

Erich Bernard, Architekturzentrum Wien (eds.), *Amt Macht Stadt. Erich Leischner und das Wiener Stadtbauamt*, exh. cat. Architekturzentrum Wien, 6/16–8/2/1999 (Vienna/Salzburg 1999).

Philipp Frankowski, Rosa Liederer, *Die Kindergärten der Stadt Wien* (Vienna 1932).

Full Recovery
pp. 266–273

Anselm Wagner, "Otto Wagners Straßenkehrer. Zum Reinigungsdiskurs der modernistischen Stadtplanung," in: *bricolage. Innsbrucker Zeitschrift für Europäische Ethnologie* 6, 2010, 36–61.

Andreas Nierhaus, *Ein Architekt als Medienstratege. Otto Wagner und die Fotografie* (Beiträge zur Geschichte der Fotografie in Österreich, vol. 19, Salzburg 2020).

Children's Town
pp. 274–281

Oliver Österreicher, "Räumliche Idealstadtmodelle und utopische Umsetzungsversuche. Versuch einer Einordnung der 'Stadt des Kindes' in Wien" (dissertation, TU Wien 2004).

Franziska Bollerey, "Anton Schweighofers 'Stadt des Kindes,'" in: Franziska Bollerey, Christoph Grafe (eds.), *Eselsohren. Journal of History of Art, Architecture and Urbanism* III, no. 1/2, Kid-Size. From Toy, to Table, to Town. Spielzeug, Möbel, Stadt (Wuppertal 2020), 305–316.

Education Initiatives
pp. 282–291

Robert Kramreiter, *Sachsenbrunn. Seminar der Erzdiözese* (Sachsenbrunn 1965).

Christa Harlander, "Der Architekt Robert Kramreiter. 1905–1965" (master's thesis, Universität Wien 2007).

Friedrich Langer, Bundesministerium für Unterricht (eds.), *Österreich baut Schulen* (Vienna 1962).

Wilhelm Hubatsch, *Der Schulbau in Österreich* (Vienna 1961).

Manfred Nehrer, Michael Wachberger, Österreichisches Institut für Schul- und Sportstättenbau (eds.), *Schulbau in Österreich von 1945 bis heute* (Vienna 1982).

Christian Kühn, "Rationalisierung und Flexibilität. Schulbaudiskurse der 1960er und -70er Jahre," in: Jeanette Böhme (ed.), *Schularchitektur im interdisziplinären Diskurs* (Wiesbaden 2009), 283–298.

Christian Dewald, "Der Wiener Schulbau Schäffergasse 1951 – gebautes Bildungsverständnis einer öffentlichen 'Wunderschule'" (bachelor's thesis, Universität Wien 2017).

Rudolf J. Boeck, Stadtbauamt der Stadt Wien (eds.), *Volks- und Hauptschule der Stadt Wien IV., Schäffergasse* (Vienna 1951).

Viktor Hufnagl, "Internationale Tendenzen im Schulbau," in: Der Aufbau 11/12, 1973, printed in: *Viktor Hufnagl, Bauten – Projekte, Erfahrungen – Erkenntnisse, Gedanken – Theorie. 1950–2000* (Vienna 2001), 81–89.

Viktor Hufnagl, "Schulbau und Pädagogik," in: architektur aktuell 68/69, 1968, printed in: *Viktor Hufnagl, Bauten – Projekte, Erfahrungen – Erkenntnisse, Gedanken – Theorie. 1950–2000* (Vienna 2001), 24–26.

Viktor Hufnagl, *Bauten – Projekte, Erfahrungen – Erkenntnisse, Gedanken – Theorie. 1950–2000* (Vienna 2001).

Otto Kapfinger, Architekturforum Tirol (eds.), *Bauen in Tirol seit 1980. Ein Führer zu 260 sehenswerten Bauten* (Salzburg 2002).

Gymnasium Ursulinen, Innsbruck, Peter Paul Steininger, Schulgeschichte: Über 300 Jahre Ursulinen in Innsbruck – Tradition und Innovation, https://ursulinen.tsn.at/schulprofil/schulgeschichte (accessed July 1, 2022).

Monika Abendstein, Architekturforum Tirol (eds.), *Josef Lackner 1931–2000* (Salzburg 2002).

Walter M. Chramosta, Magistrat der Stadt Wien (eds.), *The New Schoolhouse. Schoolchild's Universe and Urban Particle. The School Building Programme 2000 of the City of Vienna. A First Survey 1990–1996* (Vienna 1996).

Walter M. Chramosta, Stadtplanung Wien (eds.), *Ganztagshauptschule Wien 14. Kinkplatz 21 (Projekte und Konzepte, vol. 3)* (Vienna 1995).

Walter M. Chramosta, *Helmut Richter. Bauten und Projekte* (Basel 2000).

Christian Kühn, Barbara Pampe, Anna Popelka, Georg Poduschka, *Von der neuen Schule = of the new school*, exh. cat. Galerie Berlin, 11/1–12/15/2018 (Vienna 2018).

PPAG architects, *Bildungscampus Sonnwendviertel*, https://www.ppag.at/de/projects/bildungscampus/ (accessed July 1, 2022).

Universität Wien, Katharina Kniefacz, *Offener Hochschulzugang und "Massenuniversität" 1970–2015*, https://geschichte.univie.ac.at/de/themen/offener-hochschulzugang-und-massenuniversitaet (accessed July 1, 2022).

Günther Feuerstein, Bundesministerium für Bauten und Technik (eds.), *Hochschulen planen, bauen. Sonderschau des Bundesministeriums für Bauten und Technik* (Vienna 1969).

Child Friendly
pp. 292–295

Eva B. Ottillinger (ed.), *Zappel, Philipp! Kindermöbel. Eine Designgeschichte*, exh. cat. Hofmobiliendepot, 10/4/2006–1/7/2007 (Vienna 2006).

Alexander von Vegesack (ed.), *Kid Size. The Material World of Childhood*, exh. cat. Kunsthal Rotterdam, 6/28–9/28/1997 (Milan 1997).

Harald Bichler, Johannes Spalt, *Rauminhalt: Möbelklassiker 1945/60/70/85*, exh. cat. Galerie Rauminhalt, 11/7–11/29/2003 (Vienna 2003).

Image

Land of Mountains	300
Rock over Baroque	302
More than a Small Nation	306
Vienna International Centre	307
"United Nations Look à la Austria"	310
Waldheim Debate	312
Austrian Cultural Forum	314
From East to West	316
Burgenland's Brutalists	318
Vorarlberg's Baukünstler	322
Vienna/Graz	324
Re-grounded: Vienna	326
Great Hits: Graz	330
Confessional Diversity	332
What about the Synagogues?	334
The Minaret is not the Issue	338
Church as Client	342
Symbols of Power	344

Who are we?

Land of Mountains

The landscape as symbolic construct plays as important a role in how Austria views itself as in the tourism-tinged perception of it from abroad. The dismantling of the Habsburg dynasty yielded an "Alpine Republic": mountainous landscapes account for about 60 percent of Austria's territory. At the Paris International Exposition of 1937, Oswald Haerdtl's airy pavilion heightened the effect of photo collages of panoramic Alpine roads. Landscape became a symbol representing the interests of the state.

Oswald Haerdtl | Pavilion of the Republic of Austria, International Exposition | Paris, France, 1936–1937 | Exterior elevation, 1937 | Photo: Julius Scherb

The glazed front provides a frame for the monumental photo collage of Alpine roads by Robert Haas: Grossglockner High Alpine Road, Gesäuse Strasse, and Packstrasse. These were some of the most prestigious infrastructure projects to be implemented during the Austrofascist era.

Rock over Baroque

Coop Himmelb(l)au (Wolf D. Prix, Helmut Swiczinsky)
Rooftop remodeling
Falkestrasse 6, Vienna I, 1983, 1987–1988

With this addition to a law firm perched atop a Ringstrasse-era palace and consisting of a conference room and offices, Coop Himmelb(l)au made a significant contribution to the deconstructivist approach to designing buildings. It became one of the key projects in the 1988 exhibition Deconstructivist Architecture at the Museum of Modern Art in New York and constituted the architects' international breakthrough.

The glazed structure above the large, diagonally positioned conference room is supported by a combination of steel beams and reinforced-concrete beams; these structural members even break through the building envelope. The provocative treatment of the corner can be viewed as both a reinterpretation of the dome and the desire to celebrate space. Traits which, according to Wolf D. Prix, have for centuries characterized – and set apart – Austrian architecture.

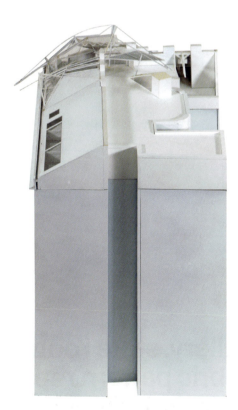

Coop Himmelb(l)au (Wolf D. Prix, Helmut Swiczinsky) | Rooftop remodeling | Falkestrasse 6, Vienna I, 1983, 1987–1988 | Presentation model | Plexiglas, styrofoam, corrugated cardboard, wood

Hans Hollein | Austriennale Milan, 1968 | Red-white-red Austria glasses | Plastic | Archive Hans Hollein, Az W and MAK, Vienna

Oswald Haerdtl | Federal chancellery, state rooms | Ballhausplatz 1, Vienna I, 1948 | Fabric pattern repeat for curtains (implemented in red/white) | Pencil and ink on paper

After regaining its independence in 1955 as small neutral nation, efforts to gain international recognition were front and center. That same year, Austria became a member of the United Nations.

More than a Small Nation

In 1959, Bruno Kreisky was named the first foreign minister. His active neutrality and peace policies provided the basis for Austria's role as bridge builder between east and west and helped propel Kurt Waldheim to the position of secretary-general of the United Nations (1971–1981).

Vienna International Centre

In 1966, the Austrian government submitted an offer to the United Nations to erect a new headquarters in Vienna. Two years later an international competition was held. The first prize went to Los Angeles-based César Pelli with Gruen Associates; second prize to the British architecture group Building Design; and third prize to the German architects Fritz Novotny and Arthur Mähner. The Austrian architect Johann Staber received fourth prize. During the revision phase, he became the beneficiary of differences of opinion between technical advisers and the United Nations. Following an intervention by Bruno Kreisky, Staber was awarded the commission. The separate wings of the Y-shaped floor plans guaranteed the adaptability of this complex building, which, instead of the originally forecast 2,600 persons would now have to accommodate 4,600 employees. In 1979, when the controversial project was inaugurated, Kreisky paid tribute to it as a cornerstone of the efforts undertaken to help Austria reenter the international stage.

Johann Staber | Vienna International Centre, UN City | Bruno-Kreisky-Platz 1, Vienna XXII, 1968–1987 | Gift to Karl Grubich, an employee, upon the inauguration on August 23, 1979 | Presentation model | Metal on plastic sheet

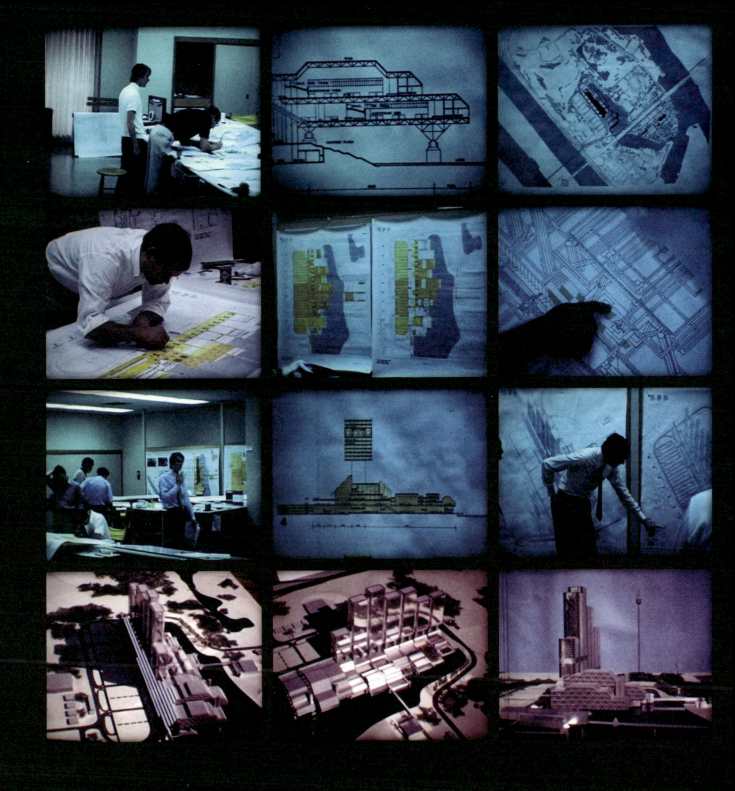

International competition Vienna International Centre, 1968 | Team: César Pelli, Partner and Gruen Associates, Los Angeles, January–June 1969 | Rylance Bird Jr., Richard Dodson, Arthur Golding, Friedrich Kastner, Douglas Meyer, Victor Schumacher, Engelbert Zobl | Film by Engelbert Zobl | Film stills

"United Nations Look à la Austria"

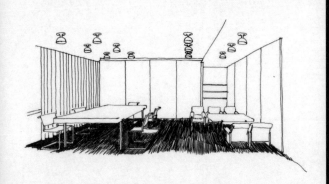

Eva Mang-Frimmel, Karl Mang | Offices of the UN Secretary-General, furnishings for Kurt Waldheim | United Nations Plaza, New York, USA, 1972–1973 | Dining room | Ink on translucent paper

Letzter Schliff an den Möbeln für den UN-Generalsekretär

UNO wird „echt" österreichisch...

Von einem original österreichischen Schreibtisch aus werden zukünftig die Geschicke der UNO gelenkt. UNO-Generalsekretär Dr. Kurt Waldheim wird nämlich jetzt eine komplette Einrichtung für sein Büro in New York bekommen. Die heimische Wirtschaft hat „gesammelt" und stellt Dr. Waldheim die Möbel als Geschenk zur Verfügung.

Wiener Geschenk für Dr. Waldheim

Von seinem Vorgänger hatte Doktor Waldheim ein eher schäbiges Büro übernommen. Bundeskammerpräsident Ing. Rudolf Sallinger hatte bei einem Besuch in New York Gelegenheit, sich über die nicht standesgemäße Einrichtung der Arbeitsräume zu ärgern. Rasch war der Plan entworfen, das Büro des UNO-Generalsekretärs mit österreichischen Möbeln auszustatten. Die Wiener Architekten Dipl.-Ing. Karl Mang und Eva Mang-Frimmel wurden mit der Planung beauftragt. Nun sind die Möbelstücke fertiggestellt und werden anfangs März nach New York transportiert. Die Gegenstände werden von einem Österreicher und UNO-Haustischlern installiert. Die Kosten belaufen sich auf eine halbe Million S.

"The UN is becoming 'truly' Austrian ...," | *Neue Kronenzeitung*, February 14, 1973

Media outlets proudly reported on Kurt Waldheim's new offices at the UN headquarters in New York. The architects Eva Mang-Frimmel and Karl Mang, who had already received acclaim for their interior designs, were commissioned to make a proposal for the interiors – a welcoming present from the Austrian Chamber of Commerce and its president Kurt Sallinger. In their reservedness, the completed furnishings – produced exclusively by Austrian firms – were consistent with the status of the high official.

Eva Mang-Frimmel, Karl Mang | Offices of the UN Secretary-General, furnishings for Kurt Waldheim | United Nations Plaza, New York, USA, 1972–1973 | Inauguration of the offices with, among others (from left to right): Karl Mang, Kurt Waldheim, Rudolf Sallinger, Elisabeth Waldheim, May 3, 1973

View into the office

Image   More than a Small Nation   311

Waldheim Debate

> **hochschule für**
> **angewandte kunst**
> **in wien**
> der rektor
>
> Betrifft: PRÄSIDENTSCHAFTSWAHL
>
> Die ohnehin eingeschränkte Entscheidungsfreiheit einer politischen Wahl mit vorgezeichneten Möglichkeiten wird derzeit durch das oberflächliche Nachholen einer 40 Jahre unterbliebenen Diskussion ad absurdum geführt.
>
> Solange die Situation dermaßen emotionsgeladen ist, müßte der Wahlkampf eingestellt und zu einem späteren Zeitpunkt neu ausgeschrieben werden, da hier in jedem Fall eine nicht mehr sachliche und demokratische Ausgangsbasis gegeben ist.
>
> Wien, 7. April 1986
>
> Oswald Oberhuber - Peter Noever - Wilhelm Holzbauer - Mario Terzic - Kurt Kalb - Hubert Schmalix - Peter Weibel - Friedrich Achleitner - Christian Reder - Erhard Suess - Heinrich Steinek - Brigitte Christoph - Boris Podrecca - Wolfgang Hutter - Edith Rosenberger - Alexandra Suess - Gerwald Rockenschaub - Heinz Adamek - Georg Fritsch - Rudolf Goessl - Heinz Kolisch - Ivo Podreka - Christian Schneider - Adolf Frohner - Nikolaus Franko - Wander Bertoni - Gabriele Koller - Willi Kopf - Erika Patka - Karl Kowanz - Eva Glück - Roland Goeschl - Franz Koglmann - Hans Koller - Walter M. Malli - Ingrid Karl - Tone Fink - Helmut Draxler - Robert Bilek - Inge Wögenstein - Julius Hummel - Alfred Vendl - Luigi Blau - Maximilian Melcher - Gloria Withalm - Franz Graf - Brigitte Kowanz - Peter Kogler - Friedrich Bastl - Wolfgang Baminger - Manfred Wagner - Peter Pongratz - Heidi Grundmann

Call to suspend Kurt Waldheim's election campaign, April 7, 1986 | Initiated by Oswald Oberhuber, rector of the University of Applied Arts, and signed by artists, architects, and other public figures | Typoscript | ÖNB

In 1985, former UN Secretary-General Kurt Waldheim announced his candidacy for president of Austria. During the campaign, a debate erupted both locally and abroad on whether the People's Party candidate had been involved in war crimes during the National Socialist era. For the first time, the "victim myth," which holds that Austria was Nazi Germany's first victim, was critically examined in a broad public discussion. By holding protests and mounting exhibitions, artists, architects, and intellectuals demanded a systematic survey of the country's own past and a new outlook for the future.

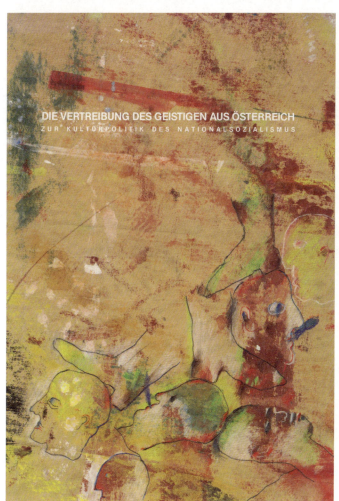

Gabriele Koller, Gloria Withalm | [The Expulsion of Intellectuality from Austria. On the Cultural Policies of National Socialism] | Vienna, 1985

Oswald Oberhuber | [Zeitgeist against Zeitgeist. A Sequence of Events from Austria's Aberration] | Vienna 1988

Austrian Cultural Forum

Image · More than a Small Nation · 314

Since the 1960s, New York's high-rise architecture has been determined by developers' pragmatism. The "artist architect" commissioned to design a new building on a site just 7.6 meters wide in the heart of Manhattan adopted a position counter to the nation's predominant commercial architecture. The stance explains why there was so much interest in this building from the very start. Correspondingly, the Museum of Modern Art organized an exhibition on Raimund Abraham's project the year after the competition. His design has two special characteristics: it merges the contemporary with the archaic to form a unified whole and, at the same time, draws attention to Austria's specific culture of building.

Raimund Abraham | Austrian Cultural Forum | 11 East 52nd Street, New York, USA, 1992–2001 | Presentation model | Wood, plastic

Günther Domenig, Eilfried Huth | Chair originally designed for the Easter Church in Oberwart, variant | Plastic, felt

From East to West

Hans Purin | Chair prototype | Wood, leather

Burgenland's Brutalists

In 1921/22, Burgenland became part of Austria as its ninth and youngest federal state, whereby Sopron, the region's bustling hub, remained with Hungary. During the National Socialist era, for a time Burgenland, as an administrative entity, had ceased to exist, and after 1945, the development of the federal state was impeded by its adjacency to the Iron Curtain. During the 1960s, the Social-Democratic-governed federal state initiated a modernization campaign which provided technical and social infrastructure such as schools, hospitals, indoor swimming pools, churches, and morgues. Burgenland is the only state in Austria to introduce cultural centers into communities. Articulated as multipurpose buildings, the typology embodies the cultural, societal, and educational policies of a welfare state and the elimination of the distinction between center and periphery. The sculptural béton brut buildings make Burgenland a focal point of Austrian Brutalism, whereby the architects Matthias Szauer and Herwig Udo Graf assumed the leading roles. The image of the buildings – which were long the recipients of bad press – has in the meantime been amended, but many buildings designed by Burgenland's Brutalists are threatened with demolition or have already been destroyed.

The five cultural centers (KUZ) of Burgenland:

Cultural Center Mattersburg, Herwig Udo Graf, 1973–1976 (Partial demolition and extension: HOLODECK Architects 2016–2021)

Cultural Center Güssing, Matthias Szauer, 1973–1977 (In 2021, a slim majority of 59 percent was in favor of renovating the KUZ.)

Cultural Center Jennersdorf (addition to an existing inn), Karl Hütter, 1974–1977

Cultural Center Oberschützen, Herwig Udo Graf, 1977–1982

Cultural Center Eisenstadt, Matthias Szauer, 1978–1982 (Refurbishment and extension: Pichler & Traupmann Architekten, 2009–2012)

Herwig Udo Graf | Cultural Center | Wulkalände 2, Mattersburg, Burgenland, 1973–1976 | Film of the topping-out ceremony | 1976 | ORF | Film stills

Herwig Udo Graf
Cultural Center
Wulkalände 2, Mattersburg, Burgenland, 1973–1976
The Cultural Center Mattersburg was the first of five cultural centers to be built in Burgenland. In combination with a middle school and a gym, the KUZ formed an urban ensemble. In the meantime, the Social Democrats' Brutalist legacy has met with resistance: the building has been partially demolished.

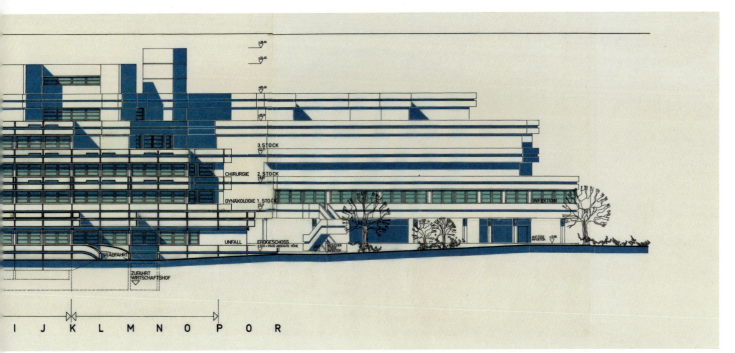

Matthias Szauer, Gottfried Fickl | State Hospital | Dornburggasse 80, Oberwart, Burgenland, 1971–1988 | West elevation | Ink on translucent paper, adhesive foil

Matthias Szauer, Gottfried Fickl
State Hospital
Dornburggasse 80, Oberwart,
Burgenland, 1971–1988

In 1971, the architects Matthias Szauer and Gottfried Fickl won the competition for the hospital in Oberwart. By taking advantage of béton brut's sculptable qualities – and alternating it with curtain walls of exposed-aggregate concrete – the architects gave shape to the building's striking exterior. They produced an expansive building whose emphasis on structural members and their geometric formal assembly adopts the aesthetics of Brutalism and enters into a dialogue with like-minded endeavors beyond Austria's borders.

Rudolf Wäger | Ruhwiesen housing estate | Waldrain 12–22, Schlins, Vorarlberg, 1971–1973 | Permit drawing, north elevation | Ink on translucent paper

Hans Purin | Halde 1 | Housing estate | Haldenweg 27–32, Bludenz, Vorarlberg, 1965–1967 | Living room | Photo: Friedrich Achleitner

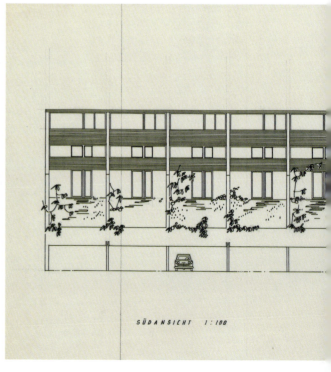

Rudolf Wäger | Ruhwiesen housing estate | Waldrain 12–22, Schlins, Vorarlberg, 1971–1973 | Living room | Photo: Friedrich Achleitner

Vorarlberg's Baukünstler

Vorarlberg, Austria's westernmost state, was one of the first to become industrialized and has an above-average population density. The emergence of the "Baukünstler" (literally: building artists) phenomenon can be traced back to the 1960s. With their built work, the young designers – often having completed apprenticeships in artisanal trades – forged a connection to both regional tradition and international design developments. As counterpoint to sprawl, Hans Purin and Rudolf Wäger – two of the movement's early protagonists – were committed to social, affordable, and communal housing models. What makes the Halde housing estate by Purin and the Ruhwiesen housing estate by Wäger exceptional is their careful insertion in the topography. Aside from the concrete-block party walls, the structural members of the two schemes are in wood – a material which at the time was not held in high esteem, as it reminded many people of wartime barracks.

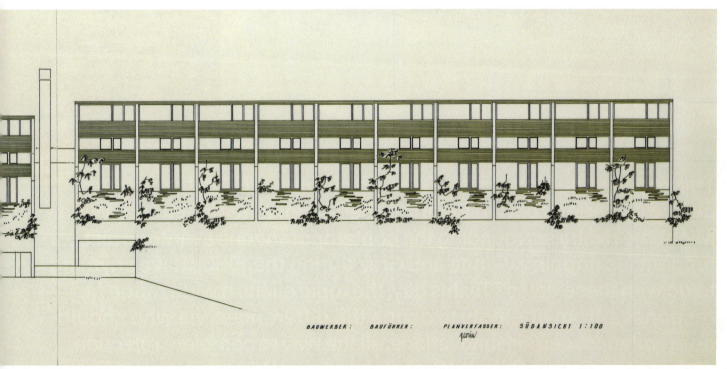

Hans Purin | Halde 2 | Housing estate | Haldenweg 42–52, Bludenz, Vorarlberg, 1965–1967 | Design plan, south elevation | Ink on translucent paper

Vienna

Hermann Czech | Kleines Café | Franziskanerplatz 3, Vienna I, 1970–1985 | Exterior

The Technische Universität Graz was founded in 1811, four years before its counterpart in Vienna – the Technische Universität Wien. Might the rivalry surrounding the contemporaneous avant-gardist tendencies gripping Vienna and Graz during the 1960s have anything to do with these dates? To this day, the topic elicits a wide range of responses, from attempts to define the differences, via who should be credited for certain innovations, all the way to complete rejection of the terms Grazer Schule [Graz School] and Wiener Schule [Vienna

Graz

Werkgruppe Graz (Eugen Gross, Friedrich Gross-Rannsbach, Werner Hollomey, Hermann Pichler) | Dormitory | Hafnerriegel 53, Graz, Styria, 1960–1963 | View of the exterior fire stair

School]. After 1945, in both locations, in connection with charismatic educators – Günter Feuerstein and Karl Schwanzer at the Technische Universität Wien; Clemens Holzmeister at the Academy of Fine Arts in Vienna; Karl Raimund Lorenz and Ferdinand Schuster at the Technische Universität Graz; and, as a "satellite," Konrad Wachsmann at the Sommerakademie in Salzburg – optimism among the students about imminent change became clearly palpable.

Re-grounded: Vienna

Eichinger oder Knechtl (Gregor Eichinger, Christian Knechtl) | Café Stein | Währinger Strasse 6–8, Vienna IX, 1985 | Interior | Photo: Margherita Spiluttini

Luigi Blau | Demmer's Tea Room | Mölker Bastei 5, Vienna I, 1981 | Interior stair | Photo: Wulf Brackrock

In the Vienna of the 1980s, the overwhelming majority of commissions for public buildings were awarded to large commercial architecture firms – competitions were almost non-existent. Excellent new architecture could only be achieved as so-called "small/minor architectures" in which furnishings and renovations, i. e. the painstaking interventions in the existing fabric, are implemented. What remained for the young architects, educated in the 1960s and 1970s during a phase of upheaval, was the opportunity to reflect on architecture. The details of such work contain ironic or historical references as well as hidden messages and are exquisitely executed.

Heidemarie Leitner | Handbag stool, 1999 | Wood, black lacquer | Production: Franz Plank GmbH

Heidemarie Leitner | Carega chair, 1999 (design 1967) | Wood, black lacquer | Production: Franz Plank GmbH

Elsa Prochazka | Bibelwerk Bookshop | Singerstrasse 7, Vienna I, 1991 | Interior | Photo: Margherita Spiluttini

Hermann Czech | Armchair, 2021 (design 1993) | Wood, black lacquer | Production: Gebrüder Thonet Vienna GmbH

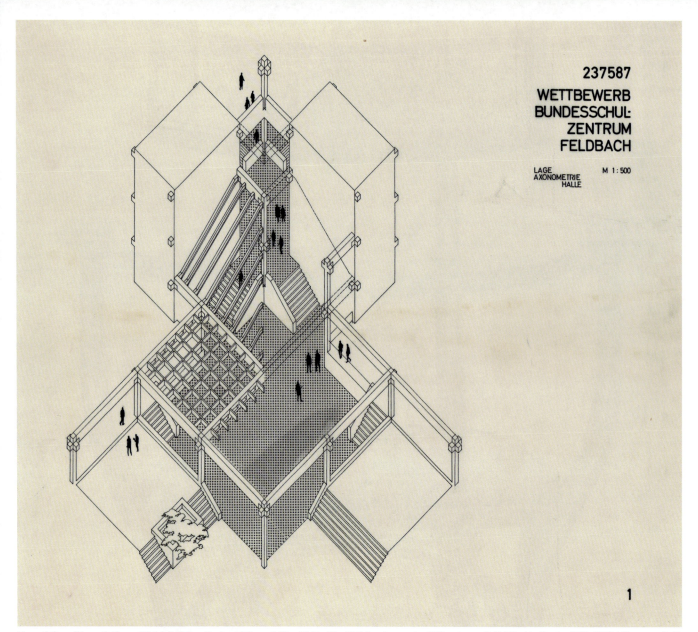

Team A Graz (Franz Cziharz, Dietrich Ecker, Herbert Missoni, Jörg Wallmüller) | School complex | Pfarrgasse 6, Feldbach, Styria, 1973–1980 | Entrance hall, axonometry | Ink on translucent paper

Szyszkowitz + Kowalski (Michael Szyszkowitz, Karla Kowalski) | Addition to Grosslobming Castle | Grosslobming 1, Styria, 1978–1981 | Sketch | Pencil, colored pencil, and felt pen on tracing paper

Great Hits: Graz

The Austrian Student Association in Graz commissioned Werkgruppe Graz to design one of the city's first high-rises. The architects built a dormitory with a sculptural exterior escape stair that self-confidently inscribed itself in the city's silhouette. With its realization of the stepped terrace housing in the St. Peter district, the same architecture firm procured a higher-than-usual urban density and a wisp of megacity.

Prophetic to this day, the architects' collective known as Team A Graz, which, in response to the proclaimed educational reforms, developed a completely new spatial concept for the new format in the education system – the Gesamtschule [comprehensive school]. It was based on a square structural unit with side lengths of 25.2 meters and a separation of the fitting out and the furniture, which would facilitate flexible usage.

Michael Szyszkowitz and Karla Kowalski looked to experimentation as a way to approach design problems in a specific context. With their expressive formal vocabulary and through the choice of materials, the architects' additions to a home economics school for girls set up a dialogue with the adjacent Grosslobming Castle.

Werkgruppe Graz (Eugen Gross, Friedrich Gross-Rannsbach, Werner Hollomey, Hermann Pichler) | Terrassenhaussiedlung [stepped terrace housing] | St. Peter Hauptstrasse 33, Graz, Styria, 1965–1978 | Exterior

Confessional Diversity

Notwithstanding the dominance of the Catholic church, the Austro-Hungarian dual monarchy was multi-denominational. There were major differences in the various regions: while in the western crown lands, far more than 90 percent of the population were Catholics, toward the south east the numbers were considerably lower. Despite their relatively small share of the overall population (4.4 percent), within the monarchy, Jews played an important role as initiators of cultural and economic development. In Galicia and in Bukovina, the Jewish segment of the population was at its largest at up to 40 percent.

In 1912, Islam was legally recognized as a religious community. With this decision, in the European context, the Habsburg monarchy had taken a leading role. At the time, 600,000 Sunnite Muslims lived in Bosnia-Herzegovina, constituting about one third of the overall population there.

The convening of the Second Vatican Council (1962–1965) led to the opening of the Catholic Church. Building new churches became a field of experimentation in the renewal of the religion. In recent decades, several factors – for instance, immigration, the opening of the former eastern bloc, and the free movement between EU countries – contributed to making Austria more denominationally diverse. Religious buildings are always also a projection surface for the images we have of ourselves and of "the other": these rely on "legibility" and "identification."

What about the Synagogues?

Image   Confessional Diversity

Arthur Grünberger, Adolf Jelletz | Neue Welt Synagogue | Eitelbergergasse 22, Vienna XIII, 1924–1929 | Model, 1994 | Wood, plastic; ceiling luminaire | Model builder: Brüll

Arthur Grünberger, Adolf Jelletz
Neue Welt Synagogue
Eitelbergergasse 22, Vienna XIII, 1924–1929

The Hietzing Synagogue was the last place of worship to be built in Vienna prior to the National Socialists' seizure of power. Arthur Grünberger and Adolf Jelletz won an international competition (1924) addressed exclusively to Jewish architects. The free-standing building symbolizes a self-assured Judaism. Longitudinally the synagogue corresponds to Reform Judaism, in which the Torah ark and the bema (holding the Torah reading table) are located together on the east wall. The Stars of David inscribed in a trefoil fulfil two functions: they communicate the building's Jewish identity outwardly and are responsible for the mystical quality of light inside. Hollywood might even have been a source of inspiration: in 1926, Grünberger moved to Los Angeles and worked as art director on film sets. During the Night of Broken Glass (November 9/10, 1938), the Hietzing Synagogue was systematically destroyed. In 1939, the last vestiges of the building were dismantled and an apartment building was erected where it had stood.

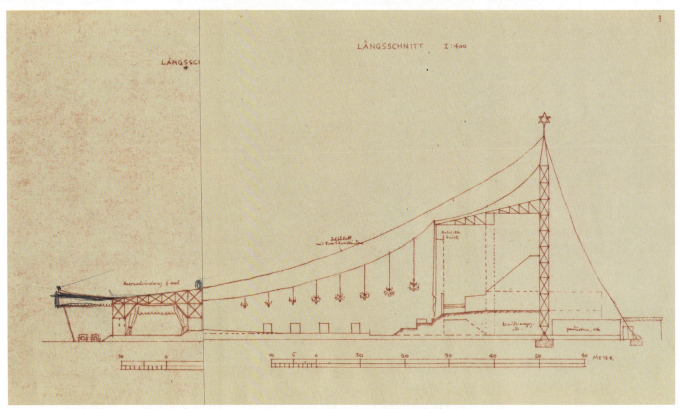

Oskar Strnad | Synagogue tent for *The Eternal Road*, an oratory | Central Park, New York, USA, 1934 | Longitudinal section | Pencil on whiteprint

Oskar Strnad
Synagogue tent for *The Eternal Road*, an oratory
Central Park, New York, USA, 1934

    Oskar Strnad's synagogue design for the Jewish oratorio *The Eternal Road* (text: Franz Werfel, music: Kurt Weill), directed by Max Reinhardt, was, on account of Strnad's death in 1935, not implemented. The design, intended for the premiere in New York City's Central Park, indirectly invoked the racist pogroms inflicted by the National Socialists. The synagogue tent, on the one hand, accommodates visitors, but, on the other hand, represents a sanctuary for the Jewish community – whose members were ultimately forced to leave the prayer house.

Friedrich Kurrent
Synagogue project
Schmerlingplatz, Vienna I, 2008

    Friedrich Kurrent's design is the product of his stance: "The city has an obligation to fulfil." The prominent site on Schmerlingplatz between the Parliament, Palais Epstein, and the Palace of Justice would offer the Jewish community – which suffered the loss of more than 40 synagogues and prayer houses in Vienna – a central location as place of worship. Kurrent based his design on an idea which originated in the late nineteenth century to develop a floor plan from the Star of David. The centrally-planned building in wood construction would accommodate 500 congregants and, at a height of 25 meters, would be almost as tall as the neighboring Parliament. Unlike in Germany, since 1945, hardly any new synagogues have been built in Austria.

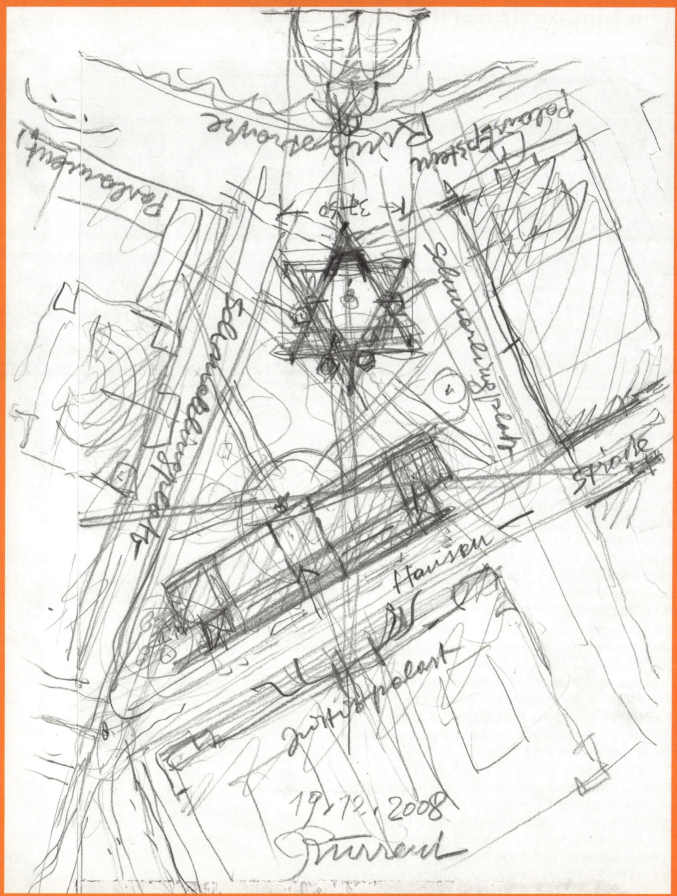

Friedrich Kurrent | Synagogue project I, Schmerlingplatz, Vienna I, 2008 | Sketch, December 19, 2008 | Pencil on paper

The Minaret is not the Issue

Vienna Islamic Centre | Am Bruckhaufen 3, Vienna XXI, 1975–1979 | "Vienna Islamic Centre (1979)", English documentation accompanying the opening on November 20, 1979 | Film, 16 mm | Wiener Stadt- und Landesarchiv, Filmarchiv der media wien | Film stills

The initiative to build a mosque on the grounds of the Türkenschanzpark can be traced back to Karl Lueger's tenure as mayor and had the support of the imperial dynasty until 1918. During the 1960s, the number of Muslims in Austria increased on account of blue-collar workers having immigrated from Turkey and the former Yugoslavia. At the start of the decade, the Muslim population was estimated at 3,000; about ten years later, it approached 20,000. The desire for a main mosque for all Muslims in the heart of the city grew. In light of ideological tensions between the different denominations of global Islam, none of the bottom-up initiatives were built. Austria's first prominent mosque was financed and administrated by Saudi Arabia and located on the city's edge: the Vienna Islamic Centre is articulated as domed structure with two minarets and is firmly rooted in the Ottoman building tradition.

Designs by Hannes Lintl, Heinz Tesar, and Bernardo Bader interpret the design problem anew, without negating the context of the cultures of origin. Few of these exceptional concepts have been erected. Bernardo Bader's superb design of the Islamic cemetery in Altach, Vorarlberg – which received the Aga Khan Award for Architecture – has yet to be followed up with new realizations.

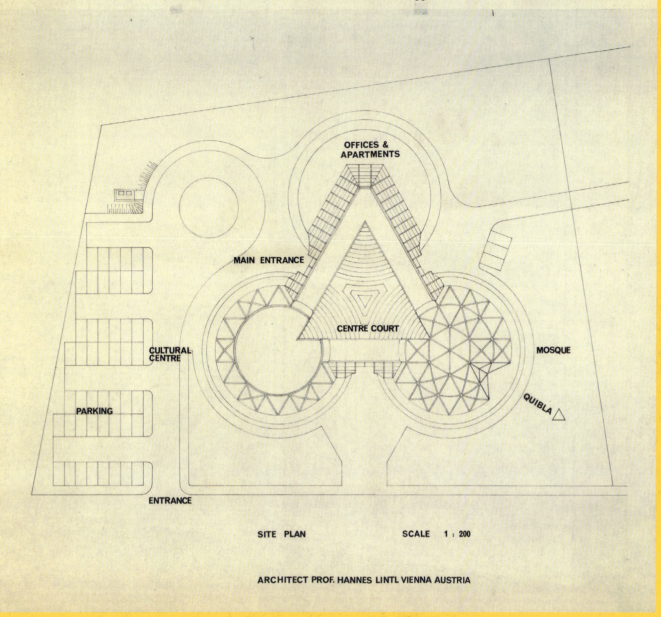

Hannes Lintl | Project for an Islamic Centre in Vienna | Design development, site plan | Print on foil

Image Confessional Diversity 339

Bernardo Bader | Islamic Cemetery | Schollenried 1, Altach, Vorarlberg, 2011–2012 | Wall element with octagon motif in wood frame | Oak | Prototype: Thomas Berchtold

Heinz Tesar | Project for the Imam Ali Center of Islamic Culture | Huttengasse 21–23, Vienna XVI, 2005 | Model | Wood, plastic

Church as Client

The "heroic phase" of Austrian church building took place primarily prior to the Second Vatican Council (1962–1965) and was marked by the ongoing discussion about renewal of the rigid liturgy. The arbeitsgruppe 4 made pioneering contributions to the implementation of liturgical innovations such as placing the altar at the center of the worship space. The architects devised solutions which pointed the way forward not only with regard to the construction of churches (desacralization), but for all of Austria's architecture of the postwar era.

KIRCHE GLANZING, WIEN 19. 1962

arbeitsgruppe 4 (Wilhelm Holzbauer, Friedrich Kurrent, Johannes Spalt) | Project for the Glanzing Church | Krottenbachstrasse 120, Vienna XIX, 1962
Model | Wood, cardboard

Symbols of Power

What do design problems as diverse as a monument to Franz Joseph I, an opera, civic center, computation center, and Hitler's birthplace have in common? In each, works of architecture, an imaginary society manifests its buildings are not a mirror-image of socio-political occurrences, do function as a socio-political means of communication. struction of the State Opera, the Second Republic consci on to its identity, seeking continuity by rebuilding box se of shifting to the more egalitarian tiered seating. By hostin petition calling for designs for a monument to Emperor Fr the Austrofascists sought to "awaken memories of" the r of the Habsburg monarchy and propagated their take on stark contrast to such attempts, a critical movement arose structed National Socialism's buildings.

The civic center and computation center tell of societal awakening after 1945. The multipurpose civic center – the S represents a new beginning for democracy, and the comp a modern, efficient municipal administration, is marked the belief in objectivity, and a can-do spirit.

peror
ocumenta-
f these
Although
s, they
the recon-
sly held
g instead
1936 com-
Joseph I,
nificence
tria. In
ich decon-

economic
dthalle –
tion center,
ptimism,

Theiss & Jaksch (Siegfried Theiss, Hans Jaksch) | Dollfussplatz competition, forecourt with Emperor Franz Joseph I Monument | Vienna IX, 1936 | Perspective | Whiteprint

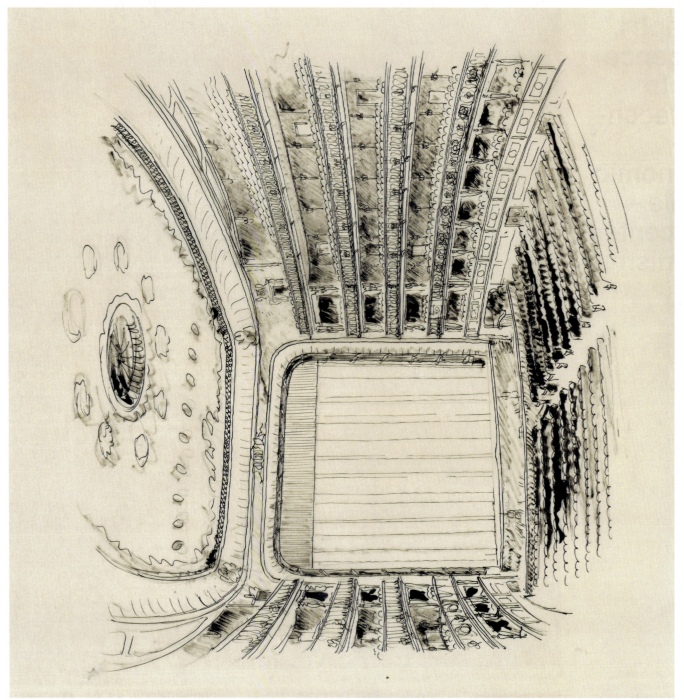

Erich Boltenstern | Reconstruction of the State Opera | Opernring 2, Vienna I, 1946–1955 | Variant, box theater, perspective | Ink on translucent paper

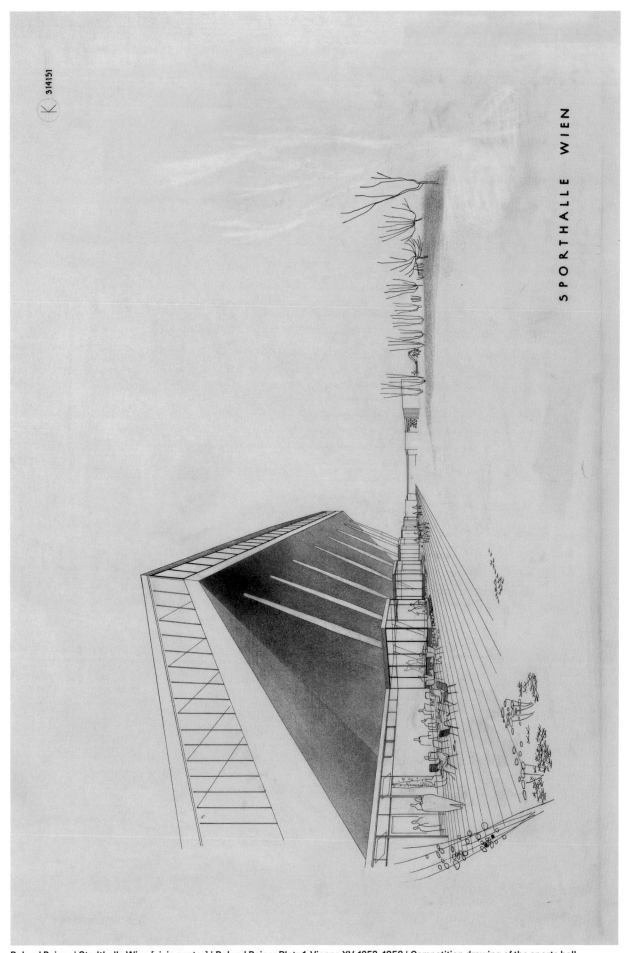

Roland Rainer | Stadthalle Wien [civic center] | Roland Rainer Platz 1, Vienna XV, 1953–1958 | Competition drawing of the sports hall, perspective | Ink and pencil on translucent paper

Harry Glück | City of Vienna Computing Center | Rathausstrasse 1, Vienna I, 1980 | Exterior | Photo: Margherita Spiluttini

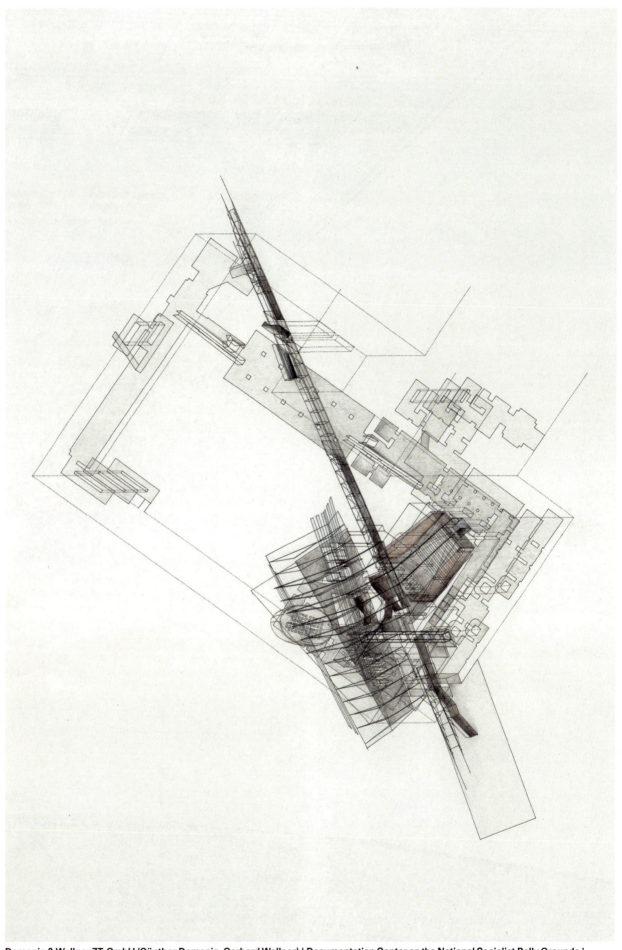

Domenig & Wallner ZT-GmbH (Günther Domenig, Gerhard Wallner) | Documentation Center on the National Socialist Rally Grounds | Bayernstrasse 110, Nuremberg, Germany, 1998–2001 | Competition drawing, axonometry | Colored pencil on printout

KABE Architekten (Birgit Kaucky, Arnold Brückner), Springer Architekten (Jörg Springer) | Competition, redesign of Adolf Hitler's birthplace | Salzburger Vorstadt 15, Braunau, Upper Austria, 2020 | Street elevation, west elevation, cross section, south elevation, east elevation | Print

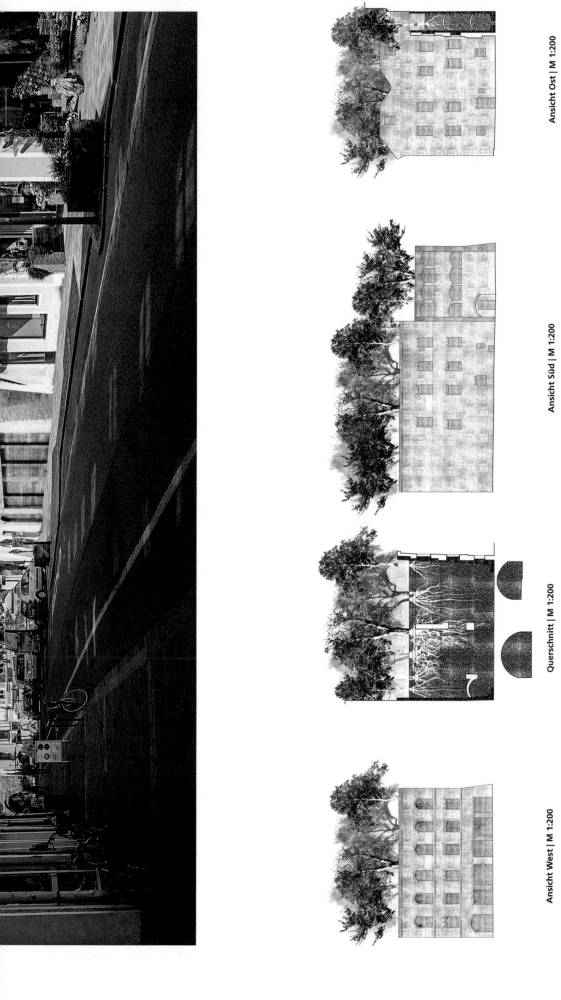

Image

Symbols of Power

Literature

Land of Mountains
pp. 300–301

Adolph Stiller, *Oswald Haerdtl. Architekt und Designer 1899–1959*, exh. cat. Ausstellungszentrum der Wiener Städtischen Allgemeinen Versicherung, Ringturm, 6/6–9/1/2000 (Salzburg 2000).

Georg Rigele, *Die Großglockner Hochalpenstraße. Zur Geschichte eines österreichischen Monuments* (Vienna 1998).

Rock over Baroque
pp. 302–305

Philip Johnson, Mark Wigley, *Deconstructivist Architecture*, exh. cat. The Museum of Modern Art, New York, 6/23–8/30/1988 (New York 1988).

Wolf D. Prix, Thomas Kramer (eds.), *Prinz Eisenbeton 6: Rock over Barock. Young and Beautiful: 7+2* (Vienna 6).

More than a Small Nation
pp. 306–315

Jakob Titz, "Wettbewerb Wiener UNO-Zentrum. Zweckbau oder Prestigeobjekt?," in: Renata Kassal-Mikula, Museum der Stadt Wien (eds.), *Das ungebaute Wien 1800–2000. Projekte für die Metropole*, exh. cat. Historisches Museum der Stadt Wien, 12/10/1999–2/20/2000 (Vienna 1999), 460–483.

Andres Lepik, Andreas Stadler, *Raimund Abraham & The Austrian Cultural Forum New York* (Ostfildern 2010).

Gudrun Hausegger, Architekturzentrum Wien (eds.), *Manhattan Austria. Die Architektur des Österreichischen Kulturinstitutes von Raimund Abraham = The Architecture of the Austrian Cultural Institute by Raimund Abraham*, exh. cat. Architekturzentrum Wien, 3/24–5/10/1999 (Salzburg 1999).

From East to West
pp. 316–323

Johann Gallis, "Bauen für das moderne Burgenland. Das Frühwerk der Architekten Matthias Szauer und Herwig Udo Graf" (master's thesis, TU Wien 2020).

Martina Pfeifer Steiner, Marina Hämmerle, vai Vorarlberger Architekturinstitut, Architekturzentrum Wien (eds.), *Rudolf Wäger. Baukünstler 1941–2019. Ein Pionier in Vorarlberg* (Basel 2021).

Otto Kapfinger, "Vorarlberger Bauschule – Zur Entstehung und Wirkung einer Schule, die nie eine war," in: *Modulør* 6 (Zurich 2012), 22–28.

Günther Prechter, *Architektur als soziale Praxis. Akteure zeitgenössischer Baukulturen: Das Beispiel Vorarlberg* (Vienna/Cologne/Weimar 2013).

Hermann Czech, *Zur Abwechslung. Ausgewählte Schriften zur Architektur in Wien*, exp. new ed. with an afterword by Arno Ritter (Vienna 1996).

Matthias Boeckl (ed.), *Architekt Luigi Blau. Häuser, Interieurs, Stadtmöbel. Beiträge zu einer Baukultur 1967–2002* (Vienna 2003).

Luigi Blau, Otto Kapfinger et al., *Luigi Blau. Architekt*, exp. new ed. (Salzburg 2018).

Elsa Prochazka, *architectureality. Raum & Designstrategien / Space & Designstrategies* (Basel 2018).

Vienna/Graz
pp. 324–331

Gregor Eichinger, Christian Knechtl, *Eichinger oder Knechtl. Projekte aus fünfundzwanzig Jahren* (Vienna 2009).

Günther Domenig, Forum Stadtpark (ed.), *Architektur – Investitionen. Grazer "Schule," 13 Standpunkte,* third exp. ed. (Graz 1986).

Anselm Wagner, Antje Senarclens de Grancy (eds.), *Was bleibt von der "Grazer Schule?" Architektur-Utopien seit den 1960ern revisited* (Berlin 2012).

Friedrich Achleitner, "Gibt es eine 'Grazer Schule?'" in: id., *Region, ein Konstrukt? Regionalismus, eine Pleite?* (Basel 1997), 79–99.

Eva Guttmann, Gabriele Kaiser, *Werkgruppe Graz 1959–1989. Architecture at the Turn of Late Modernism [Architektur am Wendepunkt der späten Moderne]* (Zurich 2013).

Simone Hain, "Studentenwohnheim Hafnerriegel: Der Erstling der Grazer Schule," in: *Architektur Steiermark*, 10/21/2021, http://www.gat.st/news/studentenwohnheim-hafnerriegel-der-erstling-der-grazer-schule (accessed July 30, 2022).

Architekturbüro Szyszkowitz-Kowalski, *Landwirtschaftliche Fachschule St. Martin, Schloß Großlobming* (Graz 1982).

Team A Graz (ed.), *Werkbericht Team A Graz. 1966–2010. Architektur und Umweltplanung* (Graz 2010).

Adam Wandruszka, Peter Urbanitsch (eds.), *Die Habsburgermonarchie 1848–1918, vol. 4, Die Konfessionen* (Vienna 1985).

Gerald Stourzh (ed.), *Die Habsburgermonarchie, vol. 3, Die Gleichberechtigung der Nationalitäten in der Verfassung und Verwaltung Österreichs 1848–1918* (Vienna 1985).

Confessional Diversity
pp. 332–343

Ulrike Unterweger, "Die Synagoge in Wien Hietzing," in: *David 70,* Sept. 2006, 34–41.

Ursula Prokop, "Arthur Grünberger und die Hietzinger Synagoge," in: *David 103*, Dec. 2014, 42–44.

Az W, Architektenlexikon 1770–1945, *Arthur Grünberger*, in: https://www.architektenlexikon.at/de/189.htm (accessed July 31, 2022).

Iris Meder, Evi Fuks (eds.), *Oskar Strnad 1879–193*5, exh. cat. Jüdisches Museum Wien, 3/28–6/24/2007 (Salzburg 2007).

Friedrich Kurrent, *Eine Synagoge für Wien. Architekt Friedrich Kurrent* (Vienna 2014).

Sonja Pisarik, Ute Waditschatka, Architekturzentrum Wien (eds.), *arbeitsgruppe 4. Wilhelm Holzbauer, Friedrich Kurrent, Johannes Spalt. 1950–1970*, exh. cat. Architekturzentrum Wien, 3/4–5/31/2010 (Salzburg 2010).

arbeitsgruppe 4, "Der neue Kirchenbau – Entwicklung und Ausblick," in: *Der Aufbau*, June 1961, 233–238.

Susanne Heine, Rüdiger Lohlker, Richard Potz, *Muslime in Österreich. Geschichte – Lebenswelt – Religion. Grundlagen für den Dialog* (Innsbruck 2012).

Ernst Fürlinger, *Moscheebaukonflikte in Österreich. Nationale Politik des religiösen Raums im globalen Zeitalter* (Wiener Forum für Theologie und Religionswissenschaft, vol. 7) (Göttingen 2013).

Islamisches Zentrum Wien, https://www.izwien.at/ (accessed July 31, 2022).

Eva Grabherr, "Häuser, Kinder und Gräber – das nennt man Heimat," in: Markus Barnay, Andreas Rudigier (eds.), *Vorarlberg. Ein Making-of in 50 Szenen. Objekte – Geschichte – Ausstellungspraxis* (Bielefeld 2022), 216–225.

Eva Grabherr, okay.zusammen leben (communal office for immigration and integration, Dornbirn), Islamischer Friedhof Altach. Geschichte des Projekts (marking the occasion of the exhibition Innenansicht Südost – Erkundungen islamischer Glaubensräume, vai Vorarlberger Architekturinstitut, 4/9–6/29/2013) (Dornbirn 2013).

Symbols of Power
pp. 344–351

Monika Platzer, Architekturzentrum Wien (eds.), *Cold War and Architecture – The Competing Forces that Reshaped Austria after 1945*, exh. cat. 10/17/2019–2/24/2020 (Zurich 2019).

Ursula Prokop, "Planen unter dem Kruckenkreuz 1934–1938," in: Renata Kassal-Mikula, Museum der Stadt Wien (eds.), *Das ungebaute Wien 1800 bis 2000. Projekte für die Metropole*, exh. cat. Historisches Museum der Stadt Wien, 12/10/1999–2/20/2020 (Vienna 1999), 320–321.

Theresa Knosp, "Sinnbild unserer Stadt in dieser unserer Zeit: Roland Rainer und die Wiener Stadthalle, 1952–1958" (master's thesis, TU Wien 2020).

Gerhard Matzig, "Bis zum Vergessen zeitlos," in: *Süddeutsche Zeitung*, 6/9/2020, https://www.sueddeutsche.de/kultur/hitler-geburtshaus-braunau-1.4930735 (accessed July 30, 2022).

Günther Domenig, "Dokumentationszentrum Reichsparteitagsgelände Nürnberg," in: Günter Schlusche (ed.), *Stiftung Denkmal für die ermordeten Juden Europas* (Berlin 2006), 64–69.

"Rechenzentrum wird abgerissen," in: *Wiener Zeitung*, 12/11/2013, https://www.wienerzeitung.at/nachrichten/chronik/wien-chronik/593709-Rechenzentrum-wird-abgerissen.html (accessed July 30, 2022).

KABE Architekten, Redesign of Hitler's birth house in Braunau, https://www.kabe.at/braunau (accessed July 31, 2022).

Springer Architekten, Braunau, Salzburger Vorstadt 15, https://springerarchitekten.de/164brn_braunau (accessed July 31, 2022).

Making

Phase 1
    Point of Departure   356
    Briefing   356
    Working with the Site   356

Phase 2
    Follies and Displays   358

Phase 3
    Color Concept   362

Phase 4
    Objects, Framing, Lettering   364

Making Hot Cold

Tracing Spaces /
Michael Hieslmair,
Michael Zinganel

seite zwei /
Christoph Schörkhuber,
Stefanie Wurnitsch

Point of Departure
The permanent exhibition Hot Questions – Cold Storage replaces the a_show, which opened in three phases starting in March 2004 and ran for 17 years. The display designed by Walking Chair Design Studios (Fidel Peugeot, Karl Emilio Pircher) consisted mainly of steel plate H-modules painted white. All ten themes shared a uniform appearance in terms of form, materiality, and color scheme, with various solid colors used for accentuation. Printed banners hung as topic headings above the low-slung theme islands.

Briefing
The Az W's wish to depart entirely from a homogeneous concept fit well with our approach to designing because it does not depend on continuously developing one's signature, but arises through our engagement with the objects and the curator's narrative threads, and in this particular case it was elaborated in several workshops with the Az W team and the designers.

Working with the Site
For the first step, our proposal was – as in religious buildings – to use materials and/or color to underscore the sculptural potential of the extant space, which consists of a barrel vault intersected by numerous lunette vaults above the archways. This we ultimately did in two ways: in order to emphasize the longitudinal direction of the barrel vault we installed continuous mounting rails for lighting along the entire length of the space, and we used a darker hue of gray to set off the side walls, niches, and lunette vaults above the window arches. These niches were furnished with structures to support rails for curtains and lighting as well as the braces for the steel tubes used for mounting the display pieces. In the niches, the curtains start just below the rounded tops of the window arches, creating a kind of display window from the outside. Inside, they resemble side chapels, becoming attractive spaces for placing and hanging display objects. In addition, the folds of the curtain add spatial structure to the background and festively frame the items on display.

The sculptural qualities of the space are highlighted through the use of color | Photo: Az W

The exhibition space and the displays set up a dialogue | Photo: Az W

Making-of Phase 1

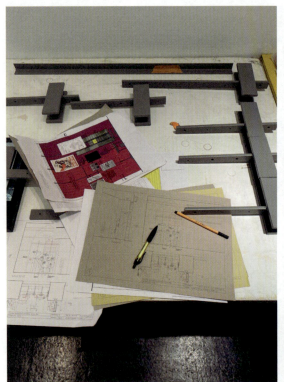
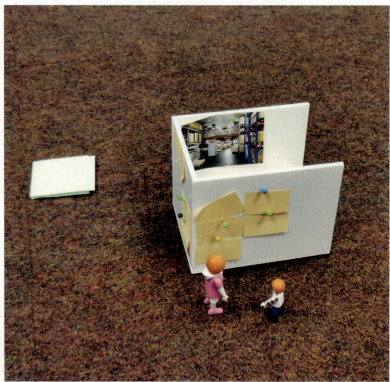

The exhibition gradually comes to life | Photos: Az W

Making-of   Phase 2   358

Follies and Displays

The concept brief for the permanent exhibition consisted in giving the visitor insight into Az W's otherwise inaccessible archive located off-site in Möllersdorf by creating a prominent display for the latter at the center of the exhibition. From this initially "cold" material collection (Cold Storage) items were metaphorically "brought out," contextualized, and bundled as "hot" narrative threads (Hot Questions) into thematic islands. In the Cold Storage display, visitors could plunge into the collection via digital interfaces, while the seven thematic islands would show "original" objects housed in an array of diversely designed structures.

In the first draft, the Cold Storage display took the form of an entirely closed-off, walk-in space within a space containing elaborate immersive media installations. In order to give the thematic islands more space and to tone down the dominance of the Cold Storage display, this space was gradually opened up, until in the end it dissolved into a pair of wings floating in space, like the pages of an open book, showing a dense, animated collage of real recordings of the archive, inventory numbers, key words, photos, models, plans, and images. For conservation purposes, high-quality reproductions took the place of "original" objects in the thematic islands – with the exception of the models – so that protective glass was no longer necessary and the objects could be better integrated into the exhibition architecture.

The design of the thematic islands and their positioning in the space follow the spatial demands of the exhibits themselves, in particular the demands of the various audiovisual displays, and take into account the sightlines within and through the islands as called for in the brief. The formal aspects of these sometimes extravagant follies, however, are also inspired by the themes, the display objects, and/or the discussions about them. For example, the role of architecture in forming an "Image" is presented in a stage set, "Elements" in archive cabinets, the "Planet" as a space station that makes reference to utopian 1960s architectural designs. The section "Habitat" is displayed in a paternoster elevator – a (housing) machine, in which models rotate past each other and temporarily give rise to various urban planning constellations. The section "Players" makes reference to Hans Hollein's Venice Biennale reproduction of Adolf Loos's proposal for the Chicago Tribune, and shows the development of the Ringstrasse in a raised circular display, whose outer surface tells of urban reconstruction and growth, while the inner surface addresses the suppressed side of fin-de-siècle society. The section "Common Good" is presented in staggered layers in front of and against the rear wall, the literal turning point of the exhibition.

Each of the thematic islands is assigned to nearby niches: irregular grids of thin steel tubing serve as the supporting structures from which display objects are suspended, as if hovering before the backdrop of various colored curtains. Similar constructions are used to brace freestanding displays and prominent display exhibits – especially large objects, projection walls, and projectors.

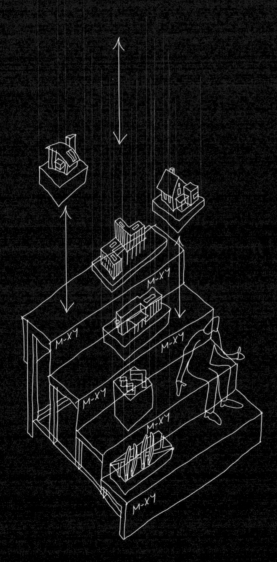

INITIAL CONCEPT,
A THEATER FOR MODELS
WITH BLEACHERS AND
FLY SYSTEM

HABITAT

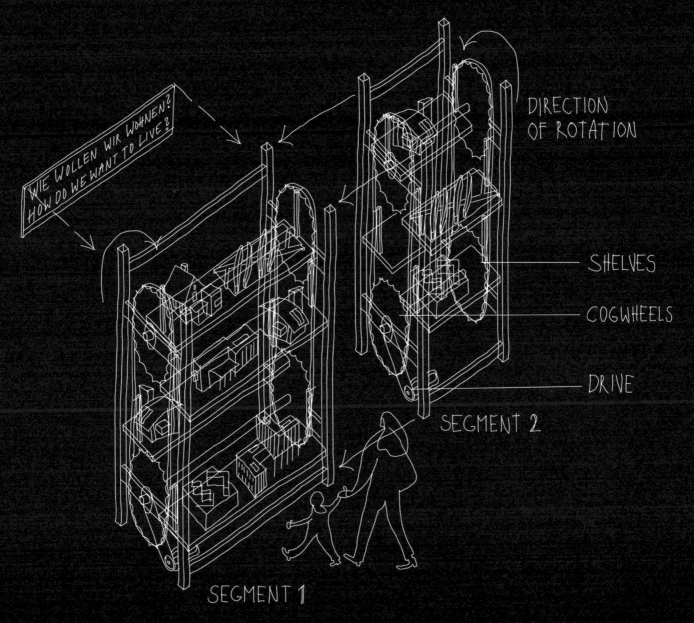

Design sketches by Michael Hieslmair

One of the exhibition team's many workshops | Photo: Az W

Color Concept

Initially, the color concept quite literally followed the dichotomy of cool and warm alluded to in the exhibition title: The materiality of the Cold Storage display was metal or glass and would utilize cool colors ranging from white to blue, while we envisioned the seven thematic islands in varying shades from yellow to red. With reference to the sequence of exhibition spaces in nineteenth-century museums in which each room was characterized by walls of a different color, our intention here was to bring all colors together in one room. We discarded this concept, however, because drawing such clear lines between the thematic islands implied zones of clearly delineated content, which to us didn't seem tenable. Instead, we divided the space into ten color zones which extend virtually across the room's entire length following the temperature color scale from warm to cold: from yellow to orange to red to violet to blue (only green is missing). The shift in color always occurs at the axis of the lunette vaults, so that the curtains also change color in the middle of the window arches, and each display, depending on its location and intersection with a virtual border, can consist of one or up to three different colors. To make the spatial experience more dynamic, some of the color shifts were consciously conceived to run straight through the middle of the sculptural display.

This handling of color from warm to cold can also be seen from outside; it jumps from niche to niche along the entire length of the facade: In each display window, illuminated curtains in different pairs of color augmented by texts affixed to the window panes in mirror foil add value to the overall facade.

Making-of   Phase 3   362

Fine-tuning the color gradation | Photo: Az W

Leftover paint following the installation of the exhibition | Photo: Az W

Fabric samples for the curtains | Photo: Az W

Making-of Phase 3 363

Objects, Framing, Lettering

In general, none of the objects are mounted directly on the walls, but are instead affixed to the structures designed specifically for each thematic island. The display images are not set behind glass. Drawings and plans are presented as reproductions in deep box frames, and photographic prints are laminated to the back of the box frames, thus adding three dimensionality to both. The frames have been painted to match the colors of the respective thematic islands.

The central themes of the exhibition are formulated as questions (Hot Questions) and rendered as illuminated signs in various styles of lettering. They are suspended above the corresponding thematic islands in the vaulted space, consciously setting up a relationship to the entire space. The plain aluminum used for the cladding of the Cold Storage display is reflected in the choice of materials for the introductory texts as well as the chapter titles, which are affixed directly to the thematic islands. The text panels describing the individual works, in contrast, were designed to match the color zone of their respective thematic islands. Finally, the typographic diversity should emphasize the different themes and text types and allow various approaches for "reading" the exhibition.

Text panels prior to installation | Photo: Az W

Options for mounting the objects | Photo: Az W

The paternoster's cogwheels await … | Photo: Az W

"Content precedes design. Design without content is decoration."
(Jeffrey Zeldman, 2008)

"Design is a relationship between form and content."
(Paul Rand)

Installation phase | Photo: Az W

Photos on this and the following pages: Lisa Rastl

Appendix

Bibliography

ABENDSTEIN Monika / ARCHITEKTURFORUM TIROL (eds.) (2002): *Josef Lackner 1931–2000.* Salzburg.

ACHLEITNER Friedrich (1980–2010): *Österreichische Architektur im 20. Jahrhundert. Ein Führer in fünf Bänden.* Salzburg.

ACHLEITNER Friedrich (1996): *Wiener Architektur. Zwischen typologischem Fatalismus und semantischem Schlamassel.* Vienna.

ACHLEITNER Friedrich (1997): "Gibt es eine 'Grazer Schule'?" in: *Region, ein Konstrukt? Regionalismus, eine Pleite?* edited by Friedrich Achleitner. Basel, 79–99.

ACHLEITNER, Friedrich / ÖGFA (eds.) (1976): *Österreichische Architektur 1945–75 [Zeitentwicklungsübersicht, Utopien-Konzeptionen, beispielhafte Objekte]* (exhibition, Secession, February 17–29, 1976), Vienna: ÖGFA.

ACHLEITNER Friedrich / TREYTL Johannes (eds.) (1969): *Neue Architektur in Österreich. 1945–1970.* Vienna.

ANGERER Alfred (2015): "Hygieia verführt Otto Wagner, Beispiele einer hygienisch motivierten Moderne" (master's thesis, TU Graz).

ANGSTER Julia (2018): "Nationalgeschichte und Globalgeschichte. Wege zu einer 'Denationalisierung' des historischen Blicks," in: *Aus Politik und Zeitgeschichte* 68, 9–16, www.bpb.de/shop/zeit schriften/apuz/280566/nationalgeschichte-und-globalgeschichte/ (accessed August 29, 2022).

ARBEITSGRUPPE 4 (1961), "Der neue Kirchenbau – Entwicklung und Ausblick," in: *Der Aufbau*, June, 233–238.

ARCHITEKTURBÜRO SZYSZKOWITZ-KOWALSKI (1982): Landwirtschaftliche Fachschule St. Martin, Schloß Großlobming. Pamphlet depicting and describing the renovated building, presented at the inauguration of the domestic science school, Graz.

ARCHITEKTURZENTRUM WIEN (ed.) (2005): *Ottokar Uhl* (exhibition catalog, Az W, March 3–June 13, 2005), Salzburg.

ARCHITEKTURZENTRUM WIEN (ed.) (2007): *Margherita Spiluttini. räumlich – spacious* (exhibition catalog, Az W, June 21–September 24, 2007), Salzburg.

ARCHITEKTURZENTRUM WIEN (ed.) (2009): *The Austrian Phenomenon. Architektur Avantgarde Österreich 1956–1973* (exhibition catalog), Basel.

ARCHITEKTURZENTRUM WIEN (ed.) (2010): Friedrich Achleitner 80 (*Hintergrund* 46/47), Vienna.

AVERMAETE Tom / CASCIATO Maristella / HOMMA Takashi / BARRADA Yto (2014): *Casablanca Chandigarh – A Report on Modernization* (exhibition catalog, Canadian Centre for Architecture, Montréal, November 26, 2013–April 20, 2014), Zurich.

AVERMAETE Tom / D'AURIA Viviana / HAVIK Klaske (eds.) (2015): "Crossing Boundaries: Transcultural Practices in Architecture and Urbanism," *OASE Architecture Journal* 95, Rotterdam.

AYRES Sara (2014): "Staging the Female Look: A Viennese Context of Display for Klimt's *Danaë*," in: *Oxford Art Journal* 37/3, December, 227–244.

BANIK-SCHWEITZER Renate (1999): "Urban Visions, Plans and Projects, 1890–1937," in: *Shaping the Great City: Modern Architecture in Central Europe, 1890–1937* edited by Eve Blau, Monika Platzer, Munich, 58–72.

BARBIERI S. Umberto / VAN DUIN Leen (2003): *A Hundred Years of Dutch Architecture, 1901–2000.* Amsterdam.

BAUMEISTER Ruth / FROSCHAUER Ruth (eds.) (2003): Die nützliche Reise (*Thesis, Wissenschaftliche Zeitschrift der Bauhaus-Universität Weimar 1*), Weimar.

BECKER Annette / STEINER Dietmar / WANG Wilfried (eds.) (1995): *Architektur im 20. Jahrhundert Österreich,* (exhibition catalog, Deutsches Architektur-Museum, Frankfurt am Main, October 14, 1995–January 14, 1996; Shedhalle St. Pölten, May 5, 1997–August 8, 1997), Munich/New York.

BENEVOLO Leonardo (1977): *History of Modern Architecture.* Cambridge MA [Ital. first edition 1960, Storia dell'architettura moderna].

BEREUTER Adolf / HIRSCHBÜHL Arnold (2014): *Bus:Stop Krumbach* edited by Verein Kultur Krumbach, Krumbach.

BERGDOLL Barry (2014): "Exhibiting History in a Period of Presentism, or Should We still be Collecting Archives?" lecture, icam 17, Montreal/New York.

BERNARD Erich / FELLER Barbara / PEYRER-HEIMSTÄTT Karl / ARCHITEKTURZENTRUM WIEN (eds.) (1999): *Amt Macht Stadt. Erich Leischner und das Wiener Stadtbauamt* (exhibition catalog, Az W, June 16– August 2, 1999), Salzburg.

BICHLER Harald / SPALT Johannes (2003): *Rauminhalt: Möbelklassiker 1945/60/70/85* (exhibition catalog, Galerie Rauminhalt, November 7–29, 2003), Vienna.

BLAU Eve (1999): *The Architecture of Red Vienna 1919–1934.* Cambridge, MA.

BLAU Luigi / KAPFINGER Otto et al. (2018): *Luigi Blau – Architekt* (expanded, reissued), Salzburg.

BOECK Rudolf J. / STADTBAUAMT DER STADT WIEN (eds.) (1951): *Volks- und Hauptschule der Stadt Wien IV., Schäffergasse.* Vienna.

BOECKL Matthias (2003): *Heinz Tesar. Zeichnungen.* Stuttgart.

BOECKL Matthias (ed.) (2003): *Architekt Luigi Blau. Häuser, Interieurs, Stadtmöbel – Beiträge zu einer Baukultur 1967–2002.* Vienna.

BOGNER Dieter (1992): *Haus-Rucker-Co. Denkräume – Stadträume 1967–1992* (exhibition catalog, Kunsthalle Wien, September 30–December 2, 1992), Klagenfurt.

BOLLEREY Franziska (2020): "Anton Schweighofer's 'Stadt des Kindes'", in: *Eselsohren. Journal of History of Art, Architecture and Urbanism* III, 1/2., Kid-Size. From Toy, to Table, to Town. Spielzeug, Möbel, Stadt edited by Franziska Bollerey, Christoph Grafe, Wuppertal, 305–316.

BORASI Giovanna / ZARDINI Mirko (2012): *Imperfect Health: The Medicalization of Architecture.* Montréal.

BORSANO Gabriella (1980): *The Presence of the Past. First International Exhibition of Architecture. The Corderia of the Arsenal. La Biennale di Venezia 1980 – Architectural Section.* London.

BOYER John W. (1995): *Political radicalism in late imperial Vienna: Origins of the Christian Social movement, 1848–1897.* Chicago.

BREITNER Hugo (1926): "Kapitalistische oder Sozialistische Steuerpolitik: Wer soll die Steuern zahlen? Die Armen oder die Reichen?" speech, Vienna.

BREITNER Hugo (n.d.): "Die Finanzpolitik der Gemeinde Wien": excerpt of a campaign speech, Vienna.

CASSAS Louis François / LEGRAND Jacques-Guillaume (1806): *Collection des chefs-d'œuvre de l'architecture des différents peuples, exécutés en modèles.* Paris.

CHING Francis D. K. / JARZOMBEK Mark M. / PRAKASH Vikramaditya (2007): *A Global History of Architecture.* Hoboken, NJ.

CHRAMOSTA Walter M. / STADTPLANUNG WIEN (eds.) (1995): *Ganztagshauptschule Wien 14, Kinkplatz 21* (Projekte und Konzepte series 3), Vienna: Stadtplanung Wien.

CHRAMOSTA Walter M. (2000): *Helmut Richter. Bauten und Projekte.* Basel.

CHRAMOSTA Walter M. / MAGISTRAT DER STADT WIEN (eds.) (1996): *The New Schoolhouse. Schoolchild's universe and urban particle. The School Building Programme 2000 of the City of Vienna. A First Survey 1990–1996.* Vienna.

COLOMINA Beatriz (ed.) (2016): *Das Andere: A Magazine for the Introduction of Occidental Culture to Austria – Written by Adolf Loos.* Zurich.

CZECH Hermann (1996): *Zur Abwechslung. Ausgewählte Schriften zur Architektur in Wien* (expanded, reissued), with an epilog by Arno Ritter. Vienna: Löcker.

CZEIKE Felix (2004): *Historisches Lexikon Wien*, vol. 5 of 6. Vienna.

DEWALD Christian (2017): "Der Wiener Schulbau Schäffergasse 1951 – gebautes Bildungsverständnis einer öffentlichen 'Wunderschule'" (bachelor's degree, Universität Wien).

DIRNHUBER Karl (1932): *Zivilarchitekt Dr. Ing. Karl Dirnhuber, zehn Jahre freischaffender Architekt 1921–1931*. Foreword by M. Eisler, Vienna/Leipzig.

DOMENIG Günther (2006): "Dokumentationszentrum Reichsparteitagsgelände Nürnberg," in: *Bericht der Stiftung Denkmal für die ermordeten Juden Europas* edited by Günter Schlusche, Berlin, 64–69.

DOMENIG Günther / FORUM STADTPARK (eds.) (1986): *Architektur – Investitionen. Grazer "Schule," 13 Standpunkte*, third edition, Graz.

DURAND Jean-Nicolas-Louis (1801): *Recueil et parallèle des édifices de tout genre, anciens et modernes, remarquables par leur beauté, par leur grandeur, ou par leur singularité, et dessinés [...]*, Paris.

DURTH Werner / SIGEL Paul (2009): *Baukultur – Spiegel gesellschaftlichen Wandels*, Berlin.

EICHINGER Gregor / KNECHTL Christian (2009): *Eichinger oder Knechtl. Projekte aus fünfundzwanzig Jahren*. Vienna.

ENDERLE-BURCEL Gertrude / REITER-ZATLOUKAL Ilse (eds.) (2018): *Antisemitismus in Österreich 1933–1938*. Vienna/Cologne/Weimar.

FANKHÄNEL Teresa / LEPIK Andres (eds.) (2020): *The Architecture Machine. The Role of Computers in Architecture* (exhibition catalog, Architekturmuseum der TU München, October 14, 2020–January 10, 2021), Basel.

FELLER Barbara (1991): "Baupolitik in Wien im Austrofaschismus" (master's thesis, Universität Wien).

FEUERSTEIN Günther (1966): "Archetypen des Bauens" (dissertation, TU Wien, 2. vols.).

FEUERSTEIN Günther / BUNDESMINISTERIUM FÜR BAUTEN UND TECHNIK (eds.) (1969): *Hochschulen planen, bauen. Sonderschau des Bundesministeriums für Bauten und Technik*. Vienna.

FIGUEIREDO Sergio M. (2016): *The Nai Effect – Creating Architecture Culture*. Rotterdam.

FISCHER Lisa (2007): *Lina Loos oder Wenn die Muse sich selbst küßt*. Vienna/Cologne/Weimar.

FISCHER Lisa (2018): "Mit Frauen bauen. Das nützliche Beziehungsmuster eines antimodernen Ehemanns," in: *Adolf Loos. Schriften, Briefe, Dokumente aus der Wienbibliothek im Rathaus* edited by Markus Kristan, Sylvia Mattl-Wurm, Gerhard Murauer. Vienna, 233–244.

FISCHER Norbert (2018): "Zur Geschichte von Feuerbestattung und Krematoriumsbau mit besonderem Hinblick auf Wien und Österreich," in: *Urne wie Sarg? Zur Unterscheidung zwischen Erd- und Feuerbestattung* edited by Ewald Volgger, Florian Wegscheider. Regensburg, 9–23.

FITZ Angelika / KRASNY Elke / ARCHITEKTURZENTRUM WIEN (eds.) (2019): *Critical Care. Architecture and Urbanism for a Broken Planet* (exhibition catalog, Az W, April 24–September 9, 2019), Cambridge, MA.

FLUSSER Vilém (2014): *Gestures* (transl.: Nancy Ann Roth), Minneapolis.

FOUCAULT Michel (1973): *Archäologie des Wissens*. Frankfurt am Main.

FOUCAULT Michel (2019): *Die Ordnung der Dinge. Eine Archäologie der Humanwissenschaften*. Frankfurt am Main.

FRANKOWSKI Philipp / LIEDERER Rosa (1932): *Die Kindergärten der Stadt Wien*. Vienna.

FREISITZER Kurt / KOCH Robert (1987): *Ottokar Uhl, Mitbestimmung im Wohnbau. Ein Handbuch*. Vienna.

FÜRLINGER Ernst (2013): *Moscheebaukonflikte in Österreich. Nationale Politik des religiösen Raums im globalen Zeitalter* (Wiener Forum für Theologie und Religionswissenschaft 7), Göttingen.

GALLIS Johann (2020): "Bauen für das moderne Burgenland. Das Frühwerk der Architekten Matthias Szauer und Herwig Udo Graf" (master's thesis, TU Wien).

GALLIS Johann / KIRCHENGAST Albert (eds.) (2022): *Brutalismus in Österreich 1960–1980. Eine Architekturtopografie der Spätmoderne in 9 Perspektiven*, Vienna/Cologne/Weimar.

GEMEINSCHAFT B.R.O.T. (2010): *20 Jahre Haus Hernals 1990–2010*, festschrift, Vienna, https://brothernals.at/wp-content/uploads/2015/06/Festschrift-20-Jahre-Gemeinschaft-BROT.pdf (accessed July 2, 2022).

GOODWIN Philip L. (1943): *Brazil Builds. Architecture New and Old 1652–1942*. New York.

GRABHERR Eva (2013): *okay.zusammen leben* (accompanying the exhibition Innenansicht Südost – Erkundungen islamischer Glaubensräume, vai Vorarlberger Architekturinstitut, April 9–June 29, 2013), Dornbirn.

GRABHERR Eva (2022): "Häuser, Kinder und Gräber – das nennt man Heimat." Der Islamische Friedhof Altach als Ausdruck und Generator der Etablierung und Beheimatung von Muslim*innen in Vorarlberg, in: *Vorarlberg. Ein Making-of in 50 Szenen. Objekte – Geschichte – Ausstellungspraxis* edited by Markus Barnay, Andreas Rudigier, Bielefeld, 216–225.

GRAF Otto Antonia (1985) *Otto Wagner* (Schriften des Instituts für Kunstgeschichte, Akademie der bildenden Künste Wien), first of seven volumes; *Das Werk des Architekten 1860–1902*; vol. 2, *Das Werk des Architekten 1903–1918*. Vienna.

GRENVILLE Anthony (2011): *Stimmen der Flucht. Österreichische Emigration nach Großbritannien ab 1938*. Vienna.

GRONVØLD Ulf (2005): "Permanent Architecture," in: Permanent Exhibitions, edited by Monika Platzer, icamprint 01, 14–23.

GRUBER Roland / NAGELER Peter / TRINANES Hernan (2007): "Temporäres Theater für die Stadt Haag," in: *ORTE. Architektur in Niederösterreich 2*, edited by Walter Zschokke, Marcus Nitschke. Basel, 30–31.

GUTTMANN Eva / KAISER Gabriele (2013): *Werkgruppe Graz 1959–1989. Architecture at the Turn of Late Modernism. Eugen Gross, Friedrich Groß-Rannsbach, Werner Hollomey, Hermann Pichler*. Zurich.

HABIAN Maya / GOSSOW Tobias (2017): *Die Ballade vom Planquadrat-Garten. Eine wahre Geschichte aus Wien. Ein Mitmach-Buch*. Vienna.

HAGLEITNER Tobias (2003): *Ort, Beziehung, Funktion. Eine Dorfstudie in Bangladesh Rudrapur*. Linz.

HARLANDER Christa (2007): "Der Architekt Robert Kramreiter 1905–1965" (master's thesis, Universität Wien).

HAUSEGGER Gudrun / ARCHITEKTURZENTRUM WIEN (eds.) (1999): *Manhattan Austria. The Architecture of the Austrian Cultural Institute by Raimund Abraham* (exhibition catalog, Az W, March 24–May 10, 1999), Salzburg.

HAUS-RUCKER-CO (1977): *Stadtgestaltung. Projekte 1970–76* (exhibition catalog), Linz.

HAYDEN Dolores (1982): *The Grand Domestic Revolution: A History of Feminist Designs for American Homes, Neighborhoods, and Cities*. Cambridge, MA.

HEINE Susanne / LOHLKER Rüdiger / POTZ Richard (2012): *Muslime in Österreich. Geschichte, Lebenswelt, Religion. Grundlagen für den Dialog*. Innsbruck.

HEMMRICH Edith / BLASCHITZ Mark / WURM Jan (2014): *The Algae House: About the First Building with a Bioreactor Facade*. Sulgen.

HERINGER Anna (2004): "School. Handmade in Bangladesh" (master's thesis, Kunstuniversität Linz).

HEYNEN Hilde / BAYDAR Gulsum (eds.) (2005): *Negotiating Domesticity. Spatial Productions of Gender in Modern Architecture*. London.

HOFER-HAGENAUER Gabriele / CONRATH-SCHOLL Gabriele (2015): *Margherita Spiluttini. Archive of Spaces* (exhibition catalog, Landesgalerie Linz, March 12–May 31, 2015), Linz.

HOLZSCHUH Ingrid / PLATZER Monika / ARCHITEKTURZENTRUM WIEN (eds.) (2015), "*Vienna. The Pearl of the Reich*" – Planning for Hitler (exhibition catalog, Az W, March 19–August 17, 2015), Zurich.

HUBATSCH Wilhelm (1961): *Der Schulbau in Österreich*. Vienna.

HUFNAGL Viktor (1968): "Schulbau und Pädagogik," in: *architektur aktuell 68/69*, printed in: *Bauten – Projekte, Erfahrungen – Erkenntnisse, Gedanken – Theorie. 1950–2000* edited by Viktor Hufnagl, Vienna, 24–26.

HUFNAGL Viktor (1968): "Internationale Tendenzen im Schulbau," in: *Der Aufbau 11/12*, printed in: *Bauten – Projekte, Erfahrungen – Erkenntnisse, Gedanken – Theorie. 1950–2000* edited by Viktor Hufnagl, Vienna, 81–89.

HUFNAGL Viktor (2001): *Bauten – Projekte, Erfahrungen – Erkenntnisse, Gedanken – Theorie. 1950–2000*. Vienna.

HUFNAGL Viktor / ÖGFA (eds.) (1969): *Österreichische Architektur 1960 bis 1970* (exhibition catalog, La-Chaux-de-Fonds, May 3–23, 1969), Vienna.

HUTH Eilfried / POLLET Doris (1977): *Beteiligung, Mitbestimmung im Wohnbau. Wohnmodell Deutschlandsberg Eschensiedlung* (progress report 1972–1976, documentation of the study), Graz.

INGERSOLL Richard / KOSTOF Spiro (2013): *World Architecture: A Cross-Cultural History*. New York.

JAMES-CHAKRABORTY Kathleen (2014): *Architecture Since 1400*. Minneapolis.

JANY Andrea (2019): *Experiment Wohnbau. Die partizipative Architektur des "Modell Steiermark,"* Berlin.

JOHNSON Philip / WIGLEY Mark (1988): *Deconstructivist Architecture* (exhibition catalog, Museum of Modern Art, New York, June 23–August 30,1988), New York.

KAINRATH Wilhelm / POTYKA Hugo / ZABRANA Rudolf (1980): *Projekt Planquadrat 4. Versuch einer "sanften" Stadterneuerung*, Stuttgart.

KAISER Gabriele (2010): "Bilanzen mit Ausblick. Die Ausstellungen der arbeitsgruppe 4," in: *arbeitsgruppe 4. Wilhelm Holzbauer, Friedrich Kurrent, Johannes Spalt*. 1950–1970 (exhibition catalog, Architekturzentrum Wien, March 4–May 31, 2010), Salzburg, 142–160.

KAISER Gabriele / PLATZER Monika / ARCHITEKTURZENTRUM WIEN (eds.) (2016): *Architecture in Austria in the Twentieth and Twenty-first Centuries*, second edition, Zurich.

KAPFINGER Otto (2012): "Vorarlberger Bauschule – Zur Entstehung und Wirkung einer Schule, die nie eine war," in: *Modulør* 6, Zurich.

KAPFINGER Otto / ARCHITEKTURFORUM TIROL (eds.) (2002*)*: *Bauen in Tirol seit 1980 – Ein Führer zu 260 sehenswerten Bauten*. Salzburg.

KAPFINGER Otto / SAUER Marko (eds.) (2017): *Martin Rauch. Gebaute Erde. Gestalten & Konstruieren mit Stampflehm*. Munich.

KNIEFACZ Katharina (ed.) (2015): *Universität – Forschung – Lehre. Themen und Perspektiven im langen 20. Jahrhundert* (650 Jahre Universität Wien – Aufbruch ins neue Jahrhundert), Vienna.

KNOSP Theresa (2020): "Sinnbild unserer Stadt in dieser unserer Zeit: Roland Rainer und die Wiener Stadthalle, 1952–1958" (master's thesis TU Wien).

KOHLBAUER-FRITZ Gabriele (ed.) (2015): *Die Ringstraße. Ein jüdischer Boulevard* (exhibition catalog, Jüdisches Museum Wien, March 25–October 4, 2015), Vienna.

KRAMREITER Robert (1965): *Sachsenbrunn. Seminar der Erzdiözese*. Sachsenbrunn.

KRASNY Elke / ARCHITEKTURZENTRUM WIEN (eds.) (2008): *The Force is in the Mind – The Making of Architecture* (exhibition catalog, Az W, October 16, 2008–February 2, 2009), Basel.

KRENN Katharina / OTTE Wolfgang (2018): *Schloss Trautenfels. Von der Burg zum Museum*, Trautenfels.

KRUFT Hanno-Walter (1991): *Geschichte der Architekturtheorie*, third edition. Munich.

KÜHN Christian (2009): "Rationalisierung und Flexibilität. Schulbaudiskurse der 1960er und -70er Jahre," in: *Schularchitektur im interdisziplinären Diskurs* edited by Jeanette Böhme. Wiesbaden, 283–298.

KÜHN Christian / PAMPE Barbara / POPELKA Anna / PODUSCHKA Georg (2018): *Von der neuen Schule* (English title: *Of the new school*, exhibition catalog, Galerie Berlin, November 1–December 15, 2018), Vienna.

KUHLMANN Dörte (December 9, 2015): "Adolf Loos: Architekt und Urbanist (oder Adolf Loos und sein Schlafzimmer)," speech, Andrassy Universität Budapest, unpublished manuscript.

KULTERMANN Udo (1967): *New Japanese Architecture*, New York.

KURRENT Friedrich (2014): *Eine Synagoge für Wien. Architekt Friedrich Kurrent*. Vienna.

KUZMICH Franz / TAVOLATO Paul / UHL Ottokar (1986): "CAD-Einsatz zur Mitbestimmung im Wohnbau," in: *Neue Automatisierungstechniken. Chancen für Klein- und Mittelbetriebe* edited by Fred Margulies. Günter Hillebrand. Vienna, 249–254.

LANGER Friedrich (1962): *Österreich baut Schulen* edited by Bundesministerium für Unterricht. Vienna.

LEPIK Andres / STADLER Andreas (2010): *Raimund Abraham & The Austrian Cultural Forum New York*. Ostfildern.

LILLIE Sophie (2003): *Was einmal war, Handbuch der enteigneten Kunstsammlungen Wiens*. Vienna.

MATTL Siegfried / PIRHOFER Gottfried / GANGELMAYER Franz J. (2018): *Wien in der nationalsozialistischen Ordnung des Raums. Lücken in der Wien-Erzählung* (VWI Studienreihe 3), Vienna.

MATTL, Siegfried (2000): *Wien im 20. Jahrhundert – Geschichte Wiens* (Geschichte Wiens, 6). Vienna.

MAYER Karoline / RITTER Katharina / FITZ Angelika / ARCHITEKTURZENTRUM WIEN (eds.) (2020): *Boden für Alle (*exhibition catalog, Az W, November 11, 2020–May 3, 2021), Zurich.

MEDER Iris / FUKS Evi (eds.) (2007): *Oskar Strnad 1879–1935* (exhibition catalog, Jüdisches Museum Wien, March 28–June 24, 2007), Salzburg.

MELINZ Gerhard (2003): "Armutspolitik und Sozialversicherungsstaat: Entwicklungsmuster in Österreich (1860 bis zur Gegenwart)," in: *Österreich in Geschichte und Literatur* 47, 136–161.

MIKOLETZKY Juliane (2003): *"Von jeher ein Hort starker nationaler Gesinnung"*. Die Technische Hochschule in Wien und der Nationalsozialismus (Veröffentlichungen des Universitätsarchivs der Technischen Universität Wien, 8), Vienna.

MIKOLETZKY Juliane / GEORGEACOPOL-WINISCHHOFER Ute / POHL Margit (1997): *"Dem Zuge der Zeit entsprechend"*. Zur Geschichte des Frauenstudiums in Österreich am Beispiel der Technischen Universität Wien (Schriftenreihe des Universitätsarchivs der TU Wien), Vienna.

MUSEEN DER STADT WIEN (ed.) (1985): *Traum und Wirklichkeit* 1870–1930 (exhibition catalog, Historisches Museum der Stadt Wien, March 28–October 6, 1985), Vienna.

N. N. (1991): "Haus Magerl. Experiment mit Solarkraft," in: *Architektur & Wohnen* 6.

N. N. (1999): "Standard Solar, Das etwas andere Fertighaus," in: *Sparen Bauen Wohnen* 2.

NERDINGER Winfried (ed.) (2005): *Heinz Tesar. Architektur* (exhibition catalog, Architekturmuseum der TU München, September 29, 2005–January 8, 2006), Milan.

NIERHAUS Andreas (ed.) (2020): *Ein Architekt als Medienstratege. Otto Wagner und die Fotografie* (Beiträge zur Geschichte der Fotografie in Österreich, vol. 19), Salzburg.

NIERHAUS Andreas / PFOSER Alfred (eds.) (2019): *Otto Wagner, Meine angebetete Louise! Das Tagebuch des Architekten 1915–1918*. Salzburg.

NOCHLIN Linda (1971): "Why Are There No Great Women Artists?," in: *Woman in Sexist Society. Studies In Power And Powerlessness* edited by Vivian Gornick, Barbara Moran, New York, 344–366.

OPEL Adolf / SCHIMEK Herbert (eds.) (2013): *Lina Loos. Das Buch ohne Titel – Erlebte Geschichten*. Vienna.

ORTNER Laurids / ORTNER Manfred (eds.) (2019), *Haus-Rucker-Co. Drawings and Objects 1969–1989*, L.O.M.O. Archive, Roc Flomar Collection, 5 vols., Cologne.

ÖSTERREICHER Oliver (2004): "Räumliche Idealstadtmodelle und utopische Umsetzungsversuche. Versuch einer Einordnung der 'Stadt des Kindes' in Wien" (dissertation, TU Wien).

OTTILLINGER Eva B. (ed.) (2006): *Zappel, Philipp! Kindermöbel. Eine Designgeschichte* (exhibition catalog, Hofmobiliendepot, October 4, 2006–January 7, 2007), Vienna.

PEVSNER Nikolaus (1949): *Pioneers of Modern Design: From William Morris to Walter Gropius*. New York.

PFEIFER Steiner Martina / HÄMMERLE Marina / VAI VORARLBERGER ARCHITEKTURINSTITUT / ARCHITEKTURZENTRUM WIEN (eds.) (2021): *Rudolf Wäger. Baukünstler 1941–2019 – Ein Pionier in Vorarlberg*. Basel.

PIRHOFER Gottfried / STIMMER Kurt (2007): *Pläne für Wien. Theorie und Praxis der Wiener Stadtplanung von 1945 bis 2005*. Vienna.

PISARIK Sonja / WADITSCHATKA Ute, ARCHITEKTURZENTRUM WIEN (eds.) (2010): *arbeitsgruppe 4. Wilhelm Holzbauer, Friedrich Kurrent, Johannes Spalt. 1950–1970.* (exhibition catalog, Az W, March 4–May 31, 2010), Salzburg.

PLATZER Monika (ed.) (January 20, 2009): ICAM 30 years, special issue, *icamprint* 03, https://icamweb.org/publications/icam-print-03/ (accessed August 29, 2022).

PLATZER Monika / ARCHITEKTURZENTRUM WIEN (eds.) (1999): *Viel zu modern. Hans Steineder Architekt. 1904–1976* (exhibition catalog, Az W, February 24–April 5, 1999), Salzburg.

PLATZER Monika / ARCHITEKTURZENTRUM WIEN (eds.) (2019): *Cold War and Architecture. The Competing Forces that Reshaped Austria after 1945* (exhibition catalog, Az W, October 17, 2019–February 24, 2020), Zurich.

PRECHTER Günther (2013): *Architektur als soziale Praxis. Akteure zeitgenössischer Baukulturen: Das Beispiel Vorarlberg*. Vienna.

PRIX Wolf D. / KRAMER Thomas (eds.) (2006): *Prinz Eisenbeton 6 – Rock over Barock. Young and Beautiful: 7 + 2*. Vienna.

PROCHAZKA Elsa (2018): *architectureality. Raum & Designstrategien/Space & Designstrategies*. Basel.

PROKOP Ursula (1999), "Planen unter dem Kruckenkreuz 1934–1938," in: *Das ungebaute Wien 1800 bis 2000. Projekte für die Metropole* (exhibition catalog, Historisches Museum der Stadt Wien, December 10, 1999–February 20, 2000), edited by Renata Kassal-Mikula, Museum der Stadt Wien. Vienna, 320–321.

PROKOP Ursula (2014): "Arthur Grünberger und die Hietzinger Synagoge," in: *David* 103, December, 42–44.

PRUSCHA Carl (1975): *Kathmandu Valley – The Preservation of Physical Environment and Cultural Heritage*. Vienna.

PURTSCHER Vera (1991): Haus Standard Solar, in: *Architektur & Bauforum* 145, 10–16.

RAINER Roland (1961): *Anonymes Bauen Nordburgenland*, Salzburg.

RAINER Roland (1962): *Planungskonzept Wien*. Vienna.

REDL Leopold / WÖSENDORFER Hans (1980): *Die Donauinsel. Ein Beispiel politischer Planung in Wien*. Vienna.

REINBERG Georg W. (2021): *Architektur für eine solare Zukunft* [English title: *Architecture for a Solar Future*]. Basel: Birkhäuser.

REINBERG Georg W. / BOECKL Matthias (eds.) (2008): *Reinberg. Ökologische Architektur. Entwurf, Planung, Ausführung* [English title: *Ecological Architecture. Design, Planning, Realization*]. Vienna.

RENDELL Jane / PENNER Barbara / BORDEN Iain (2009): *Gender Space Architecture: An Interdisciplinary Introduction*. London.

REVERON Rafael Romero / ARRÁEZ-AYBAR Luis A. (2015): "Ole Worm (1588–1654) – anatomist and antiquarian," in: *European Journal of Anatomy* 19, 299–301.

RICHARDSON Margaret / STEVENS Mary Anne (2015): *John Soane, Architect. Master of Space and Light*. London.

RISTIĆ Ivan / ARCHITEKTURZENTRUM WIEN (eds.) (2009): *Bogdan Bogdanović. Memoria und Utopie in Tito-Jugoslawien* (exhibition catalog, Az W, March 5–June 2, 2009), Vienna.

SCHERER Bernd / RENN Jürgen (eds.) (2015): *Das Anthropozän. Zum Stand der Dinge*. Berlin.

SCHWARZ Werner Michael (2018): "Die Kunst der Bewegung – Otto Wagners Theorie und Politik der Großstadt," in: *Otto Wagner 1841–1918* edited by Andreas Nierhaus, Eva-Maria Orosz (exhibition catalog, Wien Museum, March 15–October 7, 2018), Salzburg, 60–67.

SCHWARZ Werner Michael / SPITALER Georg / WIKIDAL Elke (eds.) (2019): *Das Rote Wien 1919–1934. Ideen, Debatten, Praxis* (exhibition at the Wien Museum, 426), Basel.

SCHWEITZER Renate (1970): "Der Generalregulierungsplan für Wien (1893–1920)," in: *Berichte zur Raumforschung und Raumplanung* 14, 24–41, edited by Österreichische Gesellschaft für Raumforschung und Raumplanung.

SIMIONOVICI Ana-Maria (2015): "The good wife: Lina Loos, Adolf Loos and the Making of an Idea" (dissertation, TU Wien), https://publik.tuwien.ac.at/files/Pub Dat_243383.pdf (accessed May 26, 2022).

SOTRIFFER Kristian (ed.) (1982): *Das größere Österreich. Geistiges und soziales Leben von 1880 bis zur Gegenwart. Hundert Kapitel*. Vienna.

STEGER Bernhard (ed.) (2011): *Themen der Architektur: z. B. Ottokar Uhl*, Vienna.

STILLER Adolph / ARCHITEKTURZENTRUM WIEN (eds.) (2000): *Oswald Haerdtl. Architekt und Designer 1899–1959* (exhibition catalog, Ausstellungszentrum im Ringturm, June 5–September 15, 2000), Salzburg.

STOURZH Gerald (ed.) (1985): *Die Habsburgermonarchie*, vol. 3, *Die Gleichberechtigung der Nationalitäten in der Verfassung und Verwaltung Österreichs 1848–1918*. Vienna.

STRATIGAKOS Despina (2016): *Where Are the Women Architects*, Princeton.

STÜHLINGER Harald R. / MURAUER Gerhard (2015): *Vom Werden der Wiener Ringstraße*. Vienna.

SUTTNER Andreas (2017): *Das Schwarze Wien. Bautätigkeit im Ständestaat 1934–1938*. Vienna/Köln/Weimar.

SZACKA Léa-Catherine (2016): *Exhibiting the Postmodern: The 1980 Venice Architecture Biennale*. London.

SZAMBIEN Werner (1988): *Le Musée d'Architecture*. Paris.

TAYLOR John (2011): *Soane's Cork Models*. London.

TEAM A GRAZ (ed.) (2010): *Werkbericht Team A Graz 1966–2010. Architektur und Umweltplanung*. Graz.

TENENBAUM Jeremy Eric / SCOTT BROWN Denise (2018): *Your Guide to Downtown Denise Scott Brown* edited by Angelika Fitz, Katharina Ritter, Architekturzentrum Wien. Zurich.

TESAR Heinz / WAECHTER-BÖHM Liesbeth (1995): *Heinz Tesar*. Vienna/New York.

THORNTON Peter / DOREY Helen (1992): *Sir John Soane: The Architect As Collector 1753–1837*. New York.

TITZ Jakob (1999): "Wettbewerb Wiener UNO-Zentrum. Zweckbau oder Prestigeobjekt?," in: *Das ungebaute Wien 1800–2000. Projekte für die Metropole* edited by Renata Kassal-Mikula, Museum der Stadt Wien (exhibition catalog, Historisches Museum der Stadt Wien, December 10, 1999–February 20, 2000), Vienna, 460–483.

UHL Ottokar (1984): "Eine Sprache sprechen," in: *ARCH+* 77 (topic: Computer-Aided-Design).

UNTERWEGER Ulrike (2006): "Die Synagoge in Wien Hietzing," in: *David* 70, September, 34–41.

VEGESACK Alexander von (ed.) (1997): *Kid Size. The Material World of Childhood* (exhibition catalog, Kunsthal Rotterdam, June 28–September 28, 1997), Milan.

VENTURI Robert / SCOTT BROWN Denise / IZENOUR Steven (1972): *Learning from Las Vegas*. Cambridge, MA.

VOITL Helmut / GUGGENBERGER Elisabeth / PIRKER Peter (1977): *Planquadrat. Ruhe, Grün und Sicherheit. Wohnen in der Stadt*, Vienna.

WAGNER Anselm (2010): "Otto Wagners Straßenkehrer. Zum Reinigungsdiskurs der modernistischen Stadtplanung," in: *bricolage. Innsbrucker Zeitschrift für Europäische Ethnologie* 6, 36–61.

WAGNER Anselm / SENARCLENS DE GRANCY Antje (eds.) (2012): *Was bleibt von der "Grazer Schule"? Architektur-Utopien seit den 1960ern revisited*. Berlin.

WANDRUSZKA Adam / URBANITSCH Peter (eds.) (1985): *Die Habsburgermonarchie 1848–1918*, vol. 4, *Die Konfessionen*. Vienna.

WEIBEL Peter (2011): *Car Culture – Media of Mobility* (exhibiton catalog, Zentrum für Kunst und Medientechnologie Karlsruhe, June 18, 2011–January 8, 2012), Karlsruhe.

WEIHSMANN Helmut (1998) *Bauen unterm Hakenkreuz. Architektur des Untergangs*. Vienna.

WEIHSMANN Helmut (2002): *Das Rote Wien. Sozialdemokratische Architektur und Kommunalpolitik 1919–1934*. Vienna.

WEIHSMANN Helmut (2005): *In Wien erbaut. Lexikon der Wiener Architekten des 20. Jahrhunderts*. Vienna.

WEINZIERL Erika / SKALNIK Kurt (1983): *Österreich 1918–1938, Geschichte der Ersten Republik*, 2 vols., Graz/Wien/Cologne.

WERKNER Patrick / GRESSEL Heinrich (2008): *Ich bin keine Küche. Gegenwartsgeschichten aus dem Nachlass von Margarete Schütte-Lihotzky* (exhibition catalog, Universität für angewandte Kunst Wien), Vienna.

WOLFF-PLOTTEGG Manfred (2007): *Hybrid Architektur & Hyper Funktionen*. Vienna.

WOLFF-PLOTTEGG Manfred (2015): *Plottegg – Architecture Beyond Inclusion and Identity is Exclusion and Difference from Art. The Work of Manfred Wolff-Plottegg*. Basel.

WOLFGRUBER Gudrun (2013): *Von der Fürsorge zur Sozialarbeit. Wiener Jugendwohlfahrt im 20. Jahrhundert* (Schriftenreihe zur Geschichte der Sozialarbeit und Sozialarbeitsforschung 5), Vienna.

ZUG ZENTRUM FÜR UMWELTGESCHICHTE, UNIVERSITÄT FÜR BODENKULTUR Wien (ed.) (2019): *Wasser Stadt Wien. Eine Umweltgeschichte*. Vienna.

Internet sources:

Az W, Architekt*innenlexikon, https://www.azw.at/de/artikel/sammlung/architektinnenlexikon/ (accessed August 29, 2022).

Az W, Architektenlexikon 1770–1945, Arthur Grünberger, in: https://www.architektenlexikon.at/de/189.htm (accessed July 31, 2022).

Az W, Architektur Austria Gegenwart, https://www.azw.at/de/artikel/sammlung/architektur-austria-gegenwart/ (accessed August 29, 2022).

Az W, Sowjetmoderne 1955–1991, https://www.azw.at/de/artikel/sammlung/sowjetmoderne-1955-1991/ (accessed August 29, 2022).

BAUBÖCK Rainer (1996): "'Nach Rasse und Sprache verschieden' – Migrationspolitik in Österreich von der Monarchie bis heute" (IHS Political Science Series, Working Paper, 31), in: *IRIHS, Institutional Repository at IHS Vienna*, https://irihs.ihs.ac.at/id/eprint/899/1/pw_31.pdf (accessed May 26, 2022).

Baugruppe Bikes and Rails, Verein zur Förderung gemeinschaftlichen Wohnens und nachhaltiger Mobilität, https://www.bikesandrails.org/wp/ (accessed May 26, 2022).

Bodenfreiheit, Verein zur Erhaltung von Freiräumen, https://www.bodenfreiheit.at/ueber-uns.html (accessed June 3, 2022).

einszueins architektur, Wohnprojekt Wien, https://www.einszueins.at/project/wohnprojekt-wien/ (accessed July 2, 2022).

Frauenmuseum Hittisau, Raum für Geburt und Sinne, https://www.frauenmuseum.at/geburt-sinne (accessed July 2, 2022).

FUJIMOTO Sou, Bechter Zaffignani, BUS:STOP Krumbach Bränden, May 7, 2014, in: *nextroom*, https://www.nextroom.at/building.php?id=36373 (accessed June 3, 2022).

Gartenhofverein Planquadrat, http://planquadrat.weebly.com/ (accessed June 3, 2022).

Gymnasium Ursulinen, Innsbruck, Peter Paul Steininger, Schulgeschichte: Über 300 Jahre Ursulinen in Innsbruck – Tradition und Innovation, https://ursulinen.tsn.at/schulprofil/schulgeschichte (accessed July 1, 2022).

habiTAT, Verein zur Förderung selbstverwalteter und solidarischer Wohn- und Lebensformen, https://habitat.servus.at/ (accessed May 26, 2022).

HAIN Simone, "Studentenwohnheim Hafnerriegel – Der Erstling der Grazer Schule," in: Architektur Steiermark, October 21, 2010, http://www.gat.st/news/studentenwohnheim-hafnerriegel-der-erstling-der-grazer-schule (accessed July 30, 2022).

HUNDERTWASSER Friedensreich, Verschimmelungsmanifest gegen den Rationalismus in der Architektur (1958/1959/1964), in: Die Hundertwasser Gemeinnützige Privatstiftung, https://hundertwasser.com/texte/mouldiness_manifesto_against_rationalism_in_architecture (accessed June 3, 2022).

HUNT Lynn: Against Presentism, in: Perspectives on History, 1.5.2002, https://www.historians.org/research-and-publications/perspectives-on-history/may-2002/against-presentism (accessed August 29, 2022)

IG Geburtskultur a-z, Raum für Geburt und Sinne, https://geburtskultur.com/raum-fuer-geburt-und-sinne/ (accessed July 2, 2022).

Islamisches Zentrum Wien, https://www.izwien.at/ (accessed July 31, 2022).

KABE Architekten, Redesign of Hitler's birth house in Braunau, https://www.kabe.at/braunau (31.7.2022).

LandLuft, Verein zur Förderung von Baukultur in ländlichen Räumen, http://www.landluft.at/ (accessed June 3, 2022).

Lehm Ton Erde Baukunst, https://www.lehmtonerde.at/de/ (accessed June 3, 2022).

MATZIG Gerhard, "Bis zum Vergessen zeitlos," in: *Süddeutsche Zeitung*, June 9, 2020, https://www.sueddeutsche.de/kultur/hitler-geburtshaus-braunau-1.4930735 (accessed July 30, 2022).

MEDER Iris (2008), "Von Wien nach Shanghai. Der Architekt Leopold Ponzen," in: *David. Jüdische Kulturzeitschrift* 78, September, http://david.juden.at/2008/78/14_meder.htm (accessed May 26, 2022).

nonconform, Stadt Haag: eine Tribüne, die mehr kann, https://www.nonconform.at/architektur/stadt-haag-die-wiederbelebung-eines-ortes-durch-eine-theaterbuehne/ (accessed June 3, 2022).

OSIECKI Matthias, Gelungene Vorreiter-Rolle (Ö1 radio program on August 4, 2003), in: *nextroom*, https://www.nextroom.at/article.php?id=3557 (accessed June 3, 2022).

Österreichische Nationalbibliothek, Ariadne, Frauen in Bewegung 1848–1938, Erster Wiener Frauenklub, https://fraueninbewegung.onb.ac.at/node/434 (accessed May 26, 2022).

PIRHOFER Gottfried / STIMMER Kurt (2007): "Pläne für Wien – Theorie und Praxis der Wiener Stadtplanung von 1945 bis 2005," Vienna, https://www.wien.gv.at/stadtentwicklung/studien/pdf/b008280a.pdf (accessed May 26, 2022).

PPAG architects, Bildungscampus Sonnwendviertel, https://www.ppag.at/de/projects/bildungscampus/ (accessed July 1, 2022)

Rechenzentrum wird abgerissen, in: *Wiener Zeitung*, December 11, 2013, https://www.wienerzeitung.at/nachrichten/chronik/wien-chronik/593709-Rechenzentrum-wird-abgerissen.html (accessed July 30, 2022).

Sargfabrik, Verein für integrative Lebensgestaltung, https://sargfabrik.at/ (accessed May 26, 2022).

SCHEIDL Inge, "Karl Dirnhuber," in: Az W, Architektenlexikon 1770–1945, http://www.architektenlexikon.at/de/92.htm (accessed May 26, 2022).

Schusev State Museum of Architecture, http://muar.ru/ (accessed September 25, 2022).

Splitterwerk, The Label for Fine Arts and Engineering, https://www.splitterwerk.at/database/main.php?mode=view&album=Paintings&pic=09_Adele_Bloch-Bauer.jpg&dispsize=512&start=0 (accessed May 26, 2022).

Springer Architekten, Braunau, Salzburger Vorstadt 15, https://springerarchitekten.de/164brn_braunau (31.7.2022).

Standard Solar I, in: *nextroom*, https://www.nextroom.at/building.php?id=2607# (accessed June 3, 2022).

STRATIGAKOS Despina (2011): "What I Learned from Architect Barbie," in: *Places Journal*, June, https://placesjournal.org/article/what-i-learned-from-architect-barbie/?cn-reloaded=1 (accessed July 2, 2022).

THATCHER Margaret (interview): "Aids, education and the year 2000!" in: *Woman's Own* on October 31, 1987, www.margaretthatcher.org/document/106689 (accessed August 28, 2022).

Universität Wien, Katharina Kniefacz, Offener Hochschulzugang und "Massenuniversität" 1970–2015, https://geschichte.univie.ac.at/de/themen/offener-hochschulzugang-und-massenuniversitaet (accessed July 1, 2022).

Verein Initiative Gemeinsam Bauen & Wohnen, https://www.inigbw.org/wohnprojekte-plattform (accessed June 3, 2022).

VinziRast am Land, https://www.vinzirast.at/projekte/vinzirast-am-land/ (accessed June 3, 2022).

Wohnprojekt Wien, Verein für Nachhaltiges Leben, https://wohnprojekt.wien/ (accessed July 2, 2022).

WOLFF-PLOTTEGG Manfred, http://plottegg.tuwien.ac.at/ (accessed June 2, 2022).

ZOBL Engelbert, https://www.engelbert-zobl.com/ (accessed June 2, 2022).

ZOBL Engelbert, https://www.engelbert-zobl.com/mojave-desert-city/ (accessed June 3, 2022).

Index

A
- Aalto, Alvar 276
- Abd al-Aziz, Faisal ibn 338
- Abraham, Raimund 53, 75, 157, 161, 165, 232, 315
- Achleitner, Friedrich 8, 13, 78, 96, 97, 322, 323
- Aichinger, Hermann 270
- Altmann, Maria 215
- arbeitsgruppe 4 8, 64, 110, 236, 342, 343
- Architekturbüro Reinberg 201
- Arnold, Paula 197
- ARTEC Architekten 229, 251
- Ast, Maria 212
- Atelier P + F 237, 240
- Auböck, Carl 234
- Auböck, Maria 233
- Augenfeld, Felix 207

B
- Bader, Bernardo 9, 338, 340
- Banki, Susanne 88
- Baschenow, Wassili 19
- Baudisch, Elisabeth 88
- Baumfeld, Rudolf 207
- Baumgarten, Wilhelm 207
- Baydar, Gulsum 19
- Bayer, Katharina 117, 122
- Bechter Zaffignani 163
- Behrens, Peter 88, 283
- Benevolo, Leonardo 20
- Berger, Josef 207
- Beyer, Oskar 87
- Bird Jr., Rylance 309
- BKK-2 200
- Blaschitz, Mark 129, 130, 215
- Blau, Luigi 269, 326
- Böhm, Georg 252
- Bogdanović, Bogdan 8, 56, 57, 58, 59
- Bolldorf-Reitstätter, Martha 88
- Boltenstern, Erich 208, 263, 346
- Borden, Iain 19
- Breitner, Hugo 20, 196, 198
- Breuer, Otto 207
- Briggs, Ella 14, 87, 207
- Brückner, Arnold 350, 351

C
- Cadbury Bros. 211
- Canevale, Isidore 107
- Cassas, Louis-François 19
- Cermak, Wilhelm 41
- Ching, Francis 20
- Chramosta, Walter M. 106
- Conzett, Jürgen 106
- Cook, Peter 106
- Coop Himmelb(l)au 9, 157, 164, 244, 303
- Czech, Hermann 90, 91, 112, 243, 324, 329
- Cziharz, Franz 330

D
- Dapra, Josef 75, 232
- Dashiell, Dale 158
- Deltios, Martha 285
- Dex, Josef Franz 207
- Dicker-Brandeis, Friedl 207
- Dirnhuber, Karl 9, 207, 210, 211
- Dodson, Richard 309
- Dollfuß, Engelbert 206
- Domenig & Wallner ZT-GmbH 349
- Domenig, Günther 70, 71, 92, 226, 238, 290, 291, 316, 349
- Drennig von Pietra-Rossa, Klothilde 87
- Driendl*Steixner 150, 151
- Driendl, Georg 150, 151
- Duczyńska, Helene 88
- Dür, Anka 67, 89, 94, 95
- Durand, Jean-Nicolas-Louis 19

E
- Eckenstorfer, Maria 88
- Ecker, Dietrich 330
- Ehn, Karl 256
- Eichholzer, Herbert 207
- Eichinger oder Knechtl 326
- Eichinger, Gregor 326
- einszueins architektur 117, 122
- Eisler, Martin 207
- Engelmann, Paul 207

F
- Farassat, Djamshid 8, 72
- Federle, Helmut 258
- Fehringer, Franz 236, 237, 240
- Felber, Robert 152
- Ferstel, Heinrich 189
- Feuerstein, Günther 89, 90, 325
- Fickl, Gottfried 321
- Firnberg, Hertha 290
- Fischer von Erlach, Johann Bernhard 106
- Fischer von Erlach, Joseph Emanuel 106
- Fitz, Walter 195
- Flusser, Vilém 56
- Förster, Ludwig von 179
- Foucault, Michel 7, 89
- Fournier, Colin 106
- Frank, Irmgard 88
- Frank, Josef 207
- Fricke, Olga 87
- Friedenberg, Hilda 87
- Friedler, Georg 290
- Frühwirth, Hermine 87
- Fujimoto, Sou 163

G
- Gad, Dora (previously: Goldberg), née Siegel 207
- gaupenraub +/− 154, 155
- Geiswinkler & Geiswinkler 241
- Geiswinkler, Markus 241
- Geiswinkler-Aziz, Kinayeh 241
- Gerl, Josef Ignaz 107
- Gerngross, Heidulf 227
- Glas, Hans 207
- Glöckel, Otto 88
- Glück, Harry 107, 348
- Goessler-Leirer, Irmtraud 145
- Golding, Arthur 309
- Götz, Bettina 229, 251
- Graf, Herwig Udo 318, 319
- Groag, Jacques 207
- Gross, Eugen 325, 331
- Gross, Fritz 207
- Groß-Rannsbach, Friedrich 325, 331
- Gruber, Roland 147
- Grubich, Karl 307
- Gruen, Victor, born Viktor Grünbaum 207
- Grünberger, Arthur 335
- Gsteu, Johann Georg 107
- Guggenberger, Elisabeth 144, 145
- Gulle, Dietmar 147

H
- Haas, Robert 301
- Habraken, N. John 120
- Hadid, Zaha 87
- Haerdtl, Oswald 9, 12, 62, 107, 300, 301, 304
- Hagner, Alexander 154
- Hansen, Theophil von 188
- Hartl, Isabella 88
- Hatchet, Charles 18
- Hauber, Alice 87
- Hauser, Sigrid 88
- Haus-Rucker-Co 9, 140, 141, 157, 164
- Hayden, Dolores 19
- Haydn, Florian 252
- Heimerich, Grete, md. Metzger 87
- Heltschl, Norbert 64
- Hemmrich, Edith 129, 130, 215, 228
- Henke Schreieck Architekten 107
- Herdey, Lorle 88
- Herdtle, Hermann 87
- Heringer, Anna 9, 67, 89, 94, 95, 132, 135
- Hermann & Valentiny 235
- Herzog & de Meuron 258
- Hetzendorf von Hohenberg, Johann Ferdinand 106
- Heynen, Hilde 19
- Hickmann, Anton Leo 175, 178
- Hitaller, Irene 88
- Hitler, Adolf 14, 70, 173, 344, 350
- Hoffmann, Josef 62, 87, 106, 213
- Hoffmann, Margarete 88
- Hofmann, Karl 207
- Hohenberg, F. H. von 107
- Hollein, Hans 8, 53, 92, 93, 111, 112, 114, 115, 157, 162, 304, 359
- Hollomey, Werner 325, 331
- HOLODECK Architects 318
- Holzbauer, Wilhelm 64, 110, 343
- Holzmeister, Clemens 88, 196, 285, 325
- Holzschuh, Ingrid 15
- Huber, Timo 145
- Hufnagl, Viktor 284, 285
- Hummel, S. F. 192
- Hundertwasser, Friedensreich 9, 143
- Hunt, Lynn 15
- Huth, Eilfried 92, 116, 117, 118, 238, 249, 290, 291, 316
- Hütter, Karl 318

I
- Imhof, Barbara 165
- Indrist, Waltraud P. 15
- Ingersoll, Richard 20
- Izenour, Steven 75

J
- Jack Cotton, Ballard and Blow 211
- Jaksch, Hans 211, 282, 345
- James-Chakraborty, Kathleen 20
- Janeba, Fritz 207
- Jarzombek, Mark 20
- Jelletz, Adolf 335
- Jesacher, Renate 116, 120
- Jourda, Françoise-Hélène 88
- Jung, C. G. 89
- Jurecka, Edith, md. Lassman 88
- Justin & Partner 147

K
- KABE Architekten 350
- Kainrath, Wilhelm 145
- Kaiser, Gabriele 13
- Kapfinger, Otto 13, 112
- Karplus, Arnold 207
- Karplus, Gerhard 207
- Kasakow, Matwei 19
- Kastner, Friedrich 309
- Kaucky, Birgit 350
- Kiener, Franz 52
- Kiesler, Friedrich 231
- Kirchner, Marija 107, 136, 137, 138
- Kirchner, Wilfried 107, 136, 137, 138
- Klauser, Ludwig 205
- Kleiner, Leopold 207
- Kleyhons, Wilhelm 234
- Klimt, Gustav 112, 213, 215
- Kljajic, Branimir 235
- Knechtl, Christian 326
- Koller, Gabriele 313
- Kolm, Paul 290
- König, Carl 208
- König, Kardinal Franz 283
- Kopriva, Ernestine (Erna) 87
- Kornweitz, Julius 207
- Kostof, Spiro 20
- Kowalski, Karla 330, 331
- Kramreiter, Robert 283
- Kraus, Josefine 88
- Kreisky, Bruno 20, 290, 306, 307
- Krier, Rob 52
- Krischanitz, Adolf 107, 112, 258, 259
- Kronaus, Christian 256
- Kühn, Christian 4
- Kühn, Erich 273
- Kulka, Heinrich 207
- Kundl, Brigitte, md. Muthwill 87
- Kurrent, Friedrich 64, 109, 110, 336, 337, 343
- Kuzmich, Franz 48, 49, 116, 120

L
- Lackner, Josef 230, 239, 285
- Lammerhuber, Christoph 200
- Lang, Lukas 107
- Lang, Veronika Lena 135
- Langoth, Barbara 145
- Lauder, Ronald 215
- Lautner, John 8, 52, 72
- Le Corbusier 60, 62, 72, 240
- Legrand, Jacques-Guillaume 19
- Leischner, Erich Franz 12, 182, 264
- Leitner, Heidemarie 327
- Leslie Fooks, Ernest, born Ernest Leslie Fuchs 207
- Lichtblau, Ernst 207
- Liebe, Anton 207
- Lihotzky, Margarete 14, 54, 63, 83, 86, 87, 207, 293
- Linemayr, Axel 200
- Lintl, Hannes 338, 339
- Löhr, Moritz von 179
- Loos, Adolf 66, 93, 108, 112, 212, 216, 218, 219, 243, 252, 359
- Loos, Lina 20, 216, 217, 218
- Loos, Walter 207
- Loranzi, Franz J. 242
- Lorbek, Maja 14

Lorenz, Karl Raimund	325	Preser, Gerd	283
Lueger, Karl	9, 192, 193, 194, 204, 205, 338	Prix, Wolf D.	9, 164, 244, 303
Lugner, Richard	338	Prochazka, Elsa	8, 55, 63, 66, 233, 328
Lurje, Viktor	207	Pruscha, Carl	21, 75, 242
M Mack, Karin	13	Pschill, Lilli	288, 289
Mähner, Arthur	307	Puchhammer, Hans	8, 55, 72, 250
Maier, Victoria	88	Purin, Hans	317, 322, 323
Manahl, Richard	229, 251	Putz, Oskar	62, 106, 107, 258
Mang, Karl	8, 72, 310, 311	**R** Rafelsberger, Walter	176
Mang-Frimmel, Eva	310, 311	rainer pirker architeXture	235, 247
Marx, Karl	170, 171	Rainer, Roland	8, 15, 21, 63, 72, 75, 88, 186, 187, 236, 254, 347
Masaidek, Friedrich	204	Ramsauer, Hertha	87
Mascha & Seethaler	235	Rauch, Martin	9, 67, 89, 94, 95, 152
Mayer, Josef Joachim	270	Reichl, Fritz	207
McAlonie, Kelly Hayes	85	Reinberg, Georg W.	148, 201
Meili & Peter Architekten	106	Reinhardt, Max	336
Meisel-Hess, Grete	214	Rendell, Jane	19
Melnikow, Konstantin	72	Richter, Helmut	227, 267, 271, 286
Meyer, Douglas	309	Rieder, Max	107
Missoni, Herbert	330	Riesenhuber, Jörg	148
Morgenstern, Gertrude	87	Riss, Egon	207
Moser, Koloman	87	Riss, Sabina	86
Moussavi, Farshid	88	Rodeck, Melita	207
Müller, Fritz Michael	207	Roschitz, Josef	129, 130, 215, 228
N Nadel, Otto	270	Roth, Helene	87, 207
Nageler, Peter	147	Rottleuthner-Frauneder, Hertha	88
Neuman, Friedrich August	193	Rudnicki, Evelyn	200
Neurath, Otto	176	Rudofsky, Bernard	8, 73, 246
Niedermoser, Otto	208	Rysavy, Juliana	87
Nießen, Elisabeth	87	**S** Sallinger, Rudolf	310, 311
Nobile, Peter	189	Sanzenbecker, Ilse	145
Nochlin, Linda	83	Schacherl, Franz	207
nonconform	147	Schaur, Eda	14, 86
Novotny, Fritz	307	Schlögl, Hanno	55, 107
Nuler, Julia	242	Schmalhofer, Karl	270
Nüll, Eduard van der	179, 191	Schmid, Heinrich	270
O Oberhuber, Oswald	312, 313	Schmiderer, Simon	207
Ohmann, Friedrich	88	Schmidt, Friedrich	190
Ohmann, Wilhelmine	88	Schmitz, Richard	208
Ortner, Laurids	140, 141, 164	Schönerer, Georg Ritter von	204
Ortner, Manfred	140, 141, 164	Schönthal, Otto	207
P Pacanowski, Hilary	88	Schorske, Carl E.	113
Paulas-Schuller, Erika	87	Schreieck, Marta	88, 107
Pelli, César	307, 309	Schulitz, Helmut C.	158
Penner, Barbara	19	Schumacher, Victor	309
Peretti, Liselotte	233	Schuster, Ferdinand	325
Pevsner, Nikolaus	20	Schuster, Franz	106, 293
Peyscha, Anna	87	Schütte, Wilhelm	236
Pfusterer, Andreas	242	Schütte-Lihotzky, Margarete	14, 54, 63, 83, 86, 87, 207, 293
Pichler & Traupmann Architekten	41, 44, 45, 318	Schwadron, Ernst	207
Pichler, Christoph	44, 45	Schwalm-Theiss & Gressenbauer	235
Pichler, Hermann	325, 331	Schwanzer, Karl	325
Pichler, Walter	70, 71	Schwanzer, Martin	145
Piketty, Thomas	170, 171	Schwarz, Karl	325
Piller, Wolfgang	145	Schweighofer, Anton	54, 253, 274–280
Pinter, Klaus	140, 141, 164	Scott Brown, Denise	7, 75
Pirchner, Herbert	145	Seghatoleslami, Ali	288, 289
Plischke, Ernst Anton	207	Seidler, Harry	207
Podreka, Gisela	233	Semper, Gottfried	191
Poduschka, Georg	288, 289	Seraji, Nasrine	14, 86, 88
Pogoreutz, Mirko	252	Sicard von Sicardsburg, August	179, 191
Polak-Hellwig, Otto Rudolf	207	Simony, Stephan	207
Polanyi, Karl	9, 170, 171	Singer, Franz	207, 293
Ponzen, Leopold	9, 207, 208, 209	Sloane, Hans	18
pool Architektur	235	Smekal, Hans Dieter	8, 52, 72
Popelka, Anna	288, 289	Smirke, Robert	18
Popper, Kurt	207	Soane, John	19, 20
Potyka, Hugo	145	Sobotka, Walter	207
PPAG Architects	288, 289	Spalt, Johannes	8, 54, 64, 73, 110, 245, 293, 294, 343
Prader, Herbert	236, 237, 240	Sparre, Edel	88
Prakash, Vikram	20	Spiluttini, Margherita	8, 13, 54, 104, 105
Praun, Anna-Lülja	88	SPLITTERWERK	9, 129, 130, 215, 228
Preis, Alfred	207	Springer Architekten	350
		Springer, Jörg	350
		St. Florian, Friedrich	157, 160
		Staber, Johann	20, 307
		Stangl, Norbert	145
		Steidle, Otto	258
		Steineder, Hans	12, 62
		Steiner, Dietmar	4, 12, 13
		Steiner, Klaus	14
		Steixner, Gerhard	150, 151
		Stern, Annie	211
		Stiller, Adolph	12, 13
		Storck, Josef	87
		Strache, Friedrich August von	179
		Stratigakos, Despina	85
		Strnad, Oskar	87, 208, 336
		Stübben, Josef	181
		Süß, Daniel	107
		Summer, Sabrina	67, 89, 94, 95
		Sumnitsch, Franz	200
		Swiczinsky, Helmut	164, 303
		Szauer, Matthias	318, 321
		Székely, Eugen	207
		Szyszkowitz + Kowalski	330
		Szyszkowitz, Michael	330
		T Tandler, Julius	264
		Tavolato, Paul	48, 49
		Team A Graz	330, 331
		Team Habitat	242
		Tesar, Heinz	8, 60, 61, 69, 93, 338, 341
		Tessenow, Heinrich	87
		Thatcher, Margaret	9, 171
		the POOR BOYs ENTERPRISE	235
		Theiss & Jaksch	211, 282, 345
		Theiss, Siegfried	211, 282, 345
		Traupmann, Johann	44, 45
		Trifina, Carmen	86
		Trinanes, Hernan	147
		Trinkl, Maria	87
		Tungl, Elfriede	88
		U Uhl, Ottokar	8, 41, 46, 47, 48, 49, 63, 117, 120
		Ullmann, Franziska	107, 233
		V Venturi, Robert	75
		Vetter, Hans Adolf	207
		Vogler, Paul	273
		Voitl, Helmut	144, 145
		W Wachsmann, Konrad	325
		Wäger, Rudolf	322, 323
		Wagner, Otto	106, 112, 180, 181, 205, 262, 263, 266–268, 270
		Waldheim, Elisabeth	311
		Waldheim, Kurt	20, 306, 310, 311, 312
		Wallmüller, Jörg	330
		Wallner, Gerhard	349
		Wallnöfer, Florian	200
		Wawrik, Gunther	250
		Weill, Kurt	336
		Weinfeld, Regine	87
		Weiss, Grete	88
		Welzenbacher, Lois	88, 107, 248
		Werfel, Franz	336
		Werkgruppe Graz	325, 331
		Werkstatt Wien	235
		Weschta, Ilse, md. Koci	88
		Wilhelm, Karin	88
		Winter, Johann	200
		Withalm, Gloria	313
		Wittmann, Franz	245
		Wittmann, Hermine	245
		Witzmann, Carl	208
		Wlach, Oskar	207
		Wolf D. Prix & Partner ZT GmbH	244
		Wolff-Plottegg, Manfred	8, 41, 50, 51, 65
		Worm, Ole	18, 21
		Wurnig, Martin	116, 120, 235
		X Xenakis, Iannis	72
		Z Zabrana, Rudolf	145
		Zachariadis, Nikolaos	215
		Zak, Margarete, née Hofmann	207
		Zamp Kelp, Günter	140, 141, 164
		Zangerl, Erika	88
		Zentner, Charlotte	88
		Zilker, Markus	117, 122
		Zimbler, Liane, née Juliana Fisch	207
		Zobl, Engelbert	74, 75, 158, 309
		Zotter, Fritz	88
		Zweifel, Kurt	13
		Zwingl, Christine	86

Authors

Tom Avermaete
Studied architecture in Belgium and Denmark, obtained his MSc degree and PhD in the history and theory of architecture at the University of Leuven, Belgium; lecturer in the history of architecture at the University of Copenhagen (1997), leader of the Centre for Flemish Architectural Archives at the Flemish Architecture Institute (2003), associate professor (2006) and full professor of architecture (2012) at Delft University of Technology, The Netherlands; has held several visiting professorships, amongst others at the Politecnico di Milano, Academy of Fine Arts Vienna, Tokyo Institute of Technology, and the University of Copenhagen. Since 2018 professor of history and theory of urban design at ETH Zurich's Institute for the History and Theory of Architecture (Institute gta). He has served on the editorial board of the OASE Journal for Architecture (to date), the Journal of Architectural Education (JAE, until 2015), and the Architecture in the Netherlands Yearbook (2012–2016); member of the advisory board of the Architectural Theory Review and Docomomo Journal, and a co-editor of the series "Bloomsbury Studies in Modern Architecture" (with Janina Gosseye, Bloomsbury Academic). Avermaete is a member of the scientific board of the Jaap Bakema Centre (HNI, Rotterdam), the programme committee of the Berlage Centre for Advanced Studies in Architecture and Urban Design, and the Global Architectural History Teaching Collaborative (GAHTC).

Angelika Fitz
Since 2017, director of the Az W. Prior to this she worked internationally as a curator and author in the field of architecture and urbanism. Her main focus is on the societal contextualization of architecture, ecological and social justice in building, and planetary and feminist perspectives. She lectures and serves on advisory boards and juries, among others she is a member of the IBA Expert Council of the Federal Government in Berlin and the Advisory Board of the EU Mies Award. In 2003 and 2005 she curated the Austrian contribution to the Architecture Biennale in São Paulo. Her exhibitions and publications include Capital & Karma (2002); Reserve of Form (2003); Realstadt (2010); We-Traders. Swapping Crisis for City (2014); Weltstadt. Who creates the city? (2016); and Actopolis (2017). Her work at the Az W includes Assemble. How we build (2017) and Downtown Denise Scott Brown (2018). In 2019, she co-curated the exhibition Critical Care. Architecture for a Broken Planet at the Az W with Elke Krasny. The companion book was published by MIT Press, which will also be publishing the book on the exhibition Yasmeen Lari. Architecture for the Future (2023).

Sonja Pisarik
Studied art history and culture management in Vienna; served on the Austrian Historical Commission; 2001–2002 research stays in Buenos Aires and Montevideo; since 2003, curator and scientific collaborator in the collections department at the Az W; research focus: twentieth-century Austrian architecture; curatorial work: The Unknown Loos: Walter. Paraíso Latinoamericano (2006) with publication; x projects by arbeitsgruppe 4. Holzbauer, Kurrent, Spalt. 1950–1970 (2009) with publication; In the End: Architecture. Journeys through Time 1959–2019 (2016); Brutally Beautiful! 10 Highlights from Austria (2018) with publication; Vorarlberg – An Intergenerational Dialogue (2019); scientific collaborator for various exhibitions and publications, including Az W Gold (2013) and Hot Questions – Cold Storage. The Permanent Exhibition at the Az W. She has written texts on Oskar Putz, Emil Pirchan, Brutalism in Vienna, among others, and published numerous architecturally relevant articles in Austrian newspapers and journals.

Monika Platzer
Studied art history at the University of Vienna. Since 1998, part of the Az W staff, head of collections, and curator. Research focus: twentieth-century Austrian architecture and cultural history. She has led national and international research and exhibition projects, including Hot Questions – Cold Storage. The Permanent Exhibition at the Az W; Cold War and Architecture. The Competing Forces that Reshaped Austria; "Vienna. The Pearl of the Reich." Planning for Hitler; a_show. Austrian Architecture in the 20th and 21st Centuries; Lessons from Bernard Rudofsky; Shaping the Great City: Modern Architecture in Central Europe 1890–1937; Kinetism. Vienna Discovers the Avant-Garde. Monika Platzer has taught at the University of Vienna and the Technische Universität Wien; editor of ICAM print, the journal of the International Confederation of Architectural Museums (2004–2020). In 2014, she was visiting scholar at the Center for European Studies, Harvard University, USA. Her research focuses on transnational architectural history, and she lectures and publishes extensively.

Architekturzentrum Wien
The Az W is Austria's museum of architecture. It presents, discusses, and researches the ways in which architecture and urban development influence and shape our day-to-day lives, incorporating both local and international perspectives. The Az W offers a broad range of services for researchers and anyone interested in architecture. This includes a public reference library, the online building database "Architektur Austria Gegenwart" (Architecture Austria Contemporary), the online Encyclopaedia of Architects, as well as a unique collection of material on twentieth- and twenty-first-century Austrian architecture. The Az W sees itself as an institution of the future, in which knowledge is not only collected but also shared. The focus is on the social dimension of architecture. Its broad program bridges the gap between architecture professionals and everyday experts: with international themed exhibitions, the permanent exhibition Hot Questions – Cold Storage, and hundreds of events every year ranging from symposia, workshops, and lectures to tours, city expeditions, film series, and hands-on formats. What can architecture do? This is a question of great relevance to us all.

Colophon

All rights reserved; no part of this work may be reproduced or edited using an electronic system, duplicated, or distributed in any form without previous written permission.

Architekturzentrum Wien
Museumsplatz 1
1070 Vienna, Austria
www.azw.at

Park Books
Niederdorfstrasse 54
8001 Zurich, Switzerland
www.park-books.com

ISBN 978-3-03860-318-4

This book is being published in conjunction with *Hot Questions – Cold Storage. The Permanent Exhibition at the Az W* (on show since February 3, 2022, at the Architekturzentrum Wien).

Director
Angelika Fitz

Executive director
Karin Lux

Concept
Angelika Fitz, Monika Platzer

Curator
Monika Platzer

Exhibition design
Tracing Spaces / Michael Hieslmair, Michael Zinganel
seite zwei / Christoph Schörkhuber, Stefanie Wurnitsch

Financing and remodeling
Karin Lux

Project management, exhibition
Katrin Stingl

Head of production
Andreas Kurz

Image and media production, digital management
Iris Ranzinger

Text management and scientific assistant
Sonja Pisarik

Curatorial and production assistant
Barbara Kapsammer

Copy editor
Brigitte Ott

Translation G>E
Elise Feiersinger

Exhibition set up
Philipp Aschenberger and team:
Erich Angermann, Roman Aigner, Daniel Bemberger, Heinrich Schalk, Jan Schiefermair, Alexander Sobolev, Xaver Spindler

Edited by
Angelika Fitz, Monika Platzer
Architekturzentrum Wien

Book design
seite zwei / Christoph Schörkhuber, Stefanie Wurnitsch

Project management, publication
Sonja Pisarik

Image editing and processing, media production
Iris Ranzinger

Lithography
Mario Rott

Repro- and object photography
Elmar Bertsch
Thomas Gorisek
Iris Ranzinger

Copy editor
Elise Feiersinger

Translation G>E
Elise Feiersinger
Kimi Lum

Proofreading
Elise Feiersinger
Sonja Pisarik

Printed by
Gerin Druck GmbH
Gerinstraße 1–3
2120 Wolkersdorf

© 2023 Architekturzentrum Wien and Park Books AG, Zurich

© texts by the respective authors; texts pp. 24–353: Monika Platzer, with the exception of pp. 222–259: Sonja Pisarik

© all images by the Architekturzentrum Wien unless stated otherwise in the caption.

We are grateful to all the architects and photographers for their contributions and the confidence they placed in us. Without their involvement the ongoing expansion of the Az W collection would not be possible.

We would also like to thank our public and private sponsors:

Bundesministerium
Kunst, Kultur, öffentlicher Dienst und Sport

Stadt Wien

Architekturzentrum Wien

The Architecture Lounge of the Architekturzentrum Wien is an important platform for promoting the exchange of ideas between architecture, economics, and politics.

Members:

Arwag Holding AG
BDN Fleissner & Partner
Bundesimmobiliengesellschaft m.b.H.
Buwog Group
EGW Heimstätte Gesellschaft m.b.H.
Eternit Österreich GmbH
Gesiba, Gemeinn. Siedlungs- & Bau AG
Gewog – Neue Heimat
Grohe Ges.m.b.H.
iC Projektentwicklung
Immobilien Privatstiftung
Kallco Development GmbH
Kallinger Projekte GmbH
Mischek Bauträger Service GmbH
Neues Leben Gemeinn. Bau-, Wohn- und Siedlungsgen.
Österreichisches Siedlungswerk AG
Österreichisches Volkswohnungswerk
Sozialbau AG
Strabag Real Estate GmbH
Vasko+Partner Ingenieure
WBV – GPA Wohnbauvereinigung für Privatangestellte
WKÖ – Fachverband Steine - Keramik
Wien 3420 Aspern Development AG
Wienerberger Österreich GmbH
wohnfonds_wien
WSE Wiener Standort-entwicklung GmbH